X

BEYOND
REASON

BEYOND

The True Story of a Shocking
Double Murder, a Brilliant and
Beautiful Virginia Socialite, and a
Deadly Psychotic Obsession

REASON

Ken Englade

ST. MARTIN'S PRESS   NEW YORK

Grateful acknowledgement is given to the *Lynchburg News & Daily Advance* for permission to reprint portions of the editorial "What Possible Motive for Such Brutal Slayings?" which appeared in the April 10, 1985 edition.

Cover photographs: Elizabeth Haysom courtesy Wide World Photos; Derek Haysom courtesy Abbass Studios Ltd.; Nancy Haysom courtesy The Halifax Herald Ltd.

Library of Congress Cataloging-in-Publication Data

Englade, Ken.
    Beyond reason / Ken Englade.
      p. cm.
    ISBN 0-312-04267-1
    1. Murder—Virginia—Case studies. 2. Haysom, Derek, d. 1985.
   3. Haysom, Nancy, d. 1985. 4. Haysom, Elizabeth. 5. Soering, Jens.
   I. Title.
   HV6533.V8E54 1990
   364.1'523'09755—dc20   89-77078
                                                     CIP

First Edition
10 9 8 7 6 5 4 3 2 1

For the triplets: Glad, Sal, and Sam

Author's Note

THE STORY RELATED HERE IS COMPLICATED. IT INVOLVES A NUMBER OF people and events in widely separated locations, from central Virginia to Europe—from Lynchburg to London and from Boonsboro to Bonn.

There were many who helped me compile this material, patient, considerate people who often went considerably out of their way to be of assistance. Among those who offered generously of their time and knowledge, I would particularly like to thank Jim Updike, Ricky Gardner, Chuck Reid, Ken Beever, Geoffrey Brown, Colin Nicholls, Carroll Baker, Debbie Kirkland, Jennifer Thomas, Carl Wells, Hugh Jones, and Jack Rice and his crew.

There were also those who gave freely of their time and information but who asked, for one reason or another, to remain anonymous. I promised not to name them, but that does not mean I do not appreciate what they have done. They know who they are, and I hope they know how valuable their assistance was. To all of them, I am infinitely grateful.

There are also those who helped me communicate what I had learned. To them, I am particularly indebted because they helped me control my rambling, made sure I kept things in perspective, maintained consistency, and excised the irrelevant. Among them are my wife, Sara, and David Snell, Betsy Graham, and Mitchell Shields, and Peter MacPherson—good friends all. I thank them profusely.

In a story such as this there are always some gaps and loose ends; only in fiction is everything wrapped up neatly at the end. To help keep the flow of the tale I have here and there constructed a few bridges: If this happened and that was the result, then such-and-such must have happened in between. Such instances were relatively rare. In places I have reconstructed conversations, at which, obviously, I was not present. The reader will understand that I am not asserting that those exact words were spoken, but I have endeavoured to capture the thrust of events that did occur. The basic outline of this story is well documented and as factual as I could make it. If there are errors, they occurred because of my misinterpretations. For these, I apologize in advance.

A number of people were drawn into the events related here through no fault of their own. They were involved only because they happened to be in a certain place at a certain time. I have tried to protect their names and reputations by assigning them pseudonyms. The reader will recognize them because the first time they are mentioned their names are printed in italics. Otherwise, the identifications are as they appear in documents relating to the case. There are no fictional or composite characters.

BEYOND
REASON

1

SWEAT ROLLED DOWN DEREK HAYSOM'S FACE. IT STREAMED DOWN HIS forehead, collected in his eyebrows, and dripped from the end of his nose. Every few minutes he stopped digging and wiped his brow with the back of his hand. It did not do much good. Seconds later, the perspiration was flowing as freely as before.

A few miles away, in Lynchburg, the weather bureau's protected thermometer was pushing eighty-four. But it was hotter than that in the shadeless garden where Derek and his wife, Nancy, had been working since early that morning. It was much too hot, Derek thought, for March 30. Without turning his head, he asked his wife, "How are you holding up?"

"As far as I'm concerned, we can call it a day," Nancy replied wearily.

"That's a good idea," Derek agreed, slowly straightening his stiffening back. "I think it's sundowner time."

Normally, it does not get particularly warm in the Blue Ridge Mountain country of central Virginia until much later in the year. But 1985 was an exception; the sun had been beating down relentlessly all week. It was particularly hard on Derek, who was accustomed to cooler climes.

"It's going to be just as miserable tomorrow as it was today," he grumbled as he gathered his tools and began stacking them at the side of the house. Sometimes he was as fussy as an old maid, which is about what one might expect from a man whose favorite hobby, after gardening and card games, was designing circuit boards for ham radios. "But that doesn't matter," he panted. "Palm Sunday or no, we're going to have to be out early again."

Nancy nodded silently in agreement, too exhausted to reply. Turning toward the house, she listlessly peeled off her thick cotton gloves and threw them on the ground.

As he gathered the equipment, Derek tried to make light of his fatigue, joking about his "seventy-two-year-old bones" and how it was getting harder to bounce back than it used to be. Advancing age was not something he accepted readily. To help postpone it, he kept in shape with tennis and sporadic jogs along Holcomb Rock Road, the narrow, twisting thoroughfare that ran in front of their house. But a long day of hard labor in a hot sun was enough to drain even the barrel-chested Derek.

The Haysoms had moved to Boonsboro three years before, in 1982, after Derek retired as director of a venture capital organization in Nova Scotia. An engineer by education and training, Derek had shifted into management at midcareer and worked in executive jobs on three continents. Boonsboro beckoned because it was a suburb of Lynchburg, where Nancy had grown up. They lived in relative tranquility in a modest two-story house that Nancy had named Loose Chippings, after a dwelling in an obscure British novel. In the novel, the house was called that because it served as a sort of way station for eccentrics. Nancy found that particularly applicable to their situation.

Naming houses was one of Nancy's little quirks. Another was collecting small boulders, which she used for building walls around the gardens they always planted whenever they moved to a new residence. Over the twenty-five years she and Derek had been married, wherever they lived, Nancy always built rock walls around their gardens. Now that she was into middle age, the children nagged her about it. Wrestling with outsized rocks, they argued, was not a hobby particularly conducive to her continued good health. To appease them, she promised that the wall at Loose Chippings would be her last.

"I'm for a shower," she said, running her hand through a mop of auburn hair that was just beginning to show streaks of gray.

"You go ahead," Derek muttered. "I'll finish up here and then I'll be right behind you."

"GOD, IT WAS BEASTLY OUT TODAY," NANCY SAID, LOOKING COOL AND comfortable in a royal blue dashiki she had chosen for a quiet evening at home. Her speech was clipped and sprinkled with Briticisms, which was not surprising considering she had spent the last thirty-six years, since she was seventeen, living among British expatriates in southern Africa and Canada. Despite her Virginia roots, there was hardly a hint of a southern drawl.

"Summer will be here before we know it," agreed Derek. "At times like this I wish we were back in Nova Scotia."

While Nancy's accent was affected, Derek's was legitimate. Most Americans hearing him talk, in fact, thought he *was* British. In reality, he was a South African of British descent, a native of Natal Province on the East Coast. During the years he worked and studied in the United Kingdom before returning to southern Africa after World War II, he polished his speech to the point where no one but an Englishman would notice his colonial roots.

Nancy sighed. Finishing her drink, she extended her empty glass. "Would you, please?" she asked Derek.

Derek took it and strode to the liquor cabinet. "The same?" he asked, already pouring a large shot of gin over the melting cubes.

She did not answer. Given a choice, Nancy almost always drank gin: Boodles when it was available, Gordon's when it was not. It was a sign of his exhaustion that Derek did not offer his usual lecture on the evils of her beverage of choice. Almost invariably he chided her about her love for gin. "The juniper extract used to flavor it is a perfect poison," he would say. "It produces the same feelings of aggression as amphetamines." Tonight he said nothing. Silently, he added a splash of soda and a slice of lemon to her glass and put it to the side while he refilled his own. Derek's preference was scotch, which he consumed in the British fashion: straight up—no ice, no water, no soda.

Scooping up the two glasses, he recrossed the room, handing the gin to Nancy and taking a seat across from her. As much out of habit as because of the heat, Derek had closed all the curtains so that they were sitting in the glow of a single lamp. The weak light threw Derek's craggy face into strong shadow, accentuating his nose and jutting chin, making him look positively fierce. The same light made Nancy appear soft and cuddly. At fifty-three she was still a good-looking woman, perky rather than pretty, petite with attractive, even features, a charming upturned nose, flashing brown eyes, and a fine, full figure. Plump some might say. But whenever she and Derek attended social functions, and that was often, Nancy never failed to draw stares from the men in the group. This raised conflicting emotions in Derek—pride mixed with jealousy—and usually sent him off on a tirade about how she undoubtedly would remarry quickly once he was out of the way. She laughed off those exhibitions, but as a woman with an almost insatiable need for attention and affection, she was secretly pleased with her lingering voluptuousness. Tonight, she had not bothered with makeup after her shower, and the lamplight made her appear unnaturally pale. Around her neck was a double-stranded gold choker, her only concession to formality for the evening. It glowed in the darkness.

"One more, please, dear," she said. "A little something while I'm fixing dinner."

While Derek mixed her another drink, Nancy put a pot of rice on to boil and attacked a mound of ground beef, shaping the meat into thick patties, which she slid into the oven.

NANCY RINSED THE PLATES AND STACKED THEM IN THE DISHWASHER, carefully culling the silverware because she always washed that by hand. In the dining room, Derek slumped peacefully at the table, enjoying the after-dinner quiet. It had been a long day, and he was falling victim to too much sun, too much scotch, and too much dinner. He was just about to nod off when there was a loud rapping at the door. He jerked upright. "Bloody hell," he cursed, blinking and squinting at his watch. It was just past eight o'clock.

"Are you expecting anyone?" Nancy called from the kitchen.

"No," Derek grumbled, stretching like an old dog forced to surrender his favorite napping spot.

Nancy poked her head through the serving door cut into the wall between the kitchen and dining room. "I wonder who it might be?"

"I'll soon find out," replied Derek. Carefully placing his palms flat on the sturdy table, he used his powerful arms and shoulders to push himself upright. As he moved his chair back, it scraped across the slate floor like a fingernail being dragged down a chalkboard.

"I'm coming," he yelled, setting off unsteadily across the room. After his shower Derek had changed into a pair of baggy work pants and a short-sleeved shirt, which was marked by dark half-circles under the arms. On his feet was a pair of new Indian-style moccasins, the kind in which the sole wraps around the foot to be joined to the upper by thick laces. As he walked, the leather made soft scuffling sounds on the uneven stone, the kind of soft whisking noise the barber used to make when he stropped his straight razor. The scotch had thrown Derek's internal compass askew, and he walked lopsidedly to the door.

Nancy left the kitchen and crossed the dining room, silently watching her husband's erratic progress toward the door. She was more curious than anxious. Not many people arrived unannounced on a Saturday night, and she was eager to see who it was. Unconsciously, she brought her left hand to her breast and gathered the dashiki more tightly about her. Underneath the robe she wore only a beige bra and matching panties, not exactly the attire she would have preferred for welcoming guests.

Derek paused at the door, fumbling with the light switches. The visitor thumped the knocker again. "All *right*," Derek growled. "Don't be so bloody impatient." With his right hand, he flipped the switch closest to him, turning on a set of floodlights that bathed the top half of the driveway in harsh light. Clearly visible was the Haysoms' creaky ten-year-old tan van, which Nancy had joshingly christened the Bronze Belle. To its right was their 1963 BMW sedan. Immediately in front of the door, side-by-side with the Belle, was a shiny new silver-blue subcompact that Derek had never seen before.

Reaching up, Derek flipped a second switch. It controlled a

single bulb over the doorway, and when it was lit, it threw heavy shadows on whomever happened to be standing on the stoop. Sometimes, depending on how close the caller was to the door, visual identification was tricky. But a nearly full moon eliminated that problem. Although he did not know the car, Derek immediately recognized the caller.

"Oh!" he said in surprise. "What are *you* doing here?"

"I—" the visitor started, but he stopped when Nancy's head appeared over Derek's shoulder, a puzzled look on her face.

"Is Elizabeth with you?" Nancy asked, peering into the darkness to see if she could see her daughter walking up the path.

"No," the visitor replied. "I came alone." He was wearing jeans and, despite the warm night, a gray Members Only windbreaker. It effectively hid the layer of baby fat that still clung to his five-foot-eight frame. He wore thick-lensed spectacles and offered a tentative smile.

"What's this all about?" Derek demanded in the gruff manner he used with those he did not particularly like. "What do you want?"

"Is anything the matter?" Nancy interjected. "Is Elizabeth all right?"

"She's fine," the visitor said, shuffling nervously from foot to foot, bouncing in his white running shoes like a marathoner waiting for the starting gun. "I came because I wanted to talk to you and your husband."

Derek frowned. "Talk to us? What about? Why isn't Lizzie with you?" His tone was more than mildly belligerent.

"It's all right, Derek," Nancy said soothingly. Despite her gin-induced fog she felt the visitor's tension. It was palpable, as obvious as the darkness and the heat. "I'm sure there's a good reason," she whispered, laying a calming hand on her husband's forearm.

Turning to the visitor, she flashed an airline hostess smile. "Please come in," she said, trying to project a warmth she did not feel. "We were just finishing dinner. Come in, and I'll fix you a plate."

2

ANNIE MASSIE SCREECHED TO A HALT IN FRONT OF THE MODEST TWO-STORY house that she knew almost as well as her own.

"Thank God you're here," *Jane Riggs* wailed, wringing her blue-veined hands.

"I came as quickly as I could," Annie said breathlessly, striding briskly across the greening lawn to join Jane and her two companions, *Marilyn Baker* and *Constance Johanson*.

"This is so unlike Derek," Jane sobbed. "So unlike him. I just *know* something dreadful has happened."

Every week, as regularly as a church service, Derek Haysom played bridge with the three women. Unless he was away on a business trip or he and Nancy were off on a trans-Atlantic jaunt, he never failed to miss a bridge date, certainly not when he was the host.

"We pounded on the door," Jane said, nodding at the big brass knocker that glistened flatly in the weak, late-afternoon sunlight. "It didn't do any good."

"When no one answered, we thought they had lost track of time and might still be working in the garden," interjected Constance. "But we checked, and they weren't there either."

"That's when we got really worried," added Jane. "So we went down to Mitchell's Store and called you."

"I'm glad you did," Annie replied apprehensively. "Elizabeth called just before you did," she added cautiously, anxious not to upset the three elderly women any more than they already were. But she could not smother her own strong premonitions of tragedy. "She said she hasn't been able to reach them all week, and she wanted me to come out and check on them."

They all knew it was a rarity for Derek and Nancy not to have some contact every few days with their twenty-year-old daughter, a student at the University of Virginia in Charlottesville, a ninety-minute drive away. She was the focus of their lives.

Annie looked around quickly. The bunged-up van was parked in its customary spot under the trees in the center of the circular drive. A few feet farther along was Derek's BMW. It, too, was in its normal place, backed carefully off the pavement so its nose was pointing down the steep slope. He always backed it into its parking niche: When it was time to go somewhere the impatient Derek didn't like to waste time maneuvering his vehicle.

"We didn't know what else to do," said Jane, her voice cracking. "We didn't want to have to call you, but we didn't know whom else to call."

"Don't worry," Annie said soothingly. "You did the right thing."

Digging into her purse, Annie produced a dull brass key. "Nancy gave this to me a long time ago," she explained. "When they're out of town, I come over to check the house, water the plants, and make sure everything's okay." Fingering it as reverently as a Catholic would a rosary, Annie paused, considering what to do. Nancy was her dearest and closest friend. They had been like sisters since they were children. Over the years she had come to be fond of Derek as well. She liked them both too much, was too respectful of their privacy, to go barging into their home unless she was asked to do so. But this had the earmarks of an emergency. She knew no two people more reliable than Derek and Nancy. If they made an appointment and then failed to keep it, there was a reason. In the pit of her stomach, she was sure the reason would not be pleasant.

Slowly, fearfully, she approached the door. Glancing over her shoulder, Annie read the anxiety on the three women's faces and knew that the same emotion must be painted on hers as well. Gritting her teeth, she turned the key in the lock and started when the tumblers clicked noisily into place. Holding her breath, she twisted the handle and swung the door open a crack. "Hello," she yelled more loudly than she intended. Startled by her own voice, she jumped as though a hairy spider had just crawled across her foot. When there was no reply, she tried again. "Nancy?" she called more softly. "Derek?" Again there was no response. She turned and looked at the three women. No help there. Their faces were as blank as the Virginia sky.

"Should I go in?" she asked them.

Constance shrugged. Jane, the more visibly frightened of the three, bobbed her head nervously. "Something's very wrong," she said in a quavering voice. "I feel it in my bones."

Annie threw back her shoulders and took a deep breath. Reaching out, she gave the door a gentle shove. Silently, it swung open another eight inches. Immediately, she wished she had not touched it. In the gloom, she saw a sight she knew would haunt her dreams for years to come. Just inside the door, barely two strides away, Derek was sprawled on the floor surrounded by a huge dark stain which she knew intuitively was dried blood.

"Oh my God," Annie gasped, covering her mouth.

"What is it?" Jane asked shrilly. "What is it?"

"It's Derek," Annie croaked, swallowing an urge to retch. "He's right there on the floor. He's covered with blood."

"Let me see," Marilyn said, pushing forward. "Maybe we can help."

"No!" Annie replied, quickly closing the door. "There's nothing we can do now. There's no way he could be alive. Not with that much blood. Take my word for it," she said, blocking the entrance. "You don't want to see."

"What about Nancy?" Constance asked, smothering her rising panic. "Where is she? Did you see her?"

"No," Annie said, struggling to control her own horror. "I didn't see her. I don't *want* to see her."

"Maybe she got away," Jane suggested.

"Then we would have heard from her," Annie replied. "She would have called the police."

"Maybe she's lying in there hurt," Constance added.

Annie considered that. "No," she said slowly. "I don't think so."

"Oh my God, oh my God," Jane mumbled, breaking into tears.

Annie stared at her. As a physician's wife she knew how contagious hysteria was. If she did nothing, she would very quickly have three blubbering women on her hands.

"We can't go inside," Annie said firmly. "I've read enough books to know we shouldn't go into a house in which a crime has been committed. From the quick look I got, I could tell Derek has been dead a long time. Going into the house isn't going to help him or Nancy. What we need to do is call the police."

With a decisive twist, she relocked the door, removed the key, and returned it to her purse. Then she bundled the three panic-stricken women into her car. She drove down the drive and turned right in the direction of the main highway and Mitchell's Store, the same roadside market where Jane had used the telephone to call her. They were there in three minutes.

While the women waited in the car, Annie punched at the telephone's metal keyboard, willing her hand to stop shaking long enough for her to push the right buttons. When Dr. William McK. Massie came on the line Annie explained to him in a halting voice what she had seen. He told her to stay calm; he would call the police.

LYNCHBURG IS IN CAMPBELL COUNTY, BUT THE HAYSOMS LIVED IN Bedford County, a distinction Massie did not appreciate until he was told by the LPD dispatcher that he had to contact the Bedford County Sheriff's Office. The city of Bedford, where the sheriff's office is headquartered, is about thirty miles west of Lynchburg, almost exactly halfway between that city and Roanoke. But the Bedford County line runs right up to the city limits of both places. Boonsboro is only a mile and a half outside the Lynchburg city limits and barely over the county line.

As Roanoke and Lynchburg expanded, Bedford County Sheriff C. H. Wells and his troopers were faced with more work. To help facilitate the reporting of crime on the county's borders,

Wells maintained local numbers in Lynchburg, Roanoke, and Big Island, which is on the northern border with Amherst County. Dispatchers in all the counties were scrupulous about determining who had jurisdiction.

When Massie got the Bedford dispatcher on the line, he succinctly explained his reason for calling.

"Tell your wife to go back to the house," the dispatcher said. "I'll have someone there as soon as I can."

Within minutes Deputy Joe Stanley roared up the driveway. It was 4:15.

"Tell me what you saw," Stanley ordered Annie.

As soon as she finished, Stanley took the key from her trembling hand, unlocked the door, and looked inside.

"Aw, Jesus," he said. The scene was exactly as Annie had described it: Derek was stretched out grotesquely on the floor, and he had obviously been dead for several days.

As Annie had done, Stanley backed out of the house, closed, and locked the door. Following department procedure, he radioed Bedford and told them to stand by for a telephone call, mindful that ears other than those of Bedford deputies often monitored the law enforcement frequencies. From a pay phone he confirmed what Annie had said, adding that the second person believed to be in the house was not visible from the living room and that he needed another deputy immediately.

By the time Stanley got back to the house, Deputy George Thomas was there and more help was on the way. The dispatcher had put out a call for all available investigators to report to the house on Holcomb Rock Road. The LPD and sheriff's offices in neighboring counties also were alerted.

Working as a team, Stanley and Thomas went back inside. Barely glancing at Derek, they moved to the right, across the living room and into the master bedroom. Despite bloody tracks across the floor, there was no other body there.

Retracing their path, they crossed the living room again, stepped around Derek's supine form, and went into the dining room. It looked as though someone had poured a bucket of brown paint on the slate floor, then splattered some of it around the room before swishing the remainder about with a mop. But Nancy was nowhere to be seen.

"God, would you look at that," Stanley mumbled. "You ever seen anything like that before?"

"Not in my worst nightmares," Thomas stuttered.

For a considerable time they stood there, horror-stricken, staring at the evidence of more carnage than either of them could have imagined was possible.

After what seemed a long time, Stanley shook his head and found his voice. "Where's the woman?" he said. "We still haven't found the woman."

"Oh, hell, that's right," Thomas said. "Where in hell could she be?"

Without answering, Stanley nodded slowly at the open door across the room, the passage that led to the kitchen.

Slowly, they crossed the blood-splashed dining room.

"You think she's there?" Thomas asked.

"Has to be," Stanley replied.

Cautiously, afraid of what they were going to find, they peeked into the room. Curled on the linoleum floor, in the center of a large brown stain, was Nancy Haysom. Except for the dried blood, she looked as though she may have just stretched out for a nap. She was resting on her left side, her hands tucked under her body and her legs bent slightly at the knee. Her hair fanned out gently from her face. On her feet was a pair of tan walking shoes so new that the manufacturer's logo was still clearly visible on the soles. Bending over the body, Stanley could see part of a gold necklace. Most of it, however, disappeared into a horrendous slash across her throat, a wound so deep and so large she was all but decapitated. The deputy didn't have to feel for a pulse; he knew that Nancy was far beyond help.

Retreating through the dining and living rooms, Stanley and Thomas went out the front door and carefully closed it behind them. Annie Massie and the three bridge players were waiting for them, tense and white-faced.

"Did you find Nancy?" Annie asked anxiously.

"Yeah," Stanley said, breathing deeply. "I'm afraid she's dead, too."

SERGEANT GEOFFREY BROWN, LPD'S YOUTHFUL LAB TECHNICIAN, HAD gone home that afternoon with grand plans to celebrate the early spring. He was in the backyard, grilling steaks on the barbecue, when the telephone rang. A few minutes later he came back and told his wife he was going to have to leave.

"Not again!"

"A double murder," he explained quickly, "over in Boonsboro."

"But that's Bedford County," she pointed out.

"I know," he said, "but they're activating the Regional Homicide Squad. That means me."

"What time will you be back?" she asked in resignation.

"I don't know," he said, snatching his car keys off the kitchen table, "but don't wait up."

WHEN HE GOT TO THE HOUSE, BROWN'S FIRST IMPRESSION WAS THAT HE was wading into a sea of gore. Looking around quickly, he estimated that 90 percent of the floor surface in the living room, dining room, and kitchen was smeared with blood. His second impression, once he began examining the bodies, was how terribly they had been butchered.

Moving first to Derek because his body was the closest, Brown squatted and examined the scene. Derek, he noted, was lying on his back, turned slightly to his left, with his head resting against the wooden fireplace jamb. His right hand was palm down with the right index finger extended, as though he were pointing to an object on the bloodstained floor. His left hand was palm up, exposing a deep gash that ran horizontally, a cruelly ironic, cavernous lifeline.

There was no question he had died brutally. Someone with a large, very sharp knife had slashed and stabbed Derek Haysom unmercifully. There were two large, roughly parallel horizontal gashes on the left side of Derek's face. One began near his cheekbone below the corner of his eye and angled upward and across, cutting through his ear. The other ran from the corner of his prominent chin straight across to the back of his neck. There was another slash on his right cheek that began on his chin and went upward to just below the ear. Brown figured these cuts were made by the killer in efforts to slice Derek's throat. Obviously they were preliminary attempts because the killer soon found his mark. A huge, gaping wound ran right around Dereck's neck.

A glance at Derek's hands demonstrated how desperately he had fought for his life, actually grabbing the blade in attempts to wrest the knife away from the assailant. He had six cuts on his hands, including the one that traversed his entire left palm. One of his knuckles was abraded, Brown noticed, indicating that Derek may have slugged the killer at least once.

An autopsy report would later confirm that the killer's slash had severed every major blood-carrying organ in Derek's neck. If he were alive when the wound was administered, he would have bled to death in a matter of seconds. Whether he was indeed alive at that time no one knew, because that was not the only potentially fatal injury inflicted upon the retired executive. He also was stabbed through the heart.

Besides the cuts on his cheeks, jaw, and hands, there were eleven slash wounds on Derek's chest and fourteen on his back. All told, Derek was cut, sliced, or stabbed some three dozen times.

Nancy was not sliced as terribly as her husband, but there was no question that the attacker meant to kill her. In addition to the grotesque slash across her throat, there were two stab wounds to her torso which could have killed her, one to her heart and one to her side, which penetrated the peritoneal cavity. She would not have died as quickly from those wounds as she would from the slit throat, which virtually guaranteed that she had dropped where she was cut. Besides those wounds, Nancy had a cut on her jaw, a superficial wound on her left breast, and an incised wound on her left elbow, apparently inflicted when she raised her arm to try to ward off a knife thrust.

By the time Brown had finished his cursory examinations, the first wave of what soon seemed like an army of police had begun to arrive. A deputy was posted at the door to keep out everyone who did not absolutely need to be inside until the lab technicians had a chance to collect their evidence.

Since the murder occurred in Bedford County, Sheriff C. H.

Wells would be the man responsible for the investigation. Standing in the blood-soaked dining room he quickly surveyed the scene. Three chairs were pushed back from the table, which still held a dirty plate, a bowl, a wine glass, and a neatly folded paper napkin soaked in blood. On one end of the table was a stack of books, as though someone had been using it as a desk. On the tasteful gray upholstery covering the seat of one of the chairs was a large bloody palm print looking for all the world like the cover illustration on a recent mystery novel entitled *Thinner*.

Almost immediately, Wells came to two conclusions. The first was that three people had been seated at the table. Since two of them were dead, that meant that either the third party, the guest, probably was the killer or there was another body somewhere that had not been found. His second conclusion was that the attack took place in the dining room. Nancy apparently was gravely injured early on and staggered into the kitchen to die. But the killer and Derek fought around the dining room and living room until Derek was overcome by his injuries. Both bodies apparently were left where they fell.

When no third body was found, Wells' first observation was substantiated: Nancy and Derek knew their killer at least well enough to invite him into the house and serve him a meal. From the first, Wells was thinking "him." A "her," he reasoned, would not be strong enough to fight with Derek as viciously as the killer had done, and a "her" was not as likely to slice up the bodies as badly as they had been. Nor would a "her" be likely to perform what looked to be a grisly *coup de grâce*. The chances were good that the Haysoms' throats were slit either after they were dead or when they were very close to dying. It would take an unusual woman to be able to do that.

THROUGHOUT THE NIGHT LAW ENFORCEMENT OFFICERS TOILED AT THE CRIME scene. While Brown and other technicians worked on the bodies, Wells' investigators spread out in the neighborhood to try to find some clue that might lead them to the killer or killers. Who had been friendly with the Haysoms? Who had seen them and when? Had anyone seen a stranger or strangers lurking around the neighborhood? There were hundreds of questions and very few answers. But there was one thing no one connected with the investigation ever forgot: the viciousness of the crimes. Whoever murdered Derek and Nancy Haysom must have deeply hated them.

The crime was the worst anyone could remember in normally sleepy central Virginia. One LPD officer, a veteran of twenty-five years on the force, was so disturbed by the ferocity of the crime that he did something he had never done before. As soon as he got off duty he went home and put a pistol under his pillow. It stayed there for many months.

$\boxed{3}$

SHERIFF WELLS WAS NO NEOPHYTE. HALF HARD-NOSED COUNTRY COP AND half accomplished politician—a delicate, sometimes volatile mix required to be a successful rural sheriff—Wells knew a problem when he saw one. He had no sooner screeched to a halt in front of the Haysoms' door and dashed inside the house than he knew he had trouble. It was bad enough that two apparently well-to-do members of the community had been attacked in their home and sliced almost beyond recognition. Even worse, though, was the immediate knowledge that the crimes were not going to be easily solved. As he poked gently around here and there, careful not to touch anything the lab technicians had not already examined, Wells grew increasingly dispirited about the prospect of a quick resolution. The killer—Wells had seen nothing to change his opinion that the murders were committed by one person—had covered his tracks well, leaving little if anything behind to put police on his trail. Evidence would have to be developed the hard way: by talking to people in ever widening circles until sooner or later investigators got enough clues to put together a concept of why and how the crime occurred and, most importantly, who might have done it. But that took manpower, and manpower was the rarest of commodities in the Bedford County sheriff's department, an agency that was geared more to the mundane details of rural law enforcement than to spectacular murders.

Although Bedford County, like every other county in the

United States, has its share of killings, these usually involve no great mystery. A husband kills his wife because he thinks she is playing around. A wife gets tired of her husband beating her up and puts a bullet in his head. Two drunks get in a fight and try to carve each other up. In most cases the Bedford sheriff's office has the murderer in jail in remarkably quick time. But the Haysom case was different. While suspects may be predictable in more run-of-the-mill homicides, investigators in this case had not the slightest clue about who the murderer was or why the Haysoms were killed.

There was another issue to consider as well: public opinion. Wells's political antennae vibrated like a tuning fork when he thought of the effect the murders were going to have on the residents of Bedford and Campbell counties. The Lynchburg policeman who rushed home to put a pistol under his pillow was not the only one feeling jittery. The fact that the arrest of a suspect or suspects did not appear imminent, not to mention that no one was even sure about motive, caused considerable unease in Lynchburg and Bedford. Within hours of news reports about the discovery of the bodies, rumors began building that the killings were the work of an East Coast Manson, that the Haysoms perhaps had been only the first victims of a roving band of mad thrill-seekers who could strike again at any time. Almost immediately, gun and ammunition sales skyrocketed. Strangers were examined with blatant suspicion.

Sheriff Wells had anticipated this. Moments after he arrived at the Haysom residence, he decided to activate the Regional Homicide Squad.

Several years previously, law enforcement officials from six central Virginia jurisdictions, including Bedford and Campbell counties, had agreed to form a special team that could be activated in those rare instances when the investigatory job was too big for any one of the departments to handle on its own. The Haysoms had been killed in Bedford County, but that was not to say that another murder was not already being committed somewhere else in the region. By immediately summoning the team into action, Wells was not only hoping to increase the chances for a quick arrest, but covering political bases with his constituents as well. Central Virginians would sleep better if they thought a small army of investigators was combing the countryside.

Actually, early on the public believed that the investigation was being performed more efficiently than it really was. Although cops had gone banging on doors virtually as soon as the bodies were discovered, the immediate results were depressing: Nancy and Derek were not high-profile people in the neighborhood. Derek had a reputation along Holcomb Rock Road as a gruff, sometimes tactless man who was unnecessarily abrupt much of the time. Nancy was regarded by her neighbors as snooty and pretentious and a tad quirky. But neither of them was well known along Holcomb Rock Road; most of their friends lived in Lynchburg, a twenty-minute drive away.

As the investigation broadened, police learned that among those who knew the Haysoms few of them, with the exception of Annie Massie and her husband, knew them well. Much of the investigators' early information about Derek and Nancy came from Annie Massie. But once Nancy's and Derek's offspring began arriving, profiles of the victims began to be fleshed out.

As soon as he began reading the reports, Wells knew why his men had so much trouble filling in the background: The Haysoms' lives had been far from conventional.

NANCY WAS BORN IN 1932 IN A LIZARD DUNG–SIZED SPOT ON THE MAP OF Arizona called Jerome. Her father was Platt Carico Benedict, an itchy-footed geologist who was just embarking on his life's career of following the gold trail around the world. Her mother was Nancy Langhorne Gibbes, scion of a distinguished Virginia family.

Nancy's mother was not particularly happy to be in Jerome. For one thing, she had been reared along the verdant Blue Ridge, where her daughter would settle almost exactly a half century later. More than a couple of thousand miles separated the tree-covered Appalachians and the barren Gila Mountains, where Jerome, a rough and raw mining town, lay scratched into a rocky landscape seventy-five miles north of Phoenix. More people lived on her street in Lynchburg than in the entire community of

Jerome. But Jerome had gold, at least for a while. It also had copper, silver, lead, zinc, and gypsum, all of which were becoming more vital to a booming prewar society. It was her husband's job to help find them.

Life in Jerome did not offer many comforts, especially not to a woman whose illustrious family tree went back five generations in Virginia. Nancy Haysom's maternal grandmother, Hallie Hutter Gibbes, was a first cousin to Nancy Witcher Langhorne. Students of history and politics, notably the English variety, know that Nancy Langhorne gave up Danville, Virginia, for England and the bed of Waldorf Astor, great-great-grandson of John Jacob Astor. When her husband ascended to the viscountcy after his father's death in 1919, Nancy Astor, then Lady Astor, successfully ran for his seat in the House of Commons. She was the first woman elected to such a post, which she held until she retired in 1945. During her twenty-six years in public office she became famous throughout the Empire for her intellect and her wit as well as for her efforts for women's rights and, ironically, considering Nancy Haysom's predilection for gin, temperance. Hallie Gibbes gave her daughter the middle name of Langhorne in honor of her cousin. It seemed natural, then, for Nancy Langhorne Gibbes Benedict to name *her* daughter after their famous relative as well. So Nancy Haysom started out in life as Nancy Astor Benedict, goddaughter and blood relative of the renowned Lady Astor.

Much to Nancy Benedict's relief, the family stay in Jerome was relatively brief. When the minerals started to play out five years later, her gold-fevered husband followed the scent to the Yukon. Cultural and physical isolation were marginally acceptable, she reckoned, but winter-long darkness and bitter cold were not. When Platt Benedict headed off for Alaska, Nancy Benedict packed up her children and went back to Lynchburg. In addition to her daughter, who by then had been dubbed Nancita (Little Nancy in Spanish; 'Cita for short), there were two other Benedict offspring, both boys. Risque was two years older, and there was another son two years younger, Louis. Curiously, the Benedict marriage remained intact; it was just that Platt didn't come home every night like most husbands and fathers.

Once back in Virginia, there was little remarkable about

Nancy's childhood except that her father was seldom home. She did what all upper-middle-class southern girls of the time did, except more so since her family tree included contemporary British royalty. She took ballet lessons from Floyd Ward. She shone at Garland-Rodes Elementary School, where she exhibited an early flair for the dramatic by winning the lead in every school play that was produced. Later, she went to E. C. Glass High School, where she played bass in the orchestra. She was also an accomplished pianist and violinist. For two years running, 1945 and 1946, she was named to the all-state orchestra.

In 1949, when she was seventeen and barely out of Glass High, her father summoned the family, saying it was time they all lived together again. She, her mother, and Louis dutifully sped off to Johannesburg where Platt was working for another mining company, still searching for gold. Her older brother, Risque, was entrenched at the Massachusetts Institute of Technology so he did not make the move.

By all accounts, Nancy adapted superbly from the first. Never lacking for spunk, the five-foot-three teenager confronted an intruder in their home one night and routed him by swinging at him with a silver candlestick. A strikingly pretty young woman with flashing green eyes, high cheek bones, a graceful nose, and a warm, welcoming smile, it was natural that she attracted a crowd of suitors. It was a rare treat for the dour Afrikaners and reserved British bachelors to come across such a spirited young woman.

But she was not impervious to the charms of her exotic beaus. When she was still in her teens, she fell in love with a charming young Englishman named *Ian Hall.* Unhappily for her, her parents disapproved of him. Indeed, they felt so strongly that when Nancy, barely twenty, told them of her plans to marry Ian at his family's estate near Stratford-on-Avon, they vowed they would not attend. It was some consolation to Nancy that her godmother, Lady Astor, was there.

A year after the ceremony, Nancy and Ian had a son they named Howard Henry. It was about this time, too, that Nancy began to regret that she had ignored her parents' warnings about her husband. Soon after a second son, Richard Platt (named for her father), was born, she divorced Ian and announced her determination to rear the two boys on her own, which she did for the next half dozen years, making a handsome living by investing shrewdly in South African gold stocks. She was following her own gold trail.

Then she met Derek Haysom.

At five-feet-eight and some one hundred and fifty pounds, Derek William Reginald Haysom was not physically imposing. But he exhibited a commanding, dynamic presence that gave him an air of authority. Nancy found him handsome, too, in a rugged sort of way. He had a hooked nose, steely gray eyes, a trim waist, and a powerful upper torso, which he maintained through tennis and squash. He had about him an aura of vitality and vision that was absent in many younger men. But what really appealed to Nancy about Derek Haysom was his stability.

Derek's grandfather, William Pearce, had been virtually penniless when he emigrated to South Africa from Britain in the nineteenth century. Saving his money, he invested in land on which he planted sugarcane. Over the years his holdings grew, and his plantation, Ilove Estates, prospered. He became very wealthy.

Derek, who was brought up in his grandfather's house, very early showed aptitude both as a student and an athlete. In 1917, when he was only four, his parents enrolled him in a local school. His bent was science. When he finished secondary school, he attended Howard College in Durban to study mechanical engineering. After he earned his degree, he left almost immediately for England, as was customary with young South Africans of privilege. He went to work for a large firm in Manchester and attended classes in the evenings studying electrical engineering. Soon he had earned a second degree. Before he could put his training into practice, World War II broke out, and Derek joined the British Army. His specialty was intelligence work. He was shipped off to the Middle East, where he worked with a group called the Gas Gang, which managed to take over a gasoline refinery in a major coup that deprived the Axis Powers of the refinery's assets. At some point Derek saw combat. He came back home both with scars and medals.

When Nancy met him, she was twenty-seven and still bitter about her failed marriage to Hall. He was forty-six. Nancy's first husband had been charming and handsome, but he had also been immature, cruel, and irresponsible. Derek, in contrast, was everything that Ian had not been: He was kind and conscientious, solid and dependable. It didn't matter to Nancy that he was almost old enough to be her father. That merely added to his allure. After Ian, she appreciated maturity in a mate.

The details of Derek's first marriage are a closely held family secret. All that is known to outsiders is that his first wife was a New Zealander and that she returned to her native country soon after they were divorced, leaving the children in Derek's custody. Whether Derek was still married when he met Nancy is unclear. In any case, soon after he was divorced, he married her, and she followed him to Salisbury, Rhodesia, where he was managing a steel mill. That was 1960. At the time, they had between them five children ranging in age from six to twelve. The oldest was Veryan Neil Graham Haysom, Derek's older son. He was an intense, solemn child, who grew up to be a lawyer. His brother, Julian Christopher Robert Haysom, who was eight, would be an engineer like his father. Derek's daughter, Fiona Ann Valerie Haysom, was six, the same age as Nancy's younger son, Richard. Richard became an architect and his brother, Howard, who was a year older, became a surgeon. Of the five, only Howard would come to the United States to live.

Derek and Nancy had only one child together, a girl named Elizabeth Roxanne, who was born in 1964. A bubbly, blue-eyed, brown-haired girl, Elizabeth was a delightful child with a quiet, even disposition and a winning smile. More so than most children, Elizabeth seemed from an early age to crave affection. When she was old enough to write, she frequently penned sentimental notes to her parents and shyly slipped them under their bedroom door, reaffirming with regularity her need to be noticed. For the most part, Nancy and Derek were elated to comply. Since she was a decade younger than her half-siblings, Elizabeth was reared virtually as an only child, from the beginning receiving almost the full force of her parents' attention.

For several years the Haysoms led a placid, mainly uneventful life in Rhodesia, which was still a British colony, albeit a restless one. A wave of nationalism was sweeping Africa at that time, and Rhodesia's blacks, who outnumbered whites by some twenty to one, were demanding independence. The British government seemed inclined to go along.

Determined to halt the stampede to black freedom, an obstinate farmer-turned-politician named Ian Smith convinced likeminded whites to revolt from England and beat the blacks to the punch. In 1965 the Smith-led party, the Rhodesian Front, declared its independence, an action that was widely reviled as a blatant attempt to continue suppressing blacks.

Although Derek was working for a government-owned industry, he had little sympathy with Smith's views about white dominance. In direct opposition to government policy, Derek continued to follow his practice of promoting blacks in his mill, occasionally advancing them ahead of whites. It didn't take long for this to come to the attention of Smith, who had since been named prime minister in the new government. Despite several warnings, Derek continued to follow his managerial instincts more than his government's directives. As a result of this stubborn defiance he was placed under house arrest.

Clearly, Derek no longer had a future in Rhodesia. It would be another decade and then some before the country's black nationalists would militarily defeat Smith's government and form a new government under Robert Mugabe. By the time blacks came into power and renamed the country Zimbabwe, Derek and Nancy would be solidly entrenched in eastern Canada, many thousands of miles away.

But in 1965, with a wife and six children to worry about, Derek's main interest became escaping from Smith and his cohorts. He solved the problem very expeditiously: He simply left. One day he was in Rhodesia, the next he was in Switzerland. Very quickly he landed a job as a director with a major chocolate manufacturing firm and moved to Luxembourg, then sent for Nancy and the children.

Derek may never have looked at the Luxembourg job as a career. In any case, he was there only briefly. In less than four years, he took a job with a New York steel manufacturer. Before Nancy and the children could move, he changed jobs again. En route to Calgary on business for the U.S. manufacturer, Derek stopped in Halifax to see how things were going at a steel mill that had recently been purchased by the government. When he was offered a job as an executive at the mill, he leaped at it. Within weeks Nancy and the children joined him there. That was 1968.

Sixteen years down the road, Nancy, Derek, and Elizabeth were in Virginia. Veryan and Julian were in Nova Scotia, Richard in Calgary, Fiona in Vancouver, and Howard in Houston. Nancy and Derek had come to Boonsboro because it was a comfortable place to live, and it was close to Lynchburg. Nancy felt a compulsion to return to the place where she had spent her childhood. Also, they wanted to establish residence in Virginia so their daughter, Elizabeth, could attend the University of Virginia, one of the more highly regarded state universities in the country.

4

DESPITE THE DETAIL INVESTIGATORS WERE ACCUMULATING ABOUT THE LIVES of Derek and Nancy Haysom, there was little to go on. For more than a week, Sergeant Brown and the other lab techs went through the house on hands and knees, using magnifying glasses, chemicals, powders, and the latest in electronic equipment, including a laser imported from Florida that was supposed to be able to detect fingerprints that wouldn't show up with a normal dusting. In the end, they tagged and carried away some two hundred items ranging from the kitchen linoleum and sections of the wooden floor which contained bloody footprints to a wooden mousetrap and a bloodstained gray shoe. Although those items might prove extremely valuable later in proving a particular person was there (or, almost as important, in proving someone was *not* there), they did not give investigators any leads on where to begin looking.

The most promising items were bloody shoe and foot impressions and the bloody hand print that decorated the seat of a dining room chair.

One of the foot impressions was made by the left foot of a person wearing only a sock. It was nine and a half inches long, which meant it came from either a woman who normally wore a size 6 ½ or 7 ½ shoe or a man who wore size 5 or 6. The good news was that the impression was sufficiently clear to be useful later if they could find a suspect to match it with.

There also was a full-length shoe impression ten and a half to eleven inches long. Because it came from a shoe with a wavy sole and a *U*- or *L*-shaped heel plate, investigators deduced it was from a sports shoe.

Other items included:

—A soft drink can with fingerprints on it;

—Several cigarette butts;

—A knife that was found in a drawer in the dining room table, but had no blood on it;

—One hair that did not come from either Nancy or Derek. It was found in the bedroom. In the investigator's report it was identified as "a caucasian head hair approximately one and a half inches in length from root to diagonally cut end."

Blood spots were as common as water drops after a summer shower. All told, blood stains were found in fifty-two places. They included types A, B, O, and AB. The most plentiful were A and AB. Derek was a type A; Nancy, an AB. Two small type O bloodstains, together smaller than a dime, were found in the bedroom. Considerably more type O was found on and near the front door. A single type B stain was found on a washcloth from the kitchen, but investigators felt that did not necessarily mean that a fourth person had been in the house. Because of the amount of time the stains had been exposed to the elements, it is possible that a type AB spot had deteriorated to the point where it was typed as a B.

Evidence-gathering was basically a process of elimination. Evidence that could not be traced to either Nancy or Derek would have to be assumed to have been left there by the killer. It turned out that the footprints and the blood spots were in that latter category; the soft-drink can was not. Fingerprints showed it was left at the scene by one of the police officers.

Tests on saliva traces on the cigarette butts showed they came either from Derek or from someone with the same type blood.

There were bloodstains on the handle of a pair of fireplace tongs near Derek's body, but they were type A, the same as

Derek's, indicating he may have tried to grab the tongs to use them as a weapon against his attacker.

The blood in the dramatic print on the chair seat was Derek's type.

There was no seminal fluid on swabs taken from Nancy's mouth, rectum, or vagina, indicating she was not sexually attacked. That helped because investigators could eliminate rape as a possible motive.

All told, however, the amount of evidence was disappointing.

THERE WERE OTHER DISAPPOINTMENTS AS WELL. THE LASER SYSTEM FOR detecting fingerprints did not work, at least not in this case. There was another system, too, which also proved useless.

It had been determined in other cases that chemicals in Superglue fumes would adhere to fingerprints and make them visible to the naked eye. Brown and other technicians worked for a day and a half sealing the house, caulking every window and door, plugging the fireplaces, every place where a crack might allow air in or out. Then they pumped in Superglue fumes and waited for the chemicals to go to work. After giving the fumes the required amount of time, plus a little extra for luck, they rushed in, hoping to find fingerprints they had not been able to detect previously. The procedure failed.

However, one system did work: a tried and usually successful method of doctoring a surface with a chemical that would make blood stains fluorescent. Even if the stains were no longer visible to the naked eye, they could be made visible under the right lighting conditions.

The first place Brown used the chemical, called luminol, was in the house. Painstakingly, he loaded his cameras with high-speed color film and put them on tripods along the killer's likely path. Then he set the shutters for thirty-second time exposures. Lastly, he squatted and duck-walked across the floor, spraying the tan-colored luminol liquid from a plastic bottle. As the mist settled, it reacted with the chemical traces from the blood. The killer's footprints began to glow with a spooky blue-green light. Quickly, Brown tripped the shutters since the luminescence lasts only about fifteen seconds. The result was a series of photographs showing a wavy set of ghostly footprints traveling from the living room to the bedroom and into the bathroom. That confirmed what detectives had suspected: The killer had taken a shower to try to wash off the blood that must have coated him like a second skin.

It was a little more difficult to use the chemical outside because stray light could ruin the whole experiment. Brown waited for a dark night and then prepared to spray the chemical around the doorway, the yard, and the driveway. Looking up, he noticed that the house lights were still on; they would have to be extinguished for the test to work properly.

"Would you mind going in and turning off the lights?" Brown mentioned nonchalantly to one of the investigators standing nearby.

"Not me," the man said. "I'm not going in that house alone in the dark."

Surprised, Brown turned to another detective.

"Not me, either," he said. "Why don't you go?"

"I don't want to go either," Brown admitted.

"Let's both go," the second officer suggested. "I'll carry the flashlight."

"Okay," Brown agreed.

Once the lights were out and the luminol had been sprayed, the killer's path showed up just as clearly outside as it had inside, even though it had rained several times since the murders. Footprints led from the door to the driveway and across it to two large trees. They circled the trees several times, as though the person who left the prints had sought to hide behind the trunks.

"Maybe he came out and was getting in his car and something spooked him," one of the investigators suggested.

"Could be," agreed Brown.

Interestingly, there was a second set of prints. Instead of going off to the right, the second set led to the left out into the yard. They went out about eight feet and stopped, then went back. Where they stopped there was an area several feet square that was covered by what Brown described as "swishing marks." The killer walked out into the grass, vigorously rubbed his bloody feet back and forth as though he were using a doormat, then went back to the porch.

The size and shape of the prints indicated both sets were made by the same person. To investigators, this meant one thing: The killer had been in the house twice. They theorized he attacked the Haysoms, left, and then came back. They speculated the second trip was to make sure they were dead by slitting their throats.

THOSE WERE NOT THE ONLY SURPRISES THEY HAD, THOUGH. WHEN THE LAB reports came back, they showed that both Derek and Nancy had an identical amount of alcohol in their blood: .22 percent. In most states, including Virginia, a level of .1 percent is sufficient to certify that the person is too drunk to drive. Generally speaking, a level of .3 is considered lethal, although people have different tolerance levels. A lot depends on a person's weight, height, and physical condition. Still, anyone with as much booze in his or her system as Derek and Nancy had had would be very drunk indeed.

Another surprise came when an investigator was searching Nancy's "studio," the small room above the master bedroom she used as a retreat to work on her art. There was an easel in the room and several watercolors, including one of three nude women. That was hardly surprising, but what they found in a drawer in a small chest in the room was. Carefully tucked away were five snapshots of a nude young woman. The photos were all in profile so genital areas were not exposed. But the poses were somewhat strange. In one, the woman was kneeling by a bed studying an open illustrated volume of Shakespeare. Wondering who this could be, the investigator slipped the photos into his evidence bag.

Still another surprise was not even a surprise at first. There were so many wounds on Derek's body that no one initially studied them carefully to see if they might form a pattern or design. At a glance they all appeared to be random. But when they began looking at them more closely, however, they noticed a peculiar cut on Derek's chin. It was two diagonal slices joined at one end to form a *V*. It meant nothing at the time, but it soon would figure prominently in a series of developments that would dump upon police like a cloudburst.

While the technicians were busy inside the house, investigators were working even more frantically outside. The big job was finding people who knew the Haysoms well enough to be helpful in establishing habits and routines, or in locating someone who may have seen something that could lead them to the killer. Neighbors had not been able to provide much useful information. Neither had the friends of the Haysoms who had been interviewed immediately after the bodies were discovered.

Within twenty-four hours after the first call the investigation settled into a pattern. A twelve-person team with representatives from Bedford and neighboring counties was responsible for directing the course of the investigation. They did the interviews and the legwork, tracking down leads and trying to find potential witnesses or anyone who could give them information that might help them find the killer. Their first command post was in the Boonsboro Ruritan Club, but it moved almost immediately from there to the Boonsboro Elementary School, which fortuitously was empty for the Easter holidays.

Task-force members hardly had time to get the door open for business when they got their first customer: a frizzy-haired woman in white blouse and tan walking shorts who pedaled up to the front door of the school on a new blue bicycle with big, black tires. "Hello," she said, pushing her vehicle into the lobby and knocking down the kickstand. "My name is *Margaret Louise Simmons.* I think you want to talk to me."

She did most of the talking, though—virtually nonstop for as long as anyone could stand to listen. She said she was the ex-fiancée of Julian Haysom, Derek's younger son. They had met, Margaret Louise said, the year before, when Julian, an engineer like his father, found himself between jobs and decided to come to Virginia from Nova Scotia to spend some time while he looked for work. Margaret Louise was a cousin of Nancy's, but that didn't preclude a relationship with Julian since he was Derek's son, not Nancy's. They had become engaged while Julian was still in Virginia, and the relationship continued for a time after he returned to Canada. But distance and changing circumstances apparently created too much strain. Soon after Julian returned to Nova Scotia, Margaret Louise underwent a strong resurgence of her Christian faith, and it seemed to overwhelm Julian. The summer before the murder, without telling Margaret Louise in advance, Julian married a Canadian.

From an investigator's point of view, that was pretty strong grounds for resentment. Whether the resentment was strong enough to lead to murder was something they were going to have to find out. There was one other reason for the investigators' interest in Margaret Louise. A few years before she had begun experiencing increasingly severe psychological problems, and her parents had committed her. After months of treatment she was proclaimed well enough to function in society and was released. She functioned, but no one was sure just how well.

One of those assigned to interview her was Sergeant Carroll Baker, a jolly gray-haired man whose outgoing manner seemed to contradict the fact that he was a high-ranking member of the LPD SWAT team. Soon after Margaret Louise cycled into his life, Baker found himself closeted with her in a classroom with orders to find out if she had information valuable to the investigation.

She told him what Julian looked like. She told him about Canada. She told him what she had for dinner the previous Sunday. She told him about a movie she had seen. She did *not* tell him anything that was remotely helpful in finding Derek's and Nancy's killer.

Baker coughed into his fist and rolled his eyes. Every time she wound down enough to let him get a word in, he would ask a question directly relating to the Haysoms or their murders. She would go off on a tangent about something else. Finally, he quit trying to lead the conversation and let her roam wherever she wanted to go. As she rambled, Baker looked deep into her eyes. This is like looking into a cave, he thought. There's no light there. Nobody's home.

5

A FEW DAYS AFTER THE BODIES WERE DISCOVERED, SERGEANT BROWN TOOK some of the evidence to Richmond to be analyzed by the state crime lab. While he was there, on a hunch he asked two Richmond detectives who he knew specialized in cult activities to take a look at the crime scene photos.

"What are we supposed to be looking for?" one of them asked.

"Just take a look and tell me what you think," Brown replied, handing them a thick stack of color prints.

Brown settled into a chair and watched silently as the two men spread the photos out on a desk and started picking through them. Their indifference changed to interest, which quickly changed to excitement.

"Hey, look at this," one said eagerly, pointing to a picture of a blood-stained section of floor.

"Damn."

"And this!"

"And look here!"

"Here, too. Look at these chairs."

One of them motioned to Brown. "Which way is north in this picture?" It was a photo of Derek's body taken from the doorway going into the house.

Brown told him and the man shuffled the print so the body was oriented on a north-south axis.

"And which way in this picture?" It was a picture of Nancy's body.

Again Brown showed him.

"Ummmm," he grunted, like a gypsy reading tea leaves.

"What do you think?" Brown finally asked. "Is there anything there that indicates cult activity?"

"Oh hell, yeah," one of them said. "Come here, let me show you."

"No," Brown said, "you don't have to show me. I'm not an investigator. But I would like for you to come over to Lynchburg, though, and talk to the members of the homicide squad."

"When do you want us there?"

"How about tomorrow night?"

"You got it."

WHAT THE TWO RICHMOND DETECTIVES TOLD MEMBERS OF THE SQUAD GOT their attention. Cults, particularly satanic cults, they said, were much more prevalent than most people believed; in fact, they were much more common than most law enforcement officers believed. Hotbeds of such activity in Virginia were Richmond and Charlottesville, but this did not mean it was absent from the rest of the state.

"What do you have that shows satanism in this case?" one of the investigators asked.

"Okay," said the visiting officer, "let's go down the list." Raising his right hand with his fingers pointing upward, he lowered them one at a time as he ticked off his points. "First," he said, "there is the placement of the bodies themselves. You'll notice that both are pointed in the same direction: north."

"What does north have to do with it?"

"I'll explain that later. Let me make my points first."

"What makes you think that wasn't coincidence?" asked another.

"Maybe," the visiting detective said, sounding doubtful. "Let me go on."

"Second," he said, dropping another finger, "look at the blood pattern. These bodies were outlined in blood. They didn't just happen to bleed that way."

"How do you know that?"

"I don't *know* it, but see how it looks like the bodies have been purposely traced in blood."

Everybody looked. It could indeed be interpreted that someone made a conscious effort to "paint" the blood into a specific pattern. Heretofore they had been operating under the belief that the "mopping" marks throughout the house had been made by the killer in an attempt to destroy his footprints, not to perpetuate some obscure cult ritual.

For an hour or more the Richmond detectives explained what they took to be indications of ritualistic murder. Some of them seemed pretty farfetched. There was, for example, a mousetrap found near Nancy's body. It had been sprung, but it was empty. A small piece of cheese was nearby. The odd thing, though, was that there was no blood on the bottom of the trap even though it was resting on a surface covered in blood. To investigators, that could mean only that it was put there after the blood had dried. Furthermore, the trap was pointed to the north, as was the silverware on the dining room table. Every candle in the house had been burned. Granted, they did not know *when* they had been lit, but that was just another piece to the puzzle. There was a puddle of a black waxy substance on the floor at one corner of the table, between where Nancy and Derek sat to eat dinner. The substance never was identified, nor was its presence explained. The dining room chairs seemed to have been placed in a semicircle. There was the strange V-shaped cut on Derek's chin. Further, looking closely at the blood-smeared floor, one could see what appeared to be a *6* inside a vee. Three sixes is the recognized symbol for the Antichrist. The brand name on the mousetrap was Victory, which was represented on the product with a large *V,* the letter presumably also representing the word *voodoo.*

"These things have significance in satanic rituals," one of the detectives said ominously.

"Does that mean you think this was a cult killing?" one of the homicide squad members asked.

"No," said the heftier of the two experts, "that's not what we're saying. What we're saying is we don't know for sure. Some of the signs are there, some aren't. And some of those that are are wrong. A lot of it could be coincidence. But I'll tell you this: If it was a cult-type slaying, it was done by amateurs, by a person or persons who didn't know what they were really doing."

"Like someone who just started dabbling in it."

"That's it."

"Could it be that whoever left these signs was just trying to throw us off the track?"

"Sure," the Richmond detective agreed. "There's a good possibility of that, too."

WHAT THEY HAD SAID WAS UPSETTING. IT MUDDIED THE INVESTIGATORY waters. If nothing else, it emphasized just how complicated the entire case was getting to be. The sheer brutality of the murders was bad. The fact that investigators had failed to immediately identify a suspect was worse. Worst of all was the knowledge that they did not even have a clue as to motive. And then the Richmond detectives blew more smoke at them.

The message from Richmond affected members of the homicide squad in varying degrees. None of them wanted to believe *in toto* that Derek and Nancy were killed by one or more devil worshippers. Some thought the Richmond guys had made some interesting points; some thought they had been watching too many horror movies. But a few took what they had heard very seriously indeed.

Those investigators went to their libraries and checked out every book they could find on satanism. They spent their spare time, which wasn't much considering they were working twelve to fourteen hours a day, poring over the texts in an attempt to fit the scholarly studies into the context of a local murder.

From very early in the investigation the dozen investigators involved got in the habit of meeting at the command post at eight o'clock every morning. Some would bring coffee, others would bring donuts, and for an hour or more they would sit around over sugary pastries and sticky cardboard coffee containers comparing notes and arguing theories.

The satanism hypothesis rose to prominence for lack of any better one. When all the other leads they followed turned out to be dead ends, police began looking at anything that would produce results no matter how farfetched it seemed. Even Sheriff Wells, who from the first believed the murders were committed by a single person, specifically whoever had been a guest in the Haysom house that night, began wondering if there might not be a cult connection. In guarded comments to the media, he spoke of "unusual aspects" of the murders.

One investigator became so sure that satanists were at work that he turned downright paranoid. He complained to others that he was getting mysterious telephone calls, that his house was being watched, and, more disturbing, that he was certain he was being followed by a blond youth driving a red car with "666" on the license plate. He was so convinced of this last that every time he saw a red car, he almost ran his own vehicle off the road trying to see who the driver was.

Sergeant Baker, who professed not to be a superstitious man, admitted months later that he had been spooked by the murders. A husky, steady-handed member of the department's SWAT team, Baker is not easily frightened. But the way the Haysoms had been butchered and the talk of possible cult involvement made an impression on him that wouldn't easily go away. "It all came down on me months later," he confessed, "long after the homicide squad had been disbanded. I was working the night shift and it would usually be two-thirty or three o'clock in the morning before I'd get home. I'd be fine until I got to my back door, and then it would start happening. I'd look in the house, and it would be all dark, and I'd start getting this funny feeling. I was terrified to open the door to my own kitchen. I'd hold my breath, put one hand on my pistol, and turn the lights on with the other. I just *knew* there was going to be a bloody body on my kitchen floor.

"It's much better now," he smiled, "but it took a long, long time for that feeling to go away."

The possibility that the murders were cult-inspired was later totally rejected, but for several weeks it drove the search. Numerous hours were spent tracking down leads the detectives would have laughed at under normal circumstances. As a final irony, months after investigators had returned all the books on the occult they had checked out of their local libraries, the subject *did* reenter the case. And from a very unexpected quarter. When it did, it made investigators shiver. They wondered, at least momentarily, if they had not been very far off track to begin with.

RICKY GARDNER WAS ONE OF THOSE MEN SOME PEOPLE LIKE TO CALL "baby-faced." Husky and of medium height, with wavy, dark brown hair that he parted high on the right side, Gardner easily looked five years younger than his actual age. In March 1985, he was thirty years old, but with his rosy, smooth cheeks and a pleasant, easy grin, he could have passed for a shy graduate student. Looking upon his round, unlined face, no one would have guessed that he was a veteran witness to death, destruction, and human misery.

At seventeen, straight out of high school, he had joined the Bedford County Rescue Unit where his job was to answer distress calls at bloody auto wrecks and pull bloated bodies out of rivers and lakes. At twenty-five, he left the rescue unit for the sheriff's department where his duties were much the same but the pay was better. He proved an able, intelligent, eager-to-learn officer. Five years later, in October 1984, some six months before the Haysoms were murdered, he was named an investigator. Investigators were the cream of the crop in the sheriff's department, and Gardner's appointment to that post proved he was on the fast track.

In his years of seeing Bedford County life from the violent side he had examined a lot of bodies. A year of so earlier, as a uniformed deputy, he had answered a report of an explosion, and when he arrived at the scene he found what was left of a farmer who had scattered himself over a large part of Bedford County while trying to remove a stump with too much dynamite. But in his thirteen years' experience Gardner had never seen anything like what had been done to Derek and Nancy Haysom. He was to become involved not just as a witness but as an investigator. For him, this would be a first. He had never before been part of a homicide investigation.

ABOUT THE TIME ANNIE MASSIE OPENED THE DOOR AND SAW DEREK'S body spread on the floor, Gardner had been in neighboring Botetourt County talking to deputies there about a group of men suspected of breaking into Bedford County homes. He finished up and was driving back to Bedford, intending to call it a day, when chatter on the car radio caught his attention. The Bedford dispatcher was directing a uniformed deputy to an address in Boonsboro, across the county, to investigate a possible murder.

"I've found one of 'em," Gardner had heard the deputy report from Boonsboro.

One of 'em, Gardner had said to himself. Good God, how many are there? He had turned up the volume, but there were no subsequent reports. When the silence continued, Gardner had known the deputy was communicating by telephone instead of committing details to the airwaves. He had already turned the car in the direction of the sheriff's department instead of toward his home as he had planned when the dispatcher came back on the air and ordered all available investigators to converge on Boonsboro. The message was cryptic but Gardner had noted the urgency in the deputy's voice. He had spun the wheel again and jammed the accelerator to the floor.

He and Chuck Reid, another investigator, had arrived at the Holcomb Rock Road house simultaneously.

"What's it all about?" Gardner had asked, slamming the cruiser door.

"Beats me," Reid had replied, "but it sounds pretty wild." A former weapons instructor in the Marine Corps, Reid was short and wiry, like a gymnast, with a well-muscled torso and a firm jaw. Only three years older than Gardner, he had gray flecks in his brown hair and pilot's lines around his eyes from years of squinting into the sunlight at targets at the other end of a firing range. Also a former uniformed deputy, Reid had been an investigator only six months longer than Gardner.

Together they had sprinted up the driveway.

The two had barely got their heads inside the house before they were ordered out by the lab techs. The quick glimpse, however, had been enough to give them goosebumps. Reid had taken one look at the blood-splattered living room and Derek's mangled corpse and had thought he was having a bad dream. Three nights before he had watched *Helter-Skelter* on television, and he had not yet been able to erase those images from his mind.

The sight of blood had not disturbed Gardner. The case in which a farmer had blown himself up with dynamite had inured him to the sight of large amounts of gore. But this was different. It wasn't the sight of blood that bothered him; it was the idea that one human could do that to another that made him queasy.

Captain Ronnie Lockland, the department's second in command, had quickly collared the two investigators. "Go around to the neighbors and see what you can learn," Lockland had ordered. "You go that way," he had told Reid, pointing up the road, "and you," he said, looking at Gardner, "go that way."

Since then, the hours and days had passed in a blur. They had interviewed virtually around the clock, but with very few results to show for it. By Monday, April 8, five days after the bodies had been discovered, they didn't know much more than they had the previous Wednesday.

The day before, Easter Sunday, there had been a memorial service for Derek and Nancy at St. Paul's Episcopal, *the* grand old church in Lynchburg whose members included the city's elite. David and Nancy had never attended the church, but the pastor, Reverend Alexander Robertson, readily agreed to let the family hold a memorial. There was no funeral because Derek's and Nancy's bodies had been cremated as soon as they were released by the medical examiner's office.

Reverend Robertson said a few words to the mourners and then surrendered the lectern to Richard Haysom, Nancy's thirty-one-year-old architect son from Calgary, Canada. In a voice cracking with emotion, Richard made a plea for peace. He had been only six years old when his mother and Derek were married, so he grew up thinking of Derek as his father; Nancy and Derek were his parents, not his mother and stepfather.

"I urge our family and friends to block out the memory of their death and remember their life," Richard urged, looking out at a sea of faces, some of which openly registered anger and frustration. "I beg you all to open your hearts. They would have wished for us to overcome this tragedy and find the strength to go on living, the strength to go on loving, the strength to go on forgiving." It was a moving eulogy, and when he finished, there was hardly a dry eye in the place.

Among the more than a hundred people in the audience were Richard's brother Howard, a thirty-two-year-old surgeon from Houston, and his stepbrothers, Veryan, a thirty-six-year-old criminal defense lawyer from Mahone Bay, Nova Scotia, and Julian, the thirty-three-year-old engineer who had been engaged to Margaret Louise Simmons. Standing off to the side, as though she didn't want to be noticed, was Derek and Nancy's daughter, Elizabeth, a first-year student at the University of Virginia who would be twenty-one in exactly one week. Bracing her like a set of bookends were her UVA roommate, a Korean named *Charlene Song,* and Elizabeth's boyfriend, a dark-haired, eighteen-year-old German named Jens Soering.

By THAT MONDAY, THE HOMICIDE SQUAD HAD MOVED ITS COMMAND POST from the Ruritan Club to the temporarily empty Boonsboro Elementary School. Although their business was deadly serious, the investigators found in the new location grist for a form of black humor. To see a large group of big, beefy men (no one could ever doubt they were cops) operating in an environment designed for six- to ten-year-olds was to laugh in spite of the circumstances. They shuffled from foot to foot trying to pretend they didn't feel like Gullivers in Lilliput. Around them were teeny tables with teeny chairs. Teeny desks were lined up against the wall. Coathooks hung for teeny people projected outward below waist level—a good way to ruin everything if you didn't watch where you were walking. In the hall, six-footers practically had to kneel to use the water fountains. But the scene in the restrooms was even more ludicrous: husky former tackles and linebackers trying to use urinals that were only two feet off the floor—urinals some of them couldn't even see over their beer bellies.

But if the deputies were amused by the situation, the amusement quickly disappeared. When they remembered they were there to try to catch a vicious killer, the mood turned somber.

SHORTLY BEFORE ONE O'CLOCK ON APRIL 8, THE HAYSOM'S TAN VAN, THE Bronze Belle, pulled up the school driveway with Elizabeth Haysom in the passenger seat. Her boyfriend, Jens, was driving.

Elizabeth climbed out of the vehicle, said a few words to Jens, and walked into the building. Jens waited until she was inside before he drove off.

Chuck Reid watched from the hallway as Elizabeth sauntered into the building. As he watched, the first word that popped into his mind was *hippie.* She was wearing baggy, dark slacks, a wrinkled white blouse, and scuffed, black-felt Chinese slippers. Her hair, which was stringy and needed shampooing, was of medium length, brushed back over her ears. She wore no makeup. If Reid had to guess, he would say that the clothes she was wearing happened to be the first things she saw when she woke up that morning. If there had been a large black plastic trash bag with armholes draped over a chair in her bedroom, she might have worn that.

Appearances aside, though, when she opened her mouth everyone's jaws dropped. "I'm here to see Investigator Gardner," she said in a British accent as pure, elegant, and disarming as that of a news reader on the BBC. The cops in Lynchburg had heard a voice like that only in the movies. To think that such tones were rolling out of this disreputably dressed young woman was to believe that the spring thunderheads building over the Peaks of Otter would soon be dumping diamonds upon their heads.

"He asked me to come 'round for an interview," she said softly, bringing all activity in the room to a sudden halt.

Reid, for one, was impressed by her accent if nothing else. "I could have sat there all day and just listened to her talk," he said.

He didn't know it at the time, but that is exactly what he would do in the days to follow. But that day, the privilege went to Ricky Gardner and a veteran investigator from the Lynchburg Police Department named Debbie Kirkland. To keep the word *regional* in the actions of the homicide squad, whenever possible an investigator from Bedford County, which was the department with jurisdiction, was paired with an investigator from one of the other departments.

"Let's go down here," Gardner said, gallantly rising from the chair in which he had been slumped and waving down the corridor. "Let's find an empty room where we can talk."

As it turned out, the "talk" lasted for four hours.

7

NOT ONLY HAD ELIZABETH HAYSOM BROUGHT HERSELF TO THE INTERVIEW, but she had lugged along her lunch as well. As soon as she, Gardner, and Kirkland were seated around the teacher's desk in a remote classroom, Elizabeth delved into her purse and produced a thick sandwich sealed in Saran Wrap. She laid the sandwich on the desk, unwrapped it, and broke off a chunk. Popping it into her mouth, she commenced to chew, daintily but enthusiastically.

Gardner stared at her. He looked down at the sandwich, which consisted of two pieces of stale-looking white bread separated by a generous helping of a dark, viscous substance. Then he looked back at her. "Is that good?" he asked somewhat incredulously.

"Very," she said in proper Oxbridgian tones.

"Is that what I think it is?" he asked.

"What do you think it is?" she asked.

"Chocolate pudding."

She laughed. "Chocolate pudding?"

"I've never seen anyone eat a chocolate pudding sandwich before."

"It's Marmite," she said.

"Huh?"

"Marmite," she repeated, explaining that it was a beef-flavored extract made from brewer's yeast, a very popular snack food in Britain. It could be eaten between bread, as she preferred it, or it could be used as a base in soups and stews. The consistency was more like softened ice milk than pudding, dense enough to spread and not diluted enough to dribble. It was like a Texan's definition of the silt-laden Rio Grande: too thick to drink, too thin to plow.

"It's just chock full of vitamins," she said, pronouncing the word in the British fashion: VIT-amins.

"Uh huh," Gardner mumbled, shuffling a stack of papers in front of him and giving her a wary glance. "I guess we'd better get down to it."

WHILE GARDNER SET UP HIS TAPE RECORDER AND DEBBIE KIRKLAND squared away a notebook and pen so she could make some notes as they went along, Elizabeth broke off another piece of bread and Marmite, looking as poised as Maggie Thatcher waiting for questions from Members of Parliament.

The first thing the investigators wanted to determine was where she had been at about the time her parents had been murdered. Elizabeth couldn't be helpful enough. In a carefully modulated I'm-here-to-help-anyway-I-can voice, Elizabeth told them that the last time she had seen her parents had been the weekend of March 23–24. She had taken the bus down from Charlottesville on Saturday to help her father celebrate his birthday. That night, she said, her parents went out with some friends for dinner while she stayed home alone. On Sunday Derek and Nancy had driven her back to Charlottesville. Since then she had talked to them once, on the following Thursday, just to say hello. She told them she would call again on Sunday, March 31, at about eight o'clock.

"I phoned, and I didn't get a reply, but that's not that unusual because, you know, they did what they wanted to do. Sometimes, if something came up, they'd just bypass the phone call."

She said she tried to reach them late Monday morning and twice that evening, but again there had been no answer. On Tuesday she tried at about eight o'clock in the morning and late that night with no luck. By then, she said, she was getting worried.

"On Wednesday morning, as soon as I got up, I phoned Annie Massie to try and discover if she knew what was going on."

At midmorning Wednesday she left a message with Annie's maid asking her to ask Annie to check on her parents. Soon after that, Annie went to the house, opened the door and found her father's body.

"You said y'all prearranged for you to call Sunday at eight o'clock," said Kirkland. "Is that normal? Do y'all normally do this?"

Elizabeth smiled. "Well, sometimes my parents find it quite hard to get hold of me, and I find it quite hard to get hold of them, so if it was something specific we had to discuss, we would arrange a time to call. This was something specific, so I said let's get together Sunday at eight."

"What were y'all planning on talking about?" Kirkland asked.

"I have my housing needs that I had to discuss. We had trouble with our landlady. She didn't want undergraduates in the house, and we had to go and see her and try to bring her around to the idea that we were okay. So I had to discuss with them whether that had gone all right, because if that had failed, I would be up the creek for housing. I didn't have any university housing."

Gardner interrupted, sounding a little impatient. He was interested in motive. So far the investigators had no idea *why* Derek and Nancy had been murdered. If they could find the why, the investigator reasoned, it would help them find the who. He soon discovered that was going to be difficult. To hear Elizabeth tell it, Derek had a left a number of enemies back in Canada. For the next hour virtually all he heard about was how many people had it in for the murdered executive, from fellow executives to union officials and members of the local news media.

When Derek began working for Sydney Steel, Elizabeth said, he invented a procedure called the "submerge injection process," which she claimed had revolutionized steel-making.

"It was a fabulous process," she gushed. "Almost immediately, the Americans, the Japanese, the Germans, the British all bought it."

Wasn't that good? Gardner wondered. Before he could ask the question, Elizabeth told him why it was not.

"The Canadian unions were upset with the idea," she said. "I think they felt that they were going to lose their jobs or something."

Okay, Gardner told himself, the steel unions didn't like him. Who else? She told him.

The local politicians didn't think much of him either, Elizabeth explained. "Unfortunately, the political situation in Canada changed a year after Daddy came. Since Sydney Steel was a Crown corporation, he had to deal with politicians, and that was something he didn't enjoy. He thought they were scum."

Gardner could understand how an attitude like that might not endear him to the local officials. But Elizabeth was just getting wound up. The local media didn't like Derek much either, she said. Some of them, Elizabeth claimed, criticized him sharply because he was a South African. "They were asking, 'Why do we have a South African doing this? He's obviously going to discriminate against black people.' So, in fact, Daddy got nothing. No credit at all for his invention."

"So he sort of got screwed on that deal?" Gardner suggested.

"Yes," Elizabeth said, nodding vigorously. "He got screwed big time. Once everything started to boom, everybody started saying, 'Well, now we're going fine, we can blow money on this, that, and the other,' and he was saying, 'No, the reason we're booming is because we're not doing that.' "

"I'll bet that didn't sit well," Gardner said.

"You're right," Elizabeth confirmed. "It caused a lot of strikes. Finally he just couldn't stand it any longer. They started striking left, right, and center. The abuse was quite something. I was threatened a couple of times at school. In fact, I had all my front teeth knocked out."

Gardner sat upright. "Oh," he said. "Why did this come about? Who did he make mad up there?"

"Well, as I said," Elizabeth explained, "he started the idea that if you work for the company, you had shares in the company, so as the company grew, you made more. The unions didn't like that. It was too abstract for them, so they just went on strike.

Daddy's office was ransacked. Windows were broken. There were picket lines all over the place. We got phone calls. I answered a couple of calls and some of them were threats like, 'Don't think you're going to see your Daddy tonight.' Something like that. Things like, 'You'd better move.' "

Soon after all the trouble started, she said, she was attacked. "I was at school playing in the playground during the break," she said, "and a guy smashed my jaw, knocked out my front teeth—"

"You say a guy?" interjected Kirkland. "You mean a kid or an adult?"

Elizabeth shrugged. "Sixteen. Maybe seventeen."

"What happened then?" asked Gardner.

"I guess that was the deciding factor," Elizabeth said. "Mummy and Daddy decided that I was definitely going to be sent away."

"Did the school know who did it?"

She nodded. "The school knew who did it. My parents knew who did it." She paused. "Actually, no," she said, correcting herself. "My parents did *not* know who did it. They had an idea of who was involved, but the school refused to take any action."

"What do you mean?"

"The school actually went so far as to say that it didn't happen, that I had already had a broken jaw and broken teeth when I arrived."

"How did your father take *that?*"

She smiled tightly. "My father . . . well, his initial reaction was to be just totally out for blood, you know."

"Uh huh."

"But after he calmed down, it was just as though he were saying, 'Well, this has happened, and we're never going to be able to do anything about it, and it won't do any good anyway. We're just going to have to send you away some place.' "

"Was that the end of it?" Gardner asked.

Elizabeth said no, that the incident, along with her father's growing disenchantment with politics, convinced him he should quit Sydney Steel. "He just cleaned out."

"All right," Gardner said. "He left Sydney Steel. Did he have any feelings toward the board? Towards anyone? Did anyone have bad feelings toward him?"

Elizabeth bobbed her head. "I think there was tremendous ill will," she said forcefully. "If he was given the opportunity, he would go into a rage about it. If you can see the picture, my parents had moved there and they had built their all-time house, a magnificent property, you know. It was absolutely magnificent. They put their heart and soul into it. And one day he just got up and walked out. Literally. I mean he phoned us one day and said, 'I've sold the house. I can't handle it anymore. I can't bear it.' "

THEN THE TALE GOT MORE COMPLICATED.

After Derek left Sydney Steel, he took a $75,000 a year job as chairman and president of Metropolitan Area Growth Investments, Ltd.—MAGI—a venture capital organization owned jointly by the federal and provincial governments. About eighteen months after he climbed aboard, MAGI put up almost six million Canadian dollars for a mortgage on a Bermuda-registered cruise ship named *Mercator I.* Ostensibly, the ship would be used to help boost tourism. But when the details of the deal were revealed, it caused quite a disturbance. Derek was caught in the middle.

To begin with, the ship cost about half a million dollars more than originally planned. Then MAGI came up with another one hundred thousand dollars off the top for refitting. But what really caused the fuss was that virtually none of the money being spent on the project—Canadian government money—was being spent in Canada. The refitting was performed in a German shipyard, and provisions for the ship's first cruise were bought in Britain. Worse, almost half of the 110 crew members were residents of Thailand. This was a particularly sore point because unemployment was at a near record level in Nova Scotia.

According to Nova Scotia newspapers, the scandal over the ship contributed significantly to the defeat of the then-ruling provincial government in the 1978 elections.

In the end the furor was so great that Derek resigned from MAGI. In just a few years he had left two top jobs because of politics and clashes with people in power. And he had made somebody so angry that his daughter had been horribly beaten.

Gardner had come into the interview looking for a possible motive—just one simple reason why someone would want Derek dead. Now he was being deluged with a lot of reasons, was being given a veritable shopping list of potential enemies the man had made. However, his enemies would have had to want him dead pretty badly to have killed not only him but his wife as well. There were many reasons for people having been angry with Derek Haysom. But were the reasons strong enough for murder? Would someone travel from Nova Scotia to Virginia to settle an old union dispute? Or to slice two people to ribbons because of a bad investment?

Gardner sighed and rubbed his temples. He was quickly developing a splitting headache. And Elizabeth Haysom was just hitting her stride.

8

LIKE THE STORY SHE WAS TELLING, ELIZABETH'S PERSONALITY WAS multilayered, complex, often opaque, evolving before investigators Gardner and Kirkland with more twists and turns than the Blue Ridge Parkway. They had barely begun to scratch the surface of Elizabeth Haysom.

From talking about her father's occupational history, Elizabeth moved effortlessly to the more personal side of their family life, telling the detectives that her mother and father had loved her and supported her and fought for her—that they had been the best parents in the whole wide world.

Once her parents became aware of the seriousness of threats against the family after the incident at the school in Nova Scotia, they decided to send her abroad to study. First she went to a school in Switzerland, at a place called St. George's. Then she went to a posh elementary school in Britain, Riddlesworth, the same school that Princess Di had attended. Then she went to one of the most highly regarded girl's schools in Britain, Wycombe Abbey. After that, she claimed she was destined for Cambridge University but decided to join her parents in Virginia instead and attend the University of Virginia.

In the telling, the story did not come out this lucidly. Elizabeth, like Margaret Louise Simmons, tended to wander sometimes, to go off on her own tangents and explore roads the investigators did not know were even on the map. But Margaret Louise's diversions were unintentional; Elizabeth's, they later learned, were deliberate. Talking to her could be like pulling teeth; by the time he was finished with her, Gardner would be qualified to hang out a dentist's shingle.

ONCE SHE WENT ABROAD TO STUDY, ELIZABETH SAID, SHE SAW VERY LITTLE of her parents.

"How'd you feel about that?" Gardner asked.

"Well," Elizabeth replied, looking thoughtful, "in terms of school it was awful because the school had complete authority over me. Although I did well academically, and I was involved in sports and that kind of stuff, the British are very prejudiced against foreigners. I had a *hell* of a time in school. And Mom and Dad knew that. They tried to get me out, but once you get stuck in the system it's really quite difficult to change schools. The last couple of years were really quite horrific."

Part of the reason it was so horrific, she explained, was because school officials had framed her on a drug incident. "A couple of girls were caught with drugs, and for some reason they blamed it on me," she said indignantly. "I mean, I barely knew the people. The police came in and ransacked my room, tore everything apart, questioned me, hounded me, you know, gave me a bad time. I hadn't done anything."

Gardner and Kirkland exchanged glances. Where the hell is this going? the look said. This is uncharted territory.

INVESTIGATORS HAD NOT YET LEARNED HOW TO EVALUATE ELIZABETH'S information carefully. Although Gardner and Kirkland did not know it yet, most of what she was telling them was a skillful blend of fact and fantasy, a well-woven tale craftily conceived to confuse and intimidate. Elizabeth *did,* in fact, go to St. George's; she *did* go to Riddlesworth; and she *did* go to Wycombe (pronounced "Wickham") Abbey. But her experiences were nothing like what she had described to the detectives.

All schools have their cliques and subgroups, the small coteries of students who stick closely together, pointedly excluding others from their circle. This is particularly true in boarding schools, where the students not only attend classes together but live together, existing in a vacuum in an isolated world of their own. And probably in boarding schools of no other nationality is this cliquishness as well developed as it is in supremely class-conscious Britain.

The British are infamous for their snobbery. Class is stamped on every facet of a Britisher's existence, from the choice of newspapers to the color of socks. And just in case the physical flags aren't obvious enough, there is the unmistakable banner of language. To an American ear, the speech pattern perpetuated at Oxford and Cambridge is a caricature of itself, a sometimes barely intelligible mishmash of in-group slang and strange pronounciation; a whole world of broad *A*'s, nasal exclamations, and swallowed prefixes. Especially broad *A*'s. Across the Atlantic *bath* is *baath*, *tomato* is *tomaato*, *rather* is *raather*.

Snooty British women say *raather* a lot. It is a standing joke—a not-so-gentle jab—to describe a snob as being "very raather-raather." Elizabeth Haysom got to be very raather-raather.

But she may have been telling the truth when she told the detectives that the early days abroad were tough. As a stranger from Canada, a girl without strong ties to powerful British figures, notwithstanding her relationship to Lady Astor, she may have been snubbed when she first enrolled. But as she learned the language and customs, her life became easier. By the time she got to Wycombe Abbey, just as she was going into puberty, she seemed to be adapting well to the system.

Wycombe Abbey School is in the town of High Wycombe, which is in the center of an area called the Chilterns, a forty-five-minute train ride from London's Marleybone Station. This is the heart of some of the loveliest countryside England has to offer, a picture-book landscape of rolling green fields and bubbling streams, a favorite destination for citydwellers desperate for an escape from noise and grime.

Wycombe Abbey School gets half its name from the town and

half from the centerpiece of the campus, an imposing former cloister built of cold gray stone, complete with parapets, turrets, and pointy, gothic windows. Inside the austere-looking structure are two dormitories, Ruben House and Pitt House, each one accommodating forty or more girls. There are eight other houses in the school, which also have a population of forty or more each. Five of the houses are in their own red-brick buildings, and three others are shoehorned into another large structure called Daws Hill House. Other edifices quarter laboratories, an art center, a music center, and a gymnasium. Naturally there is a chapel too. Surrounding the cluster of dormitories and school buildings are 160 acres of parklike grounds with flower-bordered walking paths criss-crossing the playing fields, broad lawns, and secluded groves of hardwoods. There is even a small lake.

The single jarring note in this Edenic setting is the ten-foot-tall brick wall that separates the school from the town. No matter how well it is camouflaged by flora, the wall goes a long way toward destroying the feeling of unbridled spaciousness that is otherwise so strong. The wall, practical though it may be, forms a psychological as well as a physical barrier. Life at Wycombe Abbey is designed to confine and constrict on the one hand while ostensibly broadening on the other. Regulations are strict, and the academic workload is demanding, going far beyond what most American students are accustomed to. School officials do not want students to feel *too* free or have *too* much time on their hands. The days are highly structured, beginning with a morning prayer service in the Church of England tradition, and continuing late into the night, which is the only time many students have to work on the exhaustive projects expected of them.

For a while, Elizabeth appeared to have no problem with this regimen. During her middle years at Wycombe Abbey, she was a classic overachiever. She authored one near book-length essay on Byron, another on the history of ancient warfare, and a monster 140,000-word treatise on the history of scientific invention. Those alone required months and months of work.

There was no escape from the school on weekends either. Only once during each of the three twelve-week school terms are students permitted an extended break. Called long leave, it amounts to an expanded weekend—three nights away from the institution. During the summer and autumn terms there also is another brief respite. Called short leave, it permits each student one absence from roughly noon on Saturday to sundown on Sunday.

Emphasis at Wycombe Abbey is and has been on education. While she was interested, Elizabeth accounted well for herself. Her specialties were English, history, and languages, which included Latin, German, French, and Greek. Her curriculum vitae shows she scored at the distinction level, which is higher than the American A, in her use of English, and in her translation capabilities in Latin, Greek and French. She had A's in history, business French, and applied math, which included courses in what the British call the A (for advanced) levels, or roughly what would compare closely with college-level work in the United States. Her lowest grade was a C.

In her entrance exams for Cambridge she scored distinctions in British history, ancient history, language translation, and general subject matter, which included science, literature, art, and music. The only nondistinction was an A in European history. Oddly—given that she was captain of both the junior and senior debating teams at Wycombe Abbey and a winner of a national public speaking contest at age fifteen—her oral exam for Cambridge was scored unsatisfactory.

Later, in Virginia, when she took the SAT, she scored a 680 in the math section and a 740 in the language section. In both categories, an 800 is a perfect score. Her combined SAT of 1,420 easily put her in the top 10 percent of the country's test-takers.

With such pressure to excel in academics at Wycombe Abbey and with such rigid rules concerning absences from the campus, the only real relief for students is through sports and school-sponsored extracurricular activities. Elizabeth dove into these as well; she was an enthusiastic joiner and doer.

She was, for instance, a world-class skier who in 1980 won a berth on a national championship ski team. She also played tennis and lacrosse at an advanced level, and one year she captained the school lacrosse team. For four years running she was the winner of Wycombe Abbey's outstanding sportsmanship prize.

In addition she was an indefatigable writer and performer. While at Wycombe Abbey, she wrote three one-act plays and two three-act plays, plus a sizable portfolio of poetry. When she was fifteen, one of her poems, which she entitled "Narcissus," won fifth prize in a Britain-wide competition. She also was a cofounder and officer of a Wycombe Abbey poetry society.

Her mother loved music and acting. So did Elizabeth. She played the piano and the cello and won certificates for performance and aptitude from the Royal Academy of Music. On the stage, she played Becket in *Becket,* Henry Higgins in *Pygmalion,* Rosalind in *As You Like It,* Cleopatra in *Antony and Cleopatra,* Faust in *Dr. Faust,* and Puck in *A Midsummer Night's Dream.* The irony would later be striking: Cleopatra was a seductress, and Faust sold his soul to the devil.

For most of her stay there officials at Wycombe Abbey must have *loved* Elizabeth Haysom. She was extremely bright, uncommonly articulate, amazingly energetic, and frightfully ambitious. In her junior year school officials thought enough of her to make her Head of House, which meant she was responsible for the more than three-dozen girls in her dormitory.

Then something happened. More accurately, a combination of things happened. The result was the spectacular crash of star-pupil Elizabeth Haysom. This was the part of her life she was trying to hide from Gardner and Kirkland.

Ironically, part of her problem was rooted in the way the dormitory system works at a British boarding school. When a girl enrolls at Wycombe Abbey, she is arbitrarily assigned to a house. Barring unusual circumstances, that is where she stays until she graduates. Since there is very little mixing among the girls from the different houses, each girl is virtually isolated within a very limited group. In practice, her friends, confidantes, and supporters come from within an extremely small circle.

When Elizabeth enrolled in Wycombe Abbey at age twelve, she was assigned to Ruben House, one of the two dormitories in the main building. At age eighteen she was still in Ruben House.

All her friends were in Ruben House. In and out of class she surrounded herself with others wearing the Ruben House colors, a distinctive pink tie. Over the years they began to look upon themselves like recruits in a Marine Corps boot camp: They suffered together, worked together, shared their successes and failures together, and together they would go forth to meet the world. Except when it came time for Elizabeth's classmates to go forth, Elizabeth did not go with them.

Without consulting her, Nancy and Derek had made arrangements with the school for Elizabeth to be enrolled in a series of high-level science and math classes. Nancy and Derek had decided that their daughter would follow in Derek's footsteps and be an engineer even though this contradicted her own desires to major in history. They thought that with a little push she would see the wisdom of their decision.

Unfortunately, they were mistaken. For Elizabeth, her parents' decision resulted in disaster. She was unable to maintain the standards she had set for herself and those her parents expected. She studied relentlessly, but her grades plummeted and her morale bottomed out. After being bombarded with complaints both from Elizabeth and the school, Nancy and Derek eventually relented. But it was too late; the damage was done. The only way Elizabeth could get back on the history track was to repeat her entire senior year.

Unhappily, the ramifications extended beyond the fact that she would have to spend an additional year at Wycombe Abbey. Not only was she *not* graduating as she had planned, but all her friends were. This was a blow to her self-esteem; she was being punished by having to stay behind while her friends went off to university. She began to resent her parents enormously for that decision, building a reservoir of ill will that would grow only larger and deeper in the coming months and years. At least that is one of the excuses she used later to explain her actions. In reality, the relationship between her and her parents, particularly her mother, had been uncomfortable for years. The decision to try to push her into engineering was, certainly to her, a hateful blow. But in her mind it also was only one of many.

For her own reasons, these were things Elizabeth Haysom was not telling Kirkland and Gardner. There were things she did not want them to know, one of them being that she was a pathological liar. It would take them a while to find that out.

9

ELIZABETH TOLD KIRKLAND AND GARDNER THAT AFTER THE DRUG INCIDENT school officials prohibited her from contacting Derek and Nancy and kept her incommunicado for several days. It was more than she could stand. "I flipped out," she said. "I went off to Europe on my own." She amended her statement. "Well, with a friend," she added. "I was away, I don't know how long, about five months or something. And by that time I was terrified to come home."

"Did you contact your parents during this period?" Gardner asked.

"No," she replied.

"Had no contact?"

"No."

"In other words," Investigator Kirkland interjected, "they didn't even know when you left?"

"No," Elizabeth repeated, looking smug. "Oh, there was a wonderful hoo-haw. I mean, just like now, you know. There was ICMP, Interpol, Scotland Yard, military intelligence in Europe—"

"You had everyone looking for you?" Gardner interrupted.

"Yes," said Elizabeth, smiling nervously. "The French Interior Department, everybody. I finally turned up on the doorstep of some Colonel Herrington and he shipped me off to London where my half-brother Julian met me and then Dad came over."

"Were you trying to be elusive?" Gardner asked.

"No, not really. But I didn't have any money and I didn't have any credit cards and I didn't have anything anybody could trace me with. I just took off."

"How did you support yourself?"

"I was really lucky," she said brightly. "I got a job in Paris. My French is good, and I got a job doing research for a law firm. And I worked for IBM in Berlin."

Investigators would later discover these assertions were totally false. In France she worked at menial jobs, earning barely enough to eat on, and in Berlin she did not work at all. When she got to Germany, she was virtually destitute and survived by moving in with a group of toughs. They kept her drugged much of the time and used her body whenever they wished. But this was not what she told Gardner and Kirkland.

Her adventure in Europe couldn't have been better, she related almost cheerfully. It was great, she said, right up to the time when she tripped on the stairs and hit her head. That frightened her, she claimed, and made her seek help.

What actually happened has never been determined. In other reports Elizabeth also claimed she was attacked and thrown down an elevator shaft.

"In other words you just sort of turned yourself in?" Gardner prompted, not yet aware of her liberties with the truth.

"Yes," said Elizabeth. "I was in severe concussion. I didn't know whether I was coming or going. I just kind of got this silly belief that I was pregnant and that I was covered in lice. I couldn't keep any food down and stuff so I decided that really the time had come to amend my life. I went to the British Consulate and they immediately notified Colonel Herrington and he was there within half an hour. He took me home, got me to a doctor, and got my head plastered up, and then I was sent off to England, where Julian met me and Dad came over."

This, at least, was partially true. But her fear that she was pregnant was not a "silly belief"; it was a very real consideration. Neither had she been imagining that she was louse-infested; she had been. Her claim that Herrington had rescued her was accurate.

What was not yet clear to investigators was just how proficient Elizabeth was at lying. In the interview with Gardner and Kirkland she made her European sojourn sound like a vacation with a few more than normal problems, a sort of How-I-Kept-My-Chin-Up-and-Survived-My-Summer-in-Europe. Gardner and Kirkland were not to blame; Elizabeth's tales would fool investigators and others for a long time to come.

ALONE IN HER ROOM IN RUBEN HOUSE AFTER ALL HER FRIENDS HAD graduated, Elizabeth began to dwell on her situation, allowing her anger toward her parents to fester. The more she brooded, the more angry and vengeful she became. She added up the wrongs she perceived they had committed against her and found that there were quite a few and that they went back a long way, all the way, in fact, to at least the attack in the Nova Scotia schoolyard.

She had told the detectives that a teenage thug, angry at her father's antiunion stance, had jumped her and smashed her face against a brick wall, knocking out her front teeth. Indeed, she *may* have been attacked; the attack *may* have been caused by her father's fight with labor; she *may* have had her face smashed against a brick wall. She did have a cut on her chin, and it left a thin scar, but her teeth were not knocked out. Damaged enough to require extensive dental work, yes, but not permanently lost. Whether she was attacked or whether she fell is known only to her.

It is true that soon after that she went abroad to school, but it could have been her idea as well as Derek and Nancy's. Nevertheless, she told herself that it was their idea, and she began to hate them for it.

There was another incident at her first overseas school, St. George's in Switzerland. Later, she swore that she, as a ten-year-old, was raped on the school grounds by two or more French youths. But she also told her brother Howard and apparently her parents that it was not a case of rape by two teenagers but an incident of genital exposure by one man. Regardless of what transpired at St. George's, she told herself that it was rape and that her parents treated her horribly afterwards. She felt her mother blamed *her* for the incident, insinuating that she provoked it and calling her a little whore. She said her father was not affected at all, that he tried to pretend it never happened. Still, it was enough to convince Nancy and Derek to change her schools. The next term she went to Riddlesworth in Britain.

THE TWO YEARS AT RIDDLESWORTH APPARENTLY WERE UNEVENTFUL, AS were her first years at Wycombe Abbey, except that during that period she and her parents became even more estranged. Although Derek and Nancy occasionally visited her in England, she usually saw them only during school holidays or summer vacations. When she was with them, she felt her mother tried to smother her with affection and hardly let her out of her sight. Back at school, she told her classmates that she was adopted.

In her last year the changes in Elizabeth became too noticeable to be ignored. It was then that she changed from a near model student into a rebellious one. She let her weight get out of control, and she chopped off her hair in a period when only riffraff wore short hair. This gave her a punkish-dykish look, which tended to set her apart from the other trend-conscious students even more. She was determined, it seemed, to make herself look as miserable as she felt.

Then, too, her drug abuse came into the open. She would later claim that her proclivity for substance abuse started even before she was sent away to boarding school. When her parents were away from their home in Nova Scotia, she said, she would raid the liquor cabinet, dipping liberally into her father's scotch, her mother's gin, and what was to become her own favorite, vodka. When she grew older and she realized it was difficult to obtain liquor at a boarding school, her taste turned to chemicals, which were much easier to secure and conceal.

About this time, in a rather desperate search for friendship, she began a furtive alliance with another eccentric student, a girl named *Melinda Duncan.* For different reasons Melinda was as unhappy with her family situation as Elizabeth had convinced herself she was with hers.

Melinda was a lesbian. Whether this played a role early in

their relationship is unknown, but it certainly was not a repellent as far as Elizabeth was concerned. Elizabeth's sexual history up to then is murky. Later, she admitted to a sexual experience with another girl when she was twelve or thirteen, but she brushed it off as unimportant, equating it to boys and girls playing doctor and nurse. Since she went to girls' schools and had no little boys to play with, she explained, it was natural for her to turn to another girl to satisfy her sexual curiosity.

Both she and Melinda were unhappy in their circumstances at the time. They both longed for freedom and adventure. But one thing kept them back: their separate but parallel plans for the future. Elizabeth had wanted to go to Trinity College at Cambridge University and major in history. Melinda had her mind set on Oxford. But before they could fulfill their ambitions, Elizabeth's drug use caught up with her. One day, virtually on the eve of the last exams she would ever take at Wycombe Abbey, she was found out. She went into the chapel, she said, to take her place in the choir, and school officials sought her out and told her she was going to have to leave. If she was not truly shocked, she did a very good job of pretending. She was already an accomplished actress.

Her parents were off on a trip to Africa when this occurred, and their inaccessibility saved her from immediate explusion. School officials agreed to let her stay through the examination period, but they said that would only postpone the punishment, not obviate it. She still would have to leave under a very dark cloud.

They wanted to send her back to Canada with a nurse, Elizabeth scornfully complained to Gardner and Kirkland. She was outraged about the idea of a nurse. Yet they never asked her if she might need some psychiatric help.

Being expelled from Wycombe Abbey scuttled her plans for attending Cambridge. With a black mark like that on her record and her unsatisfactory score on her oral entrance exam, she was not likely to be accepted at Trinity College. Meanwhile, Melinda's application to Oxford was rejected, and she faced the unhappy future of attending the University of Edinburgh in Scotland, which she considered a second-rate school. Angry and frustrated, the two decided to leave family and academia behind. On July 1, 1983, the day they finished their last exams, Elizabeth and Melinda slipped off the Wycombe Abbey campus and fled to the Continent.

Their jaunt was nothing like the carefree adventure Elizabeth described to Gardner and Kirkland.

Certain that their parents would try to track them down, they carefully laid down a smokescreen. When they left the Wycombe Abbey campus, it was ostensibly to attend a rock concert at the town of Milton Keynes, about twenty miles away. Realizing the authorities would be on their tail very quickly, they further obfuscated their maneuverings by making plans through a local travel agency to go to the English port city of Harwich, then take a ferry to Holland, and from there take a train, with one-way tickets, to West Berlin.

Instead, they took a much different route. Rather than going to Harwich, which is northeast of London, they made their way to Dover, which is southwest of London. From there they took a ferry to France and went from there to Paris. To the two former students it was a wonderful little trick to pull, a magnificent start to a grand adventure. In reality it was a noble effort for beginning an affair that ended very ignobly indeed.

THEIR FIRST STOP WAS PARIS, WHERE THEY CELEBRATED THEIR SUCCESSFUL escape. From there they went to Nice. After that, the timetable and exact itinerary becomes a little fuzzy, due in large part to the fact that both Melinda and Elizabeth were heavily into drugs.

During July, August, September, and October they moved around almost constantly, usually by hitchhiking. They took work where they could find it. For a while they picked grapes on land owned by Moët-Chandon, the champagne people. They also worked temporarily for a vintner near the town of Ay in northern France, but quickly moved on when the man made sexual advances toward Elizabeth. That must have been particularly disturbing to the pair since they had become lovers. Melinda, called "Melie" by Elizabeth, and "Bunnie," as Melinda called Elizabeth, had begun sharing a bed.

"It was too bad," Elizabeth later confided to a friend, speaking of the circumstances that forced them to leave the vineyard in Ay. "The pay was good, the room and board were paid, and we had all the champagne we could drink."

During this period, they visited, among other cities, Bonn and Trier in Germany; Luxembourg; Reims and Dijon in France; and San Remo and Genoa in Italy. In Nice they were mugged by a man armed with a knife.

When they couldn't find work, they existed by selling their blood and possibly their bodies. Melinda was hospitalized for three days while they were in Italy, suffering from anemia. They also stayed for several days at a compound run by the Hari Krishnas while she recuperated further.

In Paris Elizabeth, who had been traveling on a British visitor's passport she had obtained the night before she and Melinda left Wycombe Abbey, applied for a six-month Canadian passport. Why Elizabeth, who already had a Canadian passport that was valid for another year, did this is not known, unless it was to try to hide her trail and keep her parents from finding her. Nevertheless, a new Canadian passport, number XR 126047, was issued to her on October 6, 1983 and it was good until the following March. Long before then her odyssey would be over.

With her new passport in hand, she and Melinda took off again, this time for Germany. They entered the eastern sector and hitchhiked to Berlin, arriving on October 13. There, at least initially, they acted like ordinary tourists, traipsing from one site to another. They were especially fascinated with the wall. But they were running out of money and, since German work rules are rigid, were unable to find employment. Both had slimmed down to the point of emaciation, and they had just about exhausted their inventory of ways to keep alive. They could find no work, and they had nothing left to sell. Most of their luggage had either been stolen or deposited in a left-luggage facility in France. They did not even have coats, and winter was rapidly approaching. They had no money to pay for lodging, so they ended up in a flophouse.

Worse, they had fallen in with bad companions. One group included a group of American oddballs who enjoyed pretending they were Communists. An even more sinister crowd was a gang of Irishmen who claimed to be terrorists with the IRA. The Irishmen took them into their quarters and drugged them heavily with a variety of chemicals, including hallucinogens. For several days they kept the two girls half knocked out, passing them among themselves for their sexual pleasure. After four days of this, Elizabeth and Melinda sobered up enough to recognize what a bad predicament they were in. They decided to escape. On October 25 they slipped away from the Irishmen and went straight to the British Consulate. Still proud, they asked only for train tickets back to Britain.

By this time they looked disreputable. Elizabeth had a gash on her head. The wound was clearly visible because most of her head was shaved—in a mohawk, which she died a bright pink. Both Melinda and Elizabeth had lost considerable weight, and their skin had a gray, sickly color. Their outer clothes were in rags, but they were all they had. Everything else, including their underwear, had been stolen or destroyed.

Despite the physical changes, when they appeared at the consulate, they were immediately recognized by an official who had been half expecting them. She had been approached not long before by an American military officer named Stuart Herrington who had provided Elizabeth's and Melinda's descriptions and asked to be notified if they showed up. The woman stalled the two girls, asking them to return the next afternoon to pick up their tickets. As soon as they left, she called Herrington.

10

A COLONEL IN ARMY INTELLIGENCE, STUART HERRINGTON HAD ENTERED the search for Elizabeth Haysom in a roundabout way. When Derek and Nancy had little success in tracking down their missing daughter through conventional methods, they turned to unconventional ones.

It happened that the husband of Nancy's old friend, Annie Massie, had a friend who was with Army intelligence in Munich. On September 8, a little more than two months after Elizabeth's disappearance, Nancy wrote the Massies' friend and asked for his help. She recited the clues as she knew them, including the details of the false trail through Harwich, which she still thought to be accurate. The man, in turn, got Herrington involved.

In her letter Nancy had enclosed a detailed description of Elizabeth, which included a height for her daughter that was one and a half to two inches shorter than it actually is. She described Elizabeth as "well built" and "quick-witted" and as behaving in a way that Nancy undoubtedly found odious. She wrote that occasionally Elizabeth purposely made herself look unkempt, hiding what an "educated" and "sophisticated" person she was.

However much Nancy disliked this tendency in her daughter, her statement undoubtedly was accurate. Elizabeth's classmates later verified that she seemed to go out of her way to appear unattractive. But *unkempt* would hardly be the word to describe Elizabeth when Herrington found her. When he went initially to the British Consulate, Herrington was armed with color photos of Elizabeth supplied by Nancy. When the official called Herrington to tell him that Elizabeth had shown up, she alerted him to be prepared for her present appearance. "You're going to find what is left of her," she warned.

In a November 2 letter to Nancy that ran six single-spaced pages, Herrington confessed that he was indeed "shocked" by his first glimpse of Elizabeth. When he interviewed her for the first time, she spent most of the time staring off into space, chain-smoking borrowed cigarettes. Her hands shook uncontrollably and the expression on her face seemed to indicate she was ready to burst into tears. It was not an auspicious beginning.

Worried that if he didn't approach the two girls gently, he might spook them and send them fleeing back into the Berlin semi-underground, possibly never to reemerge, Herrington told them that Nancy was worried about them *both* and had nothing in mind except their safety.

His approached worked. Despite their initial reluctance they agreed to go home with him and his wife. The plan was for them to recuperate until arrangements could be made to get them back to their families. In retrospect Herrington admitted that the situation had been very touchy. He worried that if he had not been able to convince the pair that what he was doing was for the good of *both* of them, they would have been gone again.

When he wrote Nancy, he went out of his way to stress that not all of Elizabeth's and Melinda's experiences had been bad, that they had many pleasant episodes along with the unpleasant, and that Elizabeth had collected a thick book full of names and addresses of people she had met on her travels. The connections she made would become significant years later in a very controversial way.

Herrington also cautioned Nancy that Elizabeth had serious problems, both physical and psychological.

When Elizabeth first reported to the British Consulate, he recounted, she was hemorrhaging from the vagina. The woman at the consulate was so concerned that she took Elizabeth immediately to a physician, who diagnosed the condition as a heavy menstrual period. Up until then, Elizabeth later admitted, she had been worried that she was pregnant.

The loyalty Elizabeth and Melinda exhibited toward each other troubled Herrington, however, especially as it related to the sexual bonds that had developed between them. Herrington originally hoped to be able to put Elizabeth on a plane straight to Virginia or Nova Scotia, since Derek and Nancy had homes in both places, and send Melinda to her parents' home near London. But he realized this plan was impossible; it was too soon to expect the two girls to disattach themselves. They refused to be separated while they stayed with him, and this caused him considerable concern. Perhaps to soothe Nancy, he wrote that it was his conclusion that Melinda had been the "aggressor" in the relationship and that he felt she was destined to be a lesbian for the rest of her life, a deduction he made in part because she had a stack of lesbian pornography with her when he took them home.

Indeed, five years later that prediction seemed to be holding true: Classmates of the two girls at Wycombe Abbey breathlessly reported that Melinda was currently head of a gay and lesbian group in Edinburgh. Still, it was unclear who had seduced whom. Years later Elizabeth would deny that there had been any physical relationship, but some people were convinced there had been. Even Elizabeth admitted that Melinda was sexually aggressive.

EIGHT DAYS AFTER ELIZABETH AND MELINDA WENT HOME WITH Herrington and his wife, the colonel put them on a plane to London. They were met at the airport by Elizabeth's half-brother, Julian, who was in England on business. A few days later, as soon as he could get away, Derek flew over and Julian returned to Canada. It was not until Derek got there that a meeting was set up between Melinda and her father, a meeting which took place over dinner with Derek and Elizabeth also present. The reunion between Melinda and her father was less than joyous; after the meal, her father returned home without her, and Melinda left with Elizabeth and her father. A few days later Elizabeth talked Melinda into going home to face her parents with the understanding that if she could not work things out at home she could come to Virginia. Derek paid for her train ticket. Melinda was met at the station by another relative, who arranged for her to enroll in a local college until she could attend the University of Edinburgh.

The separation effectively ended the relationship between Elizabeth and Melinda. After she returned to Virginia, Elizabeth wrote to Melinda only once.

If there had been a miscalculation of the effects of Melinda's and Elizabeth's trip through Europe, it probably was in the depth of Elizabeth's resentment toward her parents, especially her mother. In retrospect, it was much greater than it seemed at the time. But that was not what Elizabeth told Gardner and Kirkland. What she told the detectives was that Derek and Nancy were delighted to hear from her when she surfaced at the Herringtons' and were completely understanding about her adventure. "Most parents, I think, would have been either angry or they would have tried to lay a heavy guilt complex on you. You know," she said, imitating a stern parent, " 'God, you worried us to death for the last five months,' you know, 'We spent like, I don't know, thirty thousand dollars trying to find you and, you know, this is what you're doing, you screwed up everything' . . . blah, blah, blah. And instead it was just like, 'Well, I'm glad you got that out of your system.' You know, big chuckle."

Gardner, unaware of the background of the story that Elizabeth had been weaving for them, wanted to get back to drugs, to explore that avenue a little further. He decided to back into it, to pick up *after* the incident at Wycombe Abbey to see if she would admit to more drug use than she had so far mentioned.

"You said earlier that you flipped out after being accused of possession of some drugs. When did you start doing drugs?"

"I had been doing some," Elizabeth said grudgingly. "But never in school," she added quickly. "I was far too interested in what I was doing in school. I get a great deal of pleasure out of academic work. So I never did any drugs in school." She paused. "I was smoking," she added. "I guess hash, a little grass. But that was out of school, you know. At parties and stuff like that. The usual thing."

"Cocaine?"

"No," she said emphatically.

"No coke?" Gardner pressed.

She was adamant. "No coke at all."

"Have you ever done much heroin?"

"I did heroin for a little bit," she admitted, "when I was in Italy."

"How did you do that?"

"I was injecting it."

Gardner, sensing a growing hostility, decided to leave the drug issue alone for the time being. "Okay," he said pleasantly. "You said when you took off you went with a friend?"

"Yes," Elizabeth answered guardedly.

"Did you ever leave her at any time or did y'all stay together the whole time?"

"We stayed together the whole time," Elizabeth sighed, not happy with the turn in the questions. "I went through tremendous depression. It was quite a shock. I mean I was completely spoiled. I *am* completely spoiled. I was in some ways like an only child. I was my parents' love child and my brothers are much older than I and all that attention was focused on me when I was at home and I guess the school's attention was focused on me too . . ."

"Uh huh," Kirkland prompted.

"Having to sleep, you know, in communes . . . I guess that got to me after a while, and I just did the nice cliché things, turning to something that would alleviate that."

"What did you turn to?" Kirkland asked quietly.

"Well," Elizabeth volunteered, "I started doing a lot of acid." She paused, then answered slowly, "I guess I was doing a lot of drugs. I was doing quite a lot of acid, and by the time I got to Italy—I'd never touched heroin before—and it just seemed the thing to do."

Gardner was still curious about what had happened to Elizabeth at Wycombe Abbey, whether she wasn't holding a grudge against her parents for not removing her from what she described as an extremely unpleasant situation.

"They tried to get me out," she insisted. "They couldn't have done any more. They came over to England, and they tried to get me out of it, but the situation was such that they couldn't. That was the only time I felt resentful," she said. "After that I realized that people make mistakes. They're human, and the school had everything to recommend it, and nobody knew this could happen. There was just something about me that the school couldn't handle. Or I couldn't deal with them. It wasn't my parents' fault. Whenever I came home, they were all ears and supportive."

Wasn't there anything, Gardner wanted to know, about her relationship with her parents that maybe made Elizabeth feel a little uncomfortable or that she didn't like?

Maybe there was one thing, she conceded. But it wasn't a terribly big deal.

What was that? Gardner pressed.

"My parents really did spoil me," she said. "My father certainly did. I was like his baby daughter, and what I said went. My mother tried to keep that under control, but it always ended up as hugs and kisses and a bunch of giggles."

Get to the point, Gardner thought.

"They really wanted to see me get a good education," Elizabeth continued. "My father was very much of the belief that a British education was the only one that was worth anything. Also, they were scared to death when my face was smashed up. And I think after that they felt that since I'd been away, I might as well stay in the system. But when I came home, it was tight. It was very close. There were a couple of times, you know, like when guys would come around to take me out, Dad would say, 'I'm sorry,' you know, he would say, 'I've changed my mind. I don't think it's a good idea for you to go out.' "

"What did you think about that?"

"Actually, to tell you the truth, with most of the guys concerned, it didn't bother me one way or the other. Going out was just something to do rather than me being attracted to them."

Is that all? Gardner asked himself.

"I had a fantastic relationship with my parents," Elizabeth continued. "I never went through that phase of screaming at them, saying, 'I want to take the car out,' and them saying, 'I won't give you the car' kind of stuff. It was never 'I want to go out tonight and I want to go to this party.' We had tremendous trust between us. When I went out, yeah, Daddy got a little jealous, you know. He was concerned that way. But he'd joke about it, you know. He'd say, 'You're passing your old father over for some young guy.' You know. We'd joke about it."

"Have you had many boyfriends?"

"I wouldn't say I had many *boyfriends*, but I had a lot of male friends. In fact, most of my friends are male. They used to come see me on weekends or I'd go see them on weekends. Then when I was in Lynchburg, I went out with a couple of people. But at UVA my social life is completely hectic. I don't really enjoy that. I'm fairly quiet. I mean, I like to sit home and just, you know, be quiet."

"Do you have any ambitions of marriage or anything like that?" Kirkland asked.

Elizabeth stiffened. "That's the only thing I had a row with my parents about," she said, inexplicably popping up from her chair. "My father really believed in the institution of marriage. He wasn't so concerned about premarital sex or any of that business. He was fairly liberal that way. He believed if you loved somebody, what you did was your business and nobody else's. But he really believed that if you had a gift or ability that you should have children and that you should pass the family on."

Kirkland and Gardner watched, puzzled, as Elizabeth began to pace, walking nervously around the front of the classroom.

"For a long time," she said, "I really disliked the idea of marriage. I'm still not completely happy with it. That doesn't mean to say I like the idea of living with somebody. That doesn't really appeal to me either. I value my independence tremendously. At the moment, if I were to think about getting married, I don't think it would be for a long time."

"Who did you feel closest to?" Kirkland asked. "Your Mom or Dad? As far as being able to talk to? Explain things to?"

"It really depended," Elizabeth replied nervously. "Some

things definitely were Daddy's subjects. I could talk to Daddy about sex, drugs, any of that stuff. I could talk to him about all those things, but when it came to school, I guess I talked to Mom more about that. For some reason, and this is completely unfounded, I had this tremendous feeling of pressure from my parents. I felt that I had to completely excel. Excellence was the only thing that was acceptable."

"How did you feel about this?"

"It made me want to excel."

"Did it bother you or depress you any?"

"No, it just made me a little frantic. It didn't really bother me. I enjoy pressure of some sort. I never felt depressed about it, and I never found the work sufficiently difficult to cause me any stress that way."

"Did it ever bother you that what you did in school was more important to your parents than how you felt about things?"

"No," Elizabeth emphasized. "In fact, the whole thing of pressure was completely unfounded. I mean that was something I sort of invented. It was paranoia. Something in my own head. If anything, my parents were quite carefree. All the time they used to try to get me out of school at UVA. You know, 'Just skip that,' they'd say. Then, 'Why don't you say the hell with that?' Or 'Let's have lunch.' Or 'Let's go shopping.' "

"Let's take a break," Gardner suggested, rising and stretching.

While Elizabeth went to the ladies room, Gardner turned to Kirkland.

"What do you think?"

"I think she's hiding something," Kirkland replied.

"What do you think it could be?"

"I don't know, but look how nervous she got when we started talking about marriage and pressing her about her parents."

"That seems pretty strange all right."

"I think it's pretty obvious that there's something she doesn't want us to know. I guess we just have to find out what."

11

SOMETHING ELIZABETH SAID WAS NAGGING AT GARDNER. IT WAS THE WAY she had answered his and Kirkland's questions about her boy-friends and marriage—not so much what she had said but how she had said it and the words she had used. He cautioned himself to tread carefully because he didn't want to risk making her hostile. "Now, when you say you have some question about being married," he began, "I don't know if that's because of your independence or if you are possibly gay?"

As soon as he said it, he was glad that he had not confronted her more directly. Elizabeth jumped up as though she had sat on a tack. "No!" she said loudly.

She overreacted, Gardner felt. He was sure now there was something there.

"You've strayed?" he persisted.

Elizabeth, pacing around the room, answered elliptically, conceding that after she had been attacked in the Nova Scotian schoolyard because of her father's union stance, she began to regard males with animosity, a situation all the attentions of her half-brothers could not correct.

Her statements were mostly show for Gardner and Kirkland. Elizabeth was still anxious to impress the detectives with the idea that her family was extremely close knit. To make sure they got the point, she stressed how helpful her parents had been and how grateful she was for their support.

"Nobody's like them," she said with apparent sincerity. "I

mean, my mother used to come up to my room sometimes late at night just to make sure I was okay and give me a hug. My parents were always there no matter what. No matter how dreadful I was, they were always there."

Still pacing, she glanced quickly at the two detectives, as if to see, thought Gardner and Kirkland, how they were taking her performance.

They weren't buying it at all. Not completely. But both had enough experience with people not to let their thoughts show. While they both intuited that she was not telling the truth, they weren't sure what she was lying about or why.

Elizabeth went on to explain that her parents' marriage was a model for her and that until she felt she could find someone she was as compatible with as her mother had been with Derek, she preferred not to get married.

Gardner blinked. She's been talking for five minutes, he told himself, but she still hasn't answered my question. He tried again. "The reason you don't want to get married is definitely not because you're gay?"

"Oh, no," Elizabeth said emphatically. "No, I'm *not* gay."

Gardner nodded. May as well leave it there for right now, he figured, although he was convinced he had not yet heard the truth. He started to ask another question, but Elizabeth cut him off.

"I went through a stage of that," she told him hurriedly. "I'll be honest with you. I did. Yeah."

"Yeah?" Gardner said, not really surprised. He was getting the feel of her personality now, realizing that delicacy was the key in her interrogation, not confrontation. Let her ramble long enough, and sooner or later she would tell him what he was asking. "I guess that's what happens when you go to an all-girls school," he said in mock understanding.

"Well, *that* really wasn't a thing at the school," Elizabeth explained, adding that the incident she was referring to had not occurred at school but during vacation. "It was just a holiday thing," she said.

She's getting there, Gardner told himself. That's not the whole story, but she figures that will be enough to convince me to move on to something else. But it wasn't. "What about the time you and your friend took off?" he asked. "Was she just a friend?"

That was a sore spot for Elizabeth. Her eyes flashed, and Gardner feared for a moment that he had pushed her too far too quickly, that he should have approached that subject differently.

"Melinda was gay," Elizabeth snapped, then quickly added that didn't mean she also was gay. Even though Melinda had made advances toward her, she had maintained her distance, protected her heterosexuality. "I love men, you know." Besides, she explained, it was quite fashionable in Europe at that time to be bisexual, and it would not have been unusual for a heterosexual woman to have a homosexual affair just to see what it was like.

Gardner asked if that is what had happened. Had Melinda made advances toward her believing that she might go along just to see what it was like?

"Oh, yeah," Elizabeth said, realizing she had a possible way out. "We had problems that way. But she got the idea that I didn't care if she was gay just as long as she kept her hands to herself."

Were Derek and Nancy as open-minded? Gardner asked. Did *they* worry about their daughter's sexual orientation?

As usual, Elizabeth didn't answer directly. Instead, she said that a lot of people assumed that she was gay because she had run off with a gay girl. Some other people assumed, however, that because she had no visible means of support while she and Melinda were traveling through Europe, she had been working as a prostitute. Some people even thought that she had deliberately gotten pregnant or tried to.

Most liars are convinced that the more outrageous the story, the more credible it becomes. Elizabeth tested that theory then. "Actually," she told Gardner and Kirkland with a straight face, "I had been completely celibate."

"Didn't you say earlier," Gardner pointed out, "that you thought yourself that you were pregnant?"

Elizabeth paused. How could she have forgotten that? Never at a loss for words, however, she scrambled quickly to recover.

"I just got this thing into my head that I was pregnant, you know. I mean, traveling can do strange things to your head."

Gardner rolled his eyes. But her pregnancy wasn't what interested him right then. He wanted to know more about her possible homosexual relationships. "Elizabeth—" he started, but was interrupted by the quick buzz of the recorder signaling the end of a tape. While he changed the cassette, he told Elizabeth he wanted to pick up on the homosexuality issue again when the session continued.

Forewarned, Elizabeth was ready. "I thought that the fashion of bisexuality was a scream," she began. "It amused me to dress in drag, that kind of stuff. I liked to go to gay bars and have a laugh." It was very juvenile, she confessed, but on the other hand homosexuality was not something she took very seriously.

When he had asked earlier about her parents' reaction, Elizabeth had answered evasively. So Gardner decided to try again. The homosexual issue may not have been a big deal to her, Gardner said, but it may have been one to Derek and Nancy. They must have thought she was gay. Did it bother them?

Elizabeth laughed. They had been very understanding, she said. She had just sat down with them and explained that even though Melinda was gay, that did not mean that she and Melinda had had a sexual relationship.

"Did they believe you?" Gardner asked.

"Oh, yes," Elizabeth said lightly. "They were much more concerned that I might have been pregnant."

GARDNER GLANCED OVER HIS NOTES. HE AND KIRKLAND HAD BEEN TALKING to Elizabeth for a long time, and, while the conversation was interesting, he really wasn't getting the answers he had been searching for. One of the things he had hoped Elizabeth would tell them was *why* someone may have wanted to murder her parents. So far, he hadn't even gotten close to an answer. He decided to pursue that angle more aggressively.

"Did your parents have a happy marriage?" he asked Elizabeth.

"Oh, yes," Elizabeth sighed, obviously relieved to be talking about something else.

"Very, very happy?"

"Yes."

"From day one?"

"That was the funny thing. They told me that when they got married, they made an agreement: My father said to my mother that no matter how old they got and no matter how many bits of them had been chopped off, they would always sleep together."

Gardner winced at the phrase about bits of them being chopped off. A very poor choice of words considering what happened to them, he told himself.

Elizabeth apparently did not notice. She kept right on talking, anxious to impress upon the detectives how happy her parents had been. That, too, was apparently a lie, at least according to what she would later claim. But at that stage neither Gardner nor Kirkland had sufficient background to begin weeding truth from falsehood.

"They still referred to each other by their lovers' names," Elizabeth continued. "Ruden and Druden. Those were names they had picked up in Europe somewhere." Mainly, she said, they acted like young lovers.

Gardner wanted at least to eliminate the possibility that they had been killed by a spurned lover. "Did either one of them appear jealous?"

"Oh, no," Elizabeth answered quickly.

How about the age difference? Gardner asked. Was that a problem? Nineteen years was a big gap.

"They were just like a honeymoon couple," Elizabeth insisted. Her father was very attentive. Often he came home with a bottle of champagne, or he would bring Nancy coffee in bed.

"So it would be safe to say they had a very happy marriage?" Gardner asked.

"They had a *fantastic* marriage," Elizabeth amended.

GARDNER SIGHED. ANOTHER DEAD END. TIME TO TRY ANOTHER TACK. Groping, he asked Elizabeth about her parents' financial situation.

They were very comfortable, financially speaking, she asserted. They had, in fact, paid $165,000 *in cash* for the house they were living in when they were killed. Plus, they were contemplating buying another house in North Carolina. It was priced at $225,000 and she thought they were going to pay most of that in cash.

"Were your parents very, very wealthy?" Gardner asked.

"I wouldn't say they were very, very wealthy. I would say that they had been very careful. My father was a cash man. He didn't believe in credit. He didn't buy something unless he had the money for it."

Gardner raised an eyebrow. He hadn't known about the Haysoms' penchant for cash. Did they keep a lot of money around the house? he wanted to know. Could they have been murdered by a robber? Did they have a safe?

The detective was giving Elizabeth one opportunity after another to confuse the investigation. A little slowly, because she was making it up as she went along, she told him that her mother often kept valuables, including cash, in a secret spot behind the hot water heater.

What kind of valuables? Gardner asked.

In addition to the cash, she said, her mother hid some antiques, some silver, and possibly some other things as well. She had never actually seen the hiding place, she added, because her mother was very secretive about it. But she knew it existed. Her mother told her if she ever needed money in an emergency, she could get it from there.

Who else knew about it? Gardner wanted to know.

Thinking quickly, Elizabeth spewed out the first name she could think of. Annie Massie, she said.

Gardner said nothing, but he was shocked. Why in hell did she say that? he asked himself. We've just about torn that house apart, and we didn't find any indication of a safe or a hiding place of any kind. Why is Elizabeth now trying to make us believe there was? And why did she bring Annie Massie into it? He would have to think about that, he decided. Right now he was tired. Kirkland was tired. Elizabeth was tired. It had been a long, exhausting interview. But there was one thing more he wanted to cover before he wrapped it up.

"Let's talk about Margaret Louise," Gardner said. "Are you and Margaret Louise pretty good friends?"

"Yes," Elizabeth said enthusiastically.

"I heard it through the grapevine. I may be completely off base, but I understand she had a little—"

"Oh, yes," Elizabeth interrupted. "She was put under psychiatric treatment because she needed some support. They stuck her in a home, and they gave her intense shock treatment plus a lot of drugs."

Did that affect her? Gardner asked. Permanently?

"That's bound to have an effect on anybody," Elizabeth said. Then she added quickly, "But she's completely normal when you talk to her. It's just that she's a little bit distant. She's very quiet and she thinks in a slightly different way than most people. But she's safe."

Is she unbalanced still? Gardner asked. Is she slow?

Definitely not, Elizabeth responded. "She's got a first-class mind with a degree in mathematics and computers. She has a good sense of humor. She's completely with it. She knows what's going on. She acts. She dances."

Gardner asked about Margaret Louise's relationship with Elizabeth's half-brother Julian.

They were engaged, Elizabeth said, but Julian broke it off when he met another woman in Canada. The unfortunate thing about it, she added, was that the breakup came very unexpectedly. Margaret Louise had no idea that Julian was thinking of ending the relationship until he told her that he had married someone else.

That must have been pretty traumatic, Gardner observed.

It was, Elizabeth agreed, but she had been amazed at how well Margaret Louise had taken it, how quickly she had recovered.

How had Nancy and Derek reacted? Gardner asked.

Elizabeth said her parents had been very upset with Julian because they, too, were very fond of Margaret Louise. They could not believe that Julian would have been so callous. On the whole, she said, she was impressed by how well Margaret Louise had recovered.

"I thought she'd flip out," Elizabeth said. "We were worried

12

THE NEXT MORNING, WHEN MEMBERS OF THE HOMICIDE SQUAD GOT TOgether to compare notes, Debbie Kirkland wanted to say what she thought about Elizabeth Haysom.

"I didn't like her," she began.

"Why not?" one of the officers asked.

"Maybe I'm prejudiced. I just didn't like the way she came off. She was too stuck up for me."

"Being stuck up isn't a crime," the investigator said.

"I know. I guess I just got bad feelings about her. I really got suspicious when she started that walking around bit."

"What do you mean?"

"When the questions got tough, she couldn't sit still. She had to get up and move around. I've been in this job for twelve years, and that's long enough to know that means she's hiding something. I know she was lying, I'm just not sure what about."

"Is this just personal?"

"No, it's more than that. My instincts tell me she knows a lot more than she's saying. For one thing, I guess I just didn't feel she was showing enough emotion. I mean, her parents were just killed, but you'd never know it by talking to her. There wasn't any sorrow in her eyes. There wasn't a thing there to show she felt bad about it."

"Well, you can't arrest her for that," Gardner said.

"No, I guess you can't," Kirkland agreed.

she'd commit suicide. She was extremely depressed, but she kept in contact with us. We saw her over Christmas. She had presents for us all, and it was perfectly normal and lovely."

So there was no suspicion in her mind, Gardner asked, that Margaret Louise could have been angry enough at Julian for her to take it out on Elizabeth's parents?

Elizabeth scoffed at the idea. "That would be ludicrous," she said.

TOGETHER THE THREE OF THEM LEFT THE CLASSROOM AND WALKED BACK into the main lobby. Waiting for them was the dark-haired youth who had driven Elizabeth to the interview. Elizabeth walked over to him, and the two of them climbed into the van. Kirkland and Gardner went into the principal's office, which was being used as the command post.

"Who was that?" asked Kirkland, who sensed an unpleasant arrogance about the youth who had come for Elizabeth.

"Aw, what's his name?" Gardner said, scratching his head. "I can't think of it right off. It's her boyfriend. That German kid."

THE FEELING MUST HAVE BEEN MUTUAL. AS SOON AS ELIZABETH HAD LEFT the interview with Gardner and Kirkland, she went to her brothers and reported that the police were giving her a bad time. Howard, the surgeon from Houston, called a well-known defense lawyer in Charlottesville, John Lowe. He, in turn, called Sheriff Wells and told him his investigators were not to question any members of the Haysom family without him being there.

"Come on, John," Wells told him. "You know better than that. If your clients don't want to talk to our people, *they* have to tell us that, not you."

Wells heard no more from the lawyer. Or from the Haysoms.

ON APRIL 12, FOUR DAYS AFTER THE INTERVIEW, ELIZABETH WROTE A BRIEF note to Colonel Herrington notifying him of the murders. She was writing, she said, with considerable "hostility" and a lot of "anger" about both the killings and the fact that she had been questioned. Her mother and father had been "butchered," she wrote, because of America's "savagery" and "brutality." She added that the United States is the only place where law enforcement officials would "harass" the daughter of murdered parents by treating her as a principal suspect because the victims "did not give her a car."

THE DAYS SLIPPED BY, BUT ANSWERS CONTINUED TO ELUDE THE DETECTIVES. When a week had passed and there had been no arrests, residents were starting to get antsy. Small-town gossip mills being what they are, many were already convinced that Margaret Louise was the murderer, even though officers had tried to keep secret the names of the people they were talking to. Every direction officers turned, it seemed, Margaret Louise's name came up, sometimes from the most unexpected sources.

Bedford County prosecutor Jim Updike was walking to court one day a week or so after the bodies were discovered when a lawyer from Lynchburg challenged him in the hallway.

"Why haven't you made an arrest yet?" the man demanded.

Updike stared at him in surprise.

"Everybody knows Margaret Louise did it," the lawyer continued.

Updike bit his tongue.

"You'd better arrest her and throw her in jail," the lawyer added belligerently, "before she kills someone else."

THE NEWSPAPERS WERE GETTING RESTLESS, TOO. THREE DAYS AFTER THE memorial service for the Haysoms, a week after the bodies were found, the Lynchburg *News & Daily Advance* waded into the discussion with an editorial that unintentionally reflected the same frustrations investigators were facing in trying to solve the crimes. Under the headline, "What Possible Motive for Such Brutal Slayings?" the editorial said:

> The grotesqueness of the killings is troubling, to say the least. Brutal stabbing deaths by unknown assailants of a peaceful couple is something one reads about in larger metropolitan areas—far removed from Lynchburg. This community has been spared such violence.
>
> Who would so brutally snuff out the lives of this articulate couple whose worldwide experiences had exposed them to far more dangerous settings than anything they could have anticipated in their quiet neighborhood? What beast of a human is capable of such a senseless slaughter? Why? What could possibly provoke another human or humans to inflict such punishment on fellow travelers? Revenge? Satisfying some sick desire to kill?
>
> The police are just as desperate for answers to those questions as we are. If for nothing else than peace of mind for the family and friends of the Haysoms, we hope the answers will come quickly.

While at first Sheriff Wells had assigned every man he could find in the department to the case, he soon realized it was going to be a drawn-out investigation. It didn't take him long to realize that he was going to have to cut back on the Haysom staff enough to free some officers to take care of the routine. It was time, Wells figured, to assign the case to a specific investigative team. He and his top aide, Captain Lockland, met late one afternoon to decide who it was going to be. They chose Gardner and Reid.

Late that night, when Gardner dragged in from a long day of chasing down dead-end leads, he found a note to call Lockland.

"Be sure you go by headquarters first thing in the morning," the captain told him. "There's something on your desk you need to see."

Early the next day, Gardner detoured through Bedford and went straight to his desk. Smack in the center, where he couldn't miss it, was a two-foot-tall stack of papers. He went charging into Lockland's office. "What's all that stuff?" he asked.

"That's the material to date on the Haysom case."

"What's it doing on my desk?"

"It's your case now."

"Come again?" said a surprised Gardner, the newest investigator in the department.

"You heard me," Lockland said. "It's your case. Yours and Reid's."

"Oh God," Gardner moaned. "What a way to start the day."

Lockland grinned. "Good luck and get cracking."

13

RICKY GARDNER WAS SHUFFLING THROUGH HIS NOTES FOR THE UMPTEENTH time when something he had scribbled jumped out at him. At one point in the April 8 interview Elizabeth had mentioned that she and her boyfriend had spent the weekend of the murders in Washington, D.C. It was a slow period at school, she said, and they wanted to get away for a couple of days. Knowing neither of them had a car, Gardner had asked how they got there. He had written down Elizabeth's reply. She said that they had rented a car in Charlottesville and driven up. Damn! he berated himself. Why didn't I think of that before?

The next day he drove to Charlottesville and went straight to Pantops Texaco, the local agent for National Car Rental, and asked to see the receipt for a rental to Elizabeth Haysom. When the clerk handed it over, Gardner really cursed himself.

It showed that the 1985 Chevette rented to E. R. Haysom on March 29 had 20,073 miles on the odometer when it was returned on March 31. That was 669 miles more than it had when it was checked out.

That can't be, Gardner thought at first, 669 miles? How could they rack up that much mileage on a weekend trip to Washington when it's less than 230 miles there and back?

The more he thought about it, the more likely it became that there was only one explanation. What if they didn't go just to

Washington, but instead went to Washington, then came back to Lynchburg, then went back to Washington?

He grabbed a pencil and paper. Say 120 miles from Charlottesville to Washington, more or less. He wrote down "120." Then if they went to Lynchburg, they'd have to come back to Charlottesville, so that would be another 120. He wrote another "120." Then 80, say, being generous, from Charlottesville to Lynchburg. He put down "80." Coming back, that would be 80, plus 120. Then they still had to get back to Charlottesville, so that would be another 120. He added his column of figures. Hot damn! That was 640 miles. Figure a little for driving around in Washington, and there's the 669. He put down his pencil. I think it's time to talk to Elizabeth Haysom again, he told himself.

GARDNER CALLED THE UNIVERSITY OF VIRGINIA POLICE AND ASKED THEM to contact Elizabeth and set up an interview as soon as possible.

On Tuesday, April 16, at 10:40 P.M., Gardner met Elizabeth in the UVA Police Department building on the edge of the campus. While Elizabeth still professed to want to help, the interview this time was considerably more strained. Elizabeth had carped to her brother about alleged harassment from Gardner, and Gardner knew it. It didn't make for good feelings on either side. Also, Elizabeth had sensed Debbie Kirkland's antagonism and toward the end of the last interview had become hostile. This time Gardner had another officer along, Sergeant Carroll Baker of the Lynchburg Police Department. Still, Elizabeth was not happy to see the detectives.

When they met in the tiny office at the rear of the building, Gardner abandoned much of the friendliness he displayed at the first interview; his questions became sharper, his mood less affable.

To open the interview, Gardner asked Elizabeth about her boyfriend and the period *before* the murders, intending to work up through their weekend in Washington and the issue of the excessive mileage on the rental car.

"Has your boyfriend stayed at your parents' house, too?"

"Yeah," Elizabeth replied snappishly. "A lot of people have visited from school."

"Who is 'a lot of people'?"

"I've had friends down since I've been here so it would be a steady stream of people going down for just a meal."

Gardner debated whether to push further on that. He decided against it.

"Okay," he said, "now the last time you were visiting your parents, which was your father's birthday, March 23, and you came back on the 24th, they drove you back. Was your boyfriend with you?"

"No. I was there alone."

"Okay. When was the last time—"

"That he was there?"

"Yes."

"Uh," she paused, "let's see. The week before that I went to Colorado. So it was about two or three weeks." She looked around the office. "I wish I had a calendar."

"I do," Gardner said, digging into his briefcase.

"Okay, this was the birthday," she said, pointing to the calendar. "I was in Colorado from the 9th to the 16th, the 17th, the 2nd, the 3rd." She paused again, apparently puzzled. "It must have been in February, the 23rd or the 24th, something like that. Yeah, I think it was the 23rd and 24th."

"Of February?"

"Yeah."

"When did you leave for Colorado?"

"On Friday the 8th."

"Of March?"

"Yes. And I came back on the 17th. The 17th of March."

"Okay. And on the 29th you and Jens rented a car and went to Washington?"

"Uh huh."

"And you returned on the 31st?"

"Uh huh."

"Okay. According to the mileage on the car, you drove 669 miles from the time you left Charlottesville until the time you got back to Charlottesville. Ya'll must have really driven a whole lot."

"Yeah," Elizabeth responded, looking nervous. "We did a couple of things."

Gardner raised an eyebrow.

"First we detoured."

"A detour?" Gardner asked, disbelief in his voice.

"Yeah," Elizabeth said, swinging a leg covered in dark blue Spandex tights. "We went into Warrenton. We got lost. I wasn't paying attention. We drove around there for a while and . . ." She paused. "Yeah, because we left here about . . ." She paused again. "I think we left here about three-thirty and we didn't get there until seven." She laughed nervously. "Also we drove a lot around Washington. We drove around Washington several times. And we drove around the neighboring areas, too."

Gardner said nothing.

"Where else did we go?" Elizabeth asked herself aloud. "We've rented a car several times."

Looking alert: "It must have been on that trip that we first went down to Lexington." Then she contradicted herself. "No, I don't think it was. No. We went straight to Washington. And we got lost on the way and drove around."

Gardner waited a long time before asking the next question, giving her a chance to elaborate. When she didn't, he plowed ahead. "Okay," he said, "you told us before, but why did ya'll go to Washington?"

"Oh, well, we went up just to spend the weekend together. Also, I had to go and look at a couple of things at one of the art galleries. And we went and looked at some memorials. We went to see some movies and that sort of stuff."

Again Gardner paused. "I meant to ask you this the other day, and I forgot about it. Did your parents like your boyfriend, Jens?"

Elizabeth evaded the question. "They gave me the money to go to Washington. They would come down here, and we'd all have supper together."

"But they didn't object to ya'll seeing each other, you and Jens?"

"No, not at all," she lied. But Gardner didn't know it was a lie.

Not satisfied with her answers, Gardner took her through an explanation of the Washington trip again but her story remained essentially the same. Unable to budge her, he moved on to other subjects. Who in the family owned tennis shoes? How many pairs and what sizes were they? Did her father carry a wallet? Did her mother normally offer to fix a meal for a visitor? Without warning, he switched back to Washington.

"When you stayed at the Washington Marriott, did you register in your name?"

Elizabeth thought for a minute. "I don't know quite how that worked because we used Jen's Visa card. I believe the reservation was in my name, but it was his Visa card that paid for it. And then I paid him back."

Again, Gardner switched subjects.

"Let's talk about Margaret Louise."

"That's a touchy subject with me," Elizabeth answered defensively.

"Yeah, I gathered that the other day. But Investigator Kirkland and I talked about it, and I have some more questions. Your mother really liked her, didn't she?"

"Yes, very much. They did a lot of things together."

"They had a very nice relationship?"

"My father liked her, too," Elizabeth volunteered. "But he didn't like the way Julian was handling the situation."

"Can you be more specific?"

"We all felt that Julian was, I guess, moving too quickly with Margaret Louise, that he was seeing her too much. What I mean is that Julian was aware of the fact that Margaret Louise had her problems, her emotional or psychological trouble, whatever. He knew that she had been in a home and that kind of thing, and both my parents felt that to be fair to her and fair to himself, he should take it gently and get to know her thoroughly before running off to Nova Scotia and getting engaged. My parents liked Margaret Louise, and they were very worried that Julian was going to hurt her badly and that she would flip again."

Gardner picked up on the *flip again* but let it pass.

Elizabeth added, "He dropped the engagement and got married to somebody else, and Margaret Louise was left in the lurch."

"Do you have personal knowledge of Margaret Louise's reaction when she found out that Julian had gotten married?"

"She didn't know."

"She didn't know!"

"All she knew was that Julian was perhaps living with a woman. And when she found out, she coped pretty well."

For more than thirty minutes, Gardner questioned Elizabeth about the relationship between Nancy Haysom and Margaret Louise. Elizabeth said it had been excellent up until the time she and Julian broke up, and then it had cooled. In the previous interview she had enthusiastically defended Margaret Louise, but under Gardner's questioning this time she took a patronizing stance, implying that Margaret Louise was nice, but, well, maybe she just didn't have it all together, that maybe she could be capable of a double murder.

"Had you ever known Margaret Louise to ride a bicycle to your mother's and father's?" Gardner asked.

"A bicycle?" Elizabeth asked, surprised. "No. I don't think she's coordinated enough to ride a bicycle."

"She rides," Gardner said matter-of-factly.

"She rides!" Elizabeth said. "Golly, that would be terrifying to meet her on the road. Her driving is terrifying."

"I think she got one for Christmas."

"Oh, really? I can't imagine that at all."

LEAFING THROUGH HIS NOTES FROM THE EARLIER INTERVIEW, GARDNER stopped and looked up. "It was mentioned that your mother had some valuables in a closet behind the hot water heater. Have you thought about what that could have been?"

"Well, I know absolutely, dead positive, that she had emergency cash in there. And she kept silver and some jewelry back there. She and my father lived through enough political strife and things to know anything could happen at any particular moment and you need to have some cash in the house."

"Would it be a large amount?" Gardner asked, expecting her to reply that it was a couple of hundred dollars.

"I think there was probably between five and ten thousand dollars," Elizabeth said.

Gardner was amazed. "In cash?"

Elizabeth smiled. "In cash."

"And kept in the house?"

"Yes. They were thinking about plane tickets and that kind of stuff. I don't know if it was American dollars or Canadian dollars or British pounds or whatever, but they kept a substantial sum of money back there."

Gardner's brain was whirring. despite what Elizabeth had said earlier, police had never found any sort of cache in the Haysom's house, not behind the hot water heater or anywhere else. And they had turned the house inside out. If what Elizabeth was saying was true, robbery could have been a motive even if Nancy's gold necklace and Derek's watch had not been taken.

"Did your father know about the hiding spot?"

"I think he knew it was there, but I don't think he knew *what* was there. Mummie was secretive."

"Would Margaret Louise have known? Did your mother trust her enough to tell her that it was back there?"

"I don't know," Elizabeth replied. "I know a couple of times my mother and father talked to her about looking after the house, but I don't know whether she told Margaret Louise there was something back there or not."

GARDNER WAS LEARNING ONE THING VERY QUICKLY ABOUT ELIZABETH Haysom: She was full of surprises. Talking to her was like opening one of those large Russian dolls. Inside the outer doll is another doll. Then there is another doll inside that one. And another inside that, and so forth, on and on, seemingly interminably. If Gardner asked Elizabeth what he thought was a simple question, she invariably built on it, expanding upon her answer as she went, taking it down paths that Gardner could not have suspected it could go. He thought he was looking into the murders of two members of an upper-middle-class, respectable family. Elizabeth made him shiver. If she were to be believed, her parents didn't have a skeleton or two hidden in the closet, they had a whole cemetery, a virtual Forest Lawn. At no time up until then had this phenomenon been so clear as when he asked his next question, which he thought was a straightforward query deserving of a straightforward answer. What he got stunned him as much as if he'd stuck a wet finger into an empty light socket.

"Do you know who your mother's first husband was?" he asked innocently.

Elizabeth said a name.

"Where is he?"

Elizabeth laughed. "If he's not in jail, he's probably in England."

That statement launched Elizabeth on one of the most improbable tales Gardner had ever heard. The story she was about to tell—and Gardner had no way of checking its veracity—was remarkable not only for its sheer implausibility but for its horror. What Elizabeth was trying to do, Gardner soon decided, was send investigators off on a wild goose chase by inventing a whopper so large they could not afford to ignore it. But he couldn't turn back. He had to hear what she had to say. He had to know to what lengths she would go to lay down false trails.

"Why would he be in jail?" he asked.

"He was mixed up in some very big fraud things. Kind of like going along with little old ladies and saying, 'Give me your pension, and we'll go to your apartment.' "

"Where did he and your mother meet?"

"They met in South Africa."

"What kind of problems was he giving her?"

As her story continued, it became increasingly hard to believe.

"Bad. Very bad. He beat her. He had homosexual lovers. he did a couple of real unpleasant things to the children. Really disgusting things."

"You say he had homosexual tendencies?"

"Uh huh. He was supposed to be an extremely good-looking man. Very charming. Debonair. He swept my mother off her feet. She was very young, about eighteen or nineteen. Her parents were dead set against the marriage. Her father refused to go to the wedding, and I think her mother did, too. It was very strange."

Gardner asked her when the trouble began.

"Maybe even while Mummie was pregnant. He started beating her. And he started bringing home guys."

"So he was bisexual?"

"Yeah, I guess so. He wanted children, but other than that he wasn't particularly interested in my mother. Later, he started doing fairly unpleasant things to the kids."

"Homosexual things?"

"Well, I don't know quite how you describe it." At this point, Elizabeth's unlikely account began to resemble some horrific fantasy. "My mother said the first time it happened she thought a rat had been at the kid. They took him to the hospital, and the hospital said they couldn't figure out what was going on. It wasn't an animal that had taken chunks of flesh out of the baby. Not once but several times. Four or five times. You know, we're talking about a three-month-old baby. It was so bad that the child had to go into intensive care. Because, you know, it had been eaten."

Gardner was stupefied. "Like a cannibal?" he asked incredulously.

"Yeah. It turned out that he was doing it, and my mother caught him. Then he tried to do the same thing to her."

"He was biting her?"

"Yeah. He was eating chunks out of them. You know, it's so gross that one can hardly comprehend why someone would do that."

"My first question is, you don't think this guy came back and retaliated, do you?"

"I know so little about him except for these few instances that it's hard to know if he's in jail, or if he's an alcoholic or whether he has become some sort of obsessive monster or something."

Then Elizabeth got to the point she had been trying to establish in her incredible anecdote.

"It might be worthwhile to try to locate him and find out what he's been doing," she said. "Anything is possible. I mean, if someone could do that to children at that age I guess he could go to better things like murder."

IT WAS AFTER MIDNIGHT WHEN ELIZABETH'S TALE ENDED, BUT GARDNER still had one more question. "How hard would it be to get hold of Jens?" he asked.

It was Elizabeth's turn to look rattled. "I don't know what his schedule is," she stammered.

14

AT FIRST, RICKY GARDNER HAD TROUBLE WRAPPING HIS TONGUE AROUND the strange name. He pronounced it *Jinz,* sounding the *j* as he would for *Jim* or *John.* But the German *"j"* is pronounced more like a *y* and in *Jens* the final *s* is slurred. The result is *Yence,* rhyming roughly with *prince.* The surname, too, is not what it appears to the American eye. In the United States, it may be pronounced *soaring,* but in German, the *s* becomes a soft *z* and the *oe,* which has no English equivalent, is almost a *u.* Therefore, *Soering* becomes *Zuring.* Or thereabouts.

But the pronunciation of his name was one of the least interesting details about Jens Soering.

BORN IN BANGKOK ON AUGUST 1, 1966, JENS WAS THE FIRST CHILD OF Klaus, a thirty-year-old junior officer at the German Consulate in the Thai capital, and Anne-Claire, scion of a wealthy and respected family from the northern German city of Bremen.

Klaus's family migrated to West Germany from the East in the disruptive days following World War II, and there was little stability during his early years. He joined the foreign service out of high school and used his ambition and innate talent as an administrator to work his way up the ladder. Typical of a German foreign service officer on the way up, Klaus was extremely conservative, hard-working, and demanding—a man not given to overt displays of affection. He insisted upon excellence, obedience, and efficiency. To many, he seemed callous and unfeeling, but those who knew him well said he was, at heart, a warm and compassionate man.

Anne-Claire was a product of different circumstances than her husband. A half-dozen years older than Klaus, she had grown up amid considerable wealth. Her father died when she was very young, but her mother, a strong-willed, dominating woman, quickly remarried. Her second husband was the founder of a powerful and profitable German electronics company. The family money gave Anne-Claire opportunities that had been denied to her husband. As a teenager she came to the United States and attended a prestigious prep school in the Midwest before enrolling at an American university. After she graduated, she returned to Europe and worked in a Dutch consulate, when she met Klaus. They were married in 1958, two years before Derek and Nancy Haysom. Klaus was twenty-two; Anne-Claire was closer to thirty.

In 1967, when Jens was one year old, the family moved to Cyprus. A year later Klaus and Anne-Claire had another son, Kai. The four of them remained on Cyprus until 1972, when Klaus was transferred to Bonn so he could work more closely with officials at the foreign service headquarters.

From the first the children were the focus of Klaus's and Anne-Claire's lives. They doted on them and did without to buy them fine clothes, pay for elaborate birthday parties, and send them to good schools. The younger boy, Kai, was cheerful and easy-going; he made friends easily. The older son, Jens, was an intense youth, who tended to be sharp and sarcastic with his peers. He was respected for his intelligence, but he had few friends.

In 1977, when Jens was eleven and Kai nine, Klaus was transferred to his first job in the United States, in the West German consulate in Atlanta. An administrator rather than a diplomat, Klaus became the office manager. Productivity soared, but morale dropped. Klaus pushed the staff hard, occasionally driving the women in the office to tears with his demands. Whenever that happened, however, he unfailingly apologized and for a few days afterwards the workload would be lighter.

The Soerings came to Atlanta at an opportune time. Although the Georgia capital was a backwater as far as foreign postings went, the city had definite benefits. The economy was just beginning to boom, and real estate was incredibly inexpensive. Klaus and Anne-Claire bought a comfortable, two-story brick home on Cochise Drive in a suburb called Vinings in the city's prosperous northwest quadrant, practically on the banks of the beautiful Chattahoochee River. Fortuitously, the house also was close to Lovett School, a private institution with a reputation for excellence. Unknown to Klaus and Anne-Claire, the school was pretentious to the point of caricature; its reputation was inflated. But in their determination to provide quality education for their children, they enrolled Jens in the fifth grade, Kai in the third. They lived close enough to walk to class.

Physically, Lovett School is not a lot different from Wycombe Abbey, at least in the sense that both campuses are composed of attractive buildings surrounded by pleasant grounds. While Wycombe Abbey's buildings reek of history and its campus is mainly broad, open greensward, Lovett's property is densely forested, and the physical structures—the split-level classrooms, the sleek, modern gymnasium, the football stadium, complete with lights, and the tennis courts—look as though they are only temporarily inhabiting clearings carved out of the trees, spaces that could revert to woodland overnight if the caretakers aren't careful. Wycombe Abbey resembles a rambling British estate; Lovett School looks like a well-endowed Midwestern junior college.

Intellectually, there is little room for comparison. Wycombe Abbey girls, for the most part, go off to Cambridge and Oxford, while Lovett grads are more likely to go to the University of Georgia. This is a bit of a sore spot for Lovett enthusiasts, who like to think of the institution as a first-rank prep school, a sort of Choate on the Chattahoochee.

Lovett was founded in 1926 by Eva Edwards Lovett, who is described in the school catalogue as "a Christian woman of remarkable capacities." Presumably that included a capacity for hard work since she ran the school herself for twenty-nine years,

placing great emphasis on religious instruction. After 1955 the
curriculum changed, and the school broadened its instructional
base. Despite the efforts of successive headmasters, however,
Lovett, at least up until the time Jens graduated in 1984, had
never achieved the academic recognition of most of Atlanta's
other private schools. Even some of those whose children went
there snigger quietly about the school's affectations. The father
of one of Jens's classmates said he always thought of Lovett as
a "little Southern girls' school which just happened to let some
boys in."

WHATEVER THE ACADEMIC VALUE OF LOVETT ITSELF, THERE IS NO DOUBT
that Jens Soering had a first-class intellect. "He was very, very
smart," said one of his former teachers, an instructor who is no
longer affiliated with Lovett. "His mind was very quick, and he
was very sure of himself."

Exactly how smart he was is hard to say. Lovett officials refuse
to disclose any details about Jens's academic standing, and teachers have been forbidden to discuss him under threat of losing
their jobs. Almost certainly, however, he was very near the top
of his class. He had to be. He was on the Headmaster's List every
year from the ninth grade on, and he was a member of both the
National Honor Society and the Cum Laude Society for his last
two years. In his senior year he was a semifinalist in the National
Merit Scholarship competition.

When he applied to the University of Virginia, he was se-
lected as one of only 150 freshmen to be included in the Echols
Scholars program. Another Echols Scholar in the same class was
Elizabeth Haysom.

In addition to being an Echols Scholar, Jens also was named
a Jefferson Scholar, which had a not inconsequential additional
benefit: a full four-year scholarship. The two honors definitely
placed Jens among the university's intellectual top rank. Jefferson
Scholars are the only group at UVA whose members have perfect
SAT scorers.

What Jens possessed in intellectual capability, however, he
lacked in personality. He was known as a grind. A nerd. A geek.

A student obsessed with the idea of being perfect even to the point of refusing to be corrected by a teacher.

"He'd argue with the teachers because he always thought he was right," said one high school classmate. "He was driven."

"I can hear him now," said another, five years after last seeing Jens Soering. "He always presented the attitude that he knew a lot more than anyone else, even the teachers. His tone was like, 'I know it and you don't.' "

Jens was extremely bright, but he also was arrogant, sarcastic, argumentative, haughty, and patronizing. Needless to say, he was not well liked. The fact that he was on the school Honor Council in his junior year is remarkable; that he was elected vice president of his class in the tenth grade is nothing short of amazing.

"He was real cold," commented another classmate. "He never went out of his way to be friendly."

The mother of one of his classmates succinctly summed up the attitude of many of his classmates, teachers, and the other parents: "He was a real little shit."

WHEN JENS FIRST ENROLLED AT LOVETT, HIS ENGLISH WAS STILTED AND heavily accented. As the years went by, his accent became less noticeable, and by the time he graduated, it was distinct but no longer harsh, like a pebble rubbed smooth by an Appalachian stream.

In his sophomore and junior years he was a reporter for the school newspaper. In his senior year faculty advisers appointed him editor in chief. His command of the written language, no matter the flags his speech raised, was superb.

But he had, even at that early age, more than his share of quirks. Despite his having lived in the United States for a number of years, he clung tenaciously and aggressively to his nationality. In the early grades fellow students teased him often about being a Nazi, but as time went on, the joke grew stale and the teasing stopped. That, however, did not prevent Jens from flaunting his German heritage and his nonconformist ideas. One mother vividly remembers a cover on the student literary magazine when Jens was its editor: It was a photograph of his grandfather's tombstone.

Jens was aware of his estrangement from his classmates, and he capitalized upon it. Often he would make outrageous statements just to see the effect they would have on others. One of his favorite targets was the American political system, which Jens delighted in attacking, as much for the shock value as to articulate his own beliefs. Such comments did not sit well with the other students, who, for the most part, were budding yuppies and the children of staunch Republicans. His cynicism did not fit the place or the time, which was the height of the Reagan presidency, when patriotism was not only back in favor but, in Lovett circles, mandatory.

Sometimes, though, Jens seemed to want to be one of the gang. Although his early training had been in classical music, he later switched to more mundane uses of his talents: He played guitar in a student band called "Ground Zero." His favorite rock groups were Talking Heads, the Doors, and a German group called Trio.

For a loner, an iconoclast, and a sharp-tongued foreigner who reveled in his foreignness, he joined an unusual number of school organizations. He was in the Foreign Language Club, the German Chapter (president), the Guitar Club (copresident for three years), the Photography Club, the Science and Math Club, and the Drama Club.

Drama was one of his main interests. He wasn't enthralled with the possibility of being an actor, but he liked the behind-the-scenes roles: directing, writing, and working on the sets. He sweated with the stage crew in class productions of *Jonathan* and *Arsenic and Old Lace*, but his real triumph came in his senior year, when he and some classmates decided to make a horror movie. Jens was the director. The set was the backyard of one of his classmates, chosen because it was on the Chattahoochee and when the fog rolled in off the river, it could be quite spooky.

"It was very rudimentary," said one of those who participated. "We had cardboard tombstones and a fake coffin and all kind of things. The plot called for one of the actresses to be pregnant, and she was having her baby in the graveyard. It was a *Rosemary's Baby* kind of thing. It was a hoot."

But the father of one of the participants saw it differently. "It was macabre," he said. "What really got to me was how serious

Jens was about it. I hadn't seen the other kids serious about anything."

FOR ALL HIS BRILLIANCE THERE WERE THREE THINGS JENS DID NOT HAVE. One was a sense of humor. "You might say his humor was dry," said a classmate. "Very dry. V-e-r-y dry. It was so dry it practically wasn't there." The 1984 school annual, the *Leonid,* quoted Jens in what may have been a stroke of high wit for him: "The light at the end of the tunnel is an oncoming train."

The second thing he did not have was physical strength or athletic ability. When asked to describe him physically, many of his classmates used one word: *soft.* At 5' 7" or 5' 8", he was not tall, and neither was he trim. One classmate remembers him as being almost pear-shaped. As far as any of his classmates can recall, he never took part in sports outside of PE. One classmate recollects Jens telling him he once took fencing lessons, but that undoubtedly was before his family came to the United States.

The third thing he did not have—a very important thing to an American high school student—was a girlfriend. As far as any of his classmates can remember, Jens was never involved romantically with any of his classmates. One mother recalls he had a date for the senior prom only because another mother felt sorry for him and ordered her daughter to be his companion.

"He didn't seem sexual at all," said one of his female classmates. "I never got the impression he was interested in sex. Not in me and not in any of my girlfriends."

"He may have been gay for all I know," one male classmate said. "I don't think anybody really cared."

Later someone did: Elizabeth Haysom came to care very much.

Elizabeth, as far as anyone has been able to determine, was the first female to look at him in a sexual way. For Jens it put *everything* in a new perspective.

15

ELIZABETH HAYSOM WAS INTRODUCED TO JENS SOERING AT A DORMITORY barbecue in August 1984. He was barely eighteen and looked sixteen. She was twenty and looked it.

At UVA, first-year Echols Scholars, all of whom are enrolled in the College of Arts and Sciences, are assigned to a dormitory called Watson Hall, which they share with the Rodman Scholars from the School of Engineering. Watson Hall is a brick, four-story building on the western edge of the Grounds, close enough to Scott Stadium to hear Cavalier fans cheering on bright Saturday afternoons. It is a coed dorm, women on floors one and three, men on two and four. At the beginning of each year school officials sponsor a social so the students can get acquainted.

Oddly, considering the depth of their later attachment to each other, when Elizabeth and Jens first met, there was no instant magic. When Jens's dark eyes met Elizabeth's blue ones, there were no sparks. Later, Elizabeth confided to her roommate, Charlene Song, that when she was introduced to Jens, she was convinced he was a little wimp. "No," she said, "I take that back. I thought he was an aggressive little wimp."

Around Thanksgiving her attitude began to change. Jens would sidle up to her and open a conversation about women. He was especially anxious to talk about French women, whom he held in very low regard. Amused at first, Elizabeth broadened the subject of their conversations, and soon they discovered they had a lot in common.

One of the things that attracted Elizabeth to Jens was the very thing he made such a big deal about: his foreignness. He had a European aura about him that Elizabeth found irresistible. The other thing she found compelling about him was the very thing that had made him repellant to the girls at Lovett: his weirdness. He wore it like a badge; he exulted in being different. She sopped it up.

For that matter, Elizabeth was weird, too. When she came to Virginia from Europe, she brought with her the thought patterns she had developed while growing up in England. Her ways were different from those of the American students, and, like Jens, she rejoiced in her unconventionality. She decorated her dorm room with her own drawings and hung tapestries on the walls. Invariably, she had a David Bowie album blasting in the background. Like Jens, she delighted in saying outlandish things strictly for their shock value, but could keep her dormmates entertained for hours with tales, real and imagined, of her travels through Europe with Melinda.

At twenty she was two years older than most of the other first-year-men and clearly had different ideas and goals. While most of the first-year women at UVA in that period were somewhat conscientious about their dress, Elizabeth was noticeably shabby. Her dress for the day, any day, apparently consisted of whatever she happened to put her hands on first. She favored skirts with tights underneath and loose blouses, but whether anything matched or not appeared immaterial. She was a hippie two decades too late.

In addition to her peculiar habits, the one thing that set her apart more than anything else was her accent. It was beautiful, the envy of the women of Watson. It helped make her exotic and brought her respect in the dorm as a "woman of experience."

Although she was careful about letting it show, she despised Americans. She felt infinitely superior to them. In a letter to her Berlin benefactor, Colonel Herrington, written from Yugoslavia during the Christmas holidays of 1984, her contempt was evident. She brandished her Britishness just as brazenly as Jens did his Germanness.

Elizabeth, who had always been active in extracurricular activities, talked her way onto the First-Year Judiciary Committee; knowing that only eleven students would be picked for the group out of seventy-three applicants, she went to great lengths to promote herself for the post. But once she got on the committee, she seemed to lose interest. When she participated in group proceedings, she spent much of the time passing humorous notes to other committee members and making faces behind people's backs.

While Elizabeth dated frequently and spent a lot of time with friends, Jens kept almost exclusively to himself. In Watson Hall, as at Lovett, Jens was remembered mainly for his arrogance, his belligerence in expressing his opinions, and his cynical approach to college life. At UVA football is a popular sport, second only to basketball. Yet Jens spent a lot of time denigrating Cavalier fans and making fun of the game because of its "violence." As at Lovett, his pessimism did not endear him to his fellow students. One classmate told a reporter from the student newspaper, "He irritated a lot of people with his 'I am great' kind of attitude."

Although he, along with another student, announced plans to develop a Trivial Pursuit-type game using facts about the university, the project never got off the ground. But that may have been because he started dating Elizabeth.

Once they got to know each other, Jens and Elizabeth clung together as kindred spirits, as allies in an ocean of shallow Americans. Nothing could have made Jens happier.

Elizabeth and Jens began dating seriously in November. For Jens, it was his first flesh-and-blood relationship. Elizabeth was not only good-looking and smart, she also was suave and sophisticated and worldly, a girl who could speak eloquently about literature and film and bisexualism. Even better, she knew what she was talking about. By the time classes broke for the Christmas holidays, they had decided, as Elizabeth put it, "to be in love."

THEY WERE NOT A PARTICULARLY HANDSOME COUPLE, THIS ROSY-CHEEKED eighteen-year-old and the pale, aloof twenty-year-old. Elizabeth was slightly pudgy, and her hair was short, most likely still growing out from her mohawk of the previous autumn. Jens had put himself on a weight-lifting regimen and had slimmed down. He was no longer as plump as he had been in high school, but no one was going to mistake him for a linebacker either. Still, Jens was a good three inches taller than Elizabeth, so they fit together well. She was fair with blue eyes, light hair, and well-proportioned features. Not beautiful, but definitely striking. Jens had a German's creamy skin. He wore his dark hair in bangs that hung low on his forehead, almost colliding with his heavy brows. When he smiled, his exceptionally wide mouth split his face neatly, revealing large, gappy teeth. Elizabeth's smile, on the other hand, was shy and fetching, accentuated by deep dimples. Her teeth were shining white and perfectly shaped, the handiwork of an expensive dentist.

When the two began dating regularly, Jens underwent a noticeable personality change. His cynicism and arrogance virtually evaporated. It was as though his soul had been exposed to light for the first time. At Lovett and in the dorm his classmates had found him sour and disagreeable. But after he began dating Elizabeth, he seemed like an entirely different person. He became much more tolerant, even jolly and chatty. This was especially true with Elizabeth, whom he was anxious to impress with his wit and knowledge. This was not at all the same Jens who had barely exchanged a dozen words with the girls in his high school. With Elizabeth he could hardly stop talking, rambling on for hours about literature, psychology, philosophy, science, foreign relations, and the tribulations of being an outsider in the American system. She was new to America, he told her, but he had been around long enough to know first-hand just how corrupt the system was. It probably was the only thing they discussed in which he had more experience than she.

Elizabeth, who had at first thought she would like to go to Cambridge and major in history, had changed direction. Her main interest had become writing. Not long after they met, she divulged to Jens that she was working on a novel. He was overjoyed. For hours she and Jens discussed literary works they had read and ones they wanted to write. They spent hours poring over Shakespeare, rewriting some of the master's scenes to make them more relevant, in their view, to the twentieth century.

This reawakened old urges in Jens. He had come to UVA intending to major in psychology, but as the relationship with Elizabeth grew deeper, his focus shifted to film and screenwriting. He even enrolled in an upper-level screen-writing class and announced plans to produce a movie.

But one thing seemed odd: Though they were so much alike, with such similar backgrounds, their approach to college education contrasted markedly. Elizabeth's class work was disappointing. Maybe it was because she was older, had spent an extra year in high school, and had been out of school for a year before she enrolled at UVA. Or maybe it was because, as she later swore, she was more interested in drugs than books. While she had been an outstanding student at Wycombe Abbey, at UVA she was less than mediocre. In her first semester her grades were C's with one F. Her adviser called her in for a chat and warned her she was going to have to do better. Jens, on the other hand, was on the Dean's List for his first two semesters.

While much of their shared interest was in intellectual issues, they also had two other passions. One was a desire to design a supercar. They spent weeks studying diagrams and plans for a vehicle they envisioned as a cross between a Porsche and a Ferrari. This was curious since neither showed much prior interest in automotives. Neither had a car nor appeared to have much desire in owning one except for the conveniences it could offer in the way of transportation. Elizabeth couldn't even drive a car without an automatic transmission. Nevertheless, they approached the supercar idea as design engineers, convincing each other that some day their hybrid would actually be built.

Their other passion was passion, which was rather lopsided. Although Jens talked a good game, going into extensive detail with Elizabeth about what he called his "bizarre sexual fantasies," he was a limited performer. He was impotent. But that was only a semi-impairment. Elizabeth was partial to oral sex anyway, and Jens compensated for his inability to maintain an erection by performing cunnilingus on Elizabeth. The best he could do on his own was think about her and masturbate.

THEY ALSO SPENT HOURS, AS YOUNG LOVERS DO, TALKING ABOUT THEIR families, their hopes, their goals. Not surprisingly, Jens bared his soul, confessing his most secret thoughts. He confided to her how he clashed with his father, whom he described as a hot-tempered martinet, an intolerant, work-obsessed drone, who had driven his mother to alcoholism and the brink of suicide. He felt sorry for his mother, he admitted, because of the abuse she had to take from his father.

He did not escape this abuse either, he said, explaining how his father was always critical of him because he wanted to express his individuality. The verbal abuse also extended to his younger brother, Jens said, who was an artist at heart but who had been disillusioned by his father.

Although he spoke harshly about Klaus, Jens's real venom was reserved for his maternal grandmother, whom he said he hated because of the way she treated Anne-Claire. "My mother wanted to divorce my father and go live with her, but she said no," Jens told Elizabeth. "Then she asked her mother to give her some money so she could get started on her own, but the old lady wouldn't do it."

"Maybe she couldn't afford to," Elizabeth suggested.

"Oh, she could afford it all right," Jens said bitterly. "She has about a million dollars in the bank, and that doesn't include God knows how much money she's wasted over the years. A share of that is due my mother and me. Someday," he vowed, "we'll get it."

Elizabeth eagerly reciprocated in this fervor to expose family skeletons. She guessed that she loved her parents, she said, especially her father, but her affection was tempered with anger because of the way they had treated her when she was young. Often, Elizabeth said, Derek and Nancy would leave her by herself while they partied or visited with friends. Once, before she was ten years old, Derek and Nancy went away for the afternoon, leaving her alone with her large, rambunctious puppy. The dog bit her, opening a horrible wound on her cheek. "See," she told Jens, pointing to her face, "the scar is still there."

With blood streaming down her face, she ran to a neighbor's house screaming for help. The neighbor took her to the hospital, where the wound was sewn up. But the incident was not quickly forgotten. It provoked an investigation by the child welfare agency, Elizabeth said, and the social worker handling the case recommended that she be removed from Derek and Nancy's custody.

Soon after that, Elizabeth continued, they sent her away to boarding school, where she was exposed to more damaging things than a dog bite. In her first school, an institution in Switzerland, she was raped by three Frenchmen, she claimed. More injurious than the attack, however, were her parents' reactions. Derek tried to pretend the incident never happened while Nancy called her a whore and accused her of provoking the rape.

From then on, Elizabeth added, her relationship with her mother deteriorated. Whenever she was home from school for vacation her mother would come into her bedroom every night, disrobe, and climb into bed with her. Then, Elizabeth said, Nancy would make sexual advances toward her.

Elizabeth told a flabbergasted Jens that the situation worsened when she came home after her adventure with Melinda. Not long after she moved in with Nancy and Derek in Virginia, Nancy cornered her in her bedroom one afternoon and forced her to strip. Nancy then ordered her to assume strange poses and photographed her in the nude. Later, Elizabeth said, Nancy delighted in showing the pictures to her women friends, one of whom backed her in a corner at a party and leeringly confessed how much she had enjoyed seeing the photos. While her mouth was hanging open in astonishment, Elizabeth said, the woman, with a wink and a laugh, reached out and tweaked her nipple.

"How have you been able to stand it?" Jens asked. "Your parents sound like monsters."

"They are," Elizabeth said solemnly. "I wish they were dead."

16

THE SOUL-BARING INCREASED IN TEMPO OVER THE CHRISTMAS HOLIDAYS. Only then it was by post instead of face to face.

For weeks Elizabeth had been busy building Jens's ego. Despite his arrogance, Jens, at the core, was remarkably insecure. Elizabeth played to his weakness, telling him he was intelligent, witty, and urbane. At the same time she appealed to his German machismo, trying to convince him how much she depended on him, particularly as an escape from her parents, who were treating her more cruelly than ever.

Just as she had fed off her bitterness toward Derek and Nancy in her last year at Wycombe Abbey, she encouraged Jens to be angry toward them. Tentatively at first, she began hinting about how much better their lives would be without her parents. As long as they were alive, she said, she and Jens would never be happy. She said they felt he was not good enough for her. According to Elizabeth, they wanted her to break up with him. She said they resented her enrolling in German classes because it formed another bond between them. As a clincher, she said they were even considering sending her away again just to destroy the relationship.

More and more, the words death and murder crept into their conversations. At first, they dealt with the subject in the hypothetical sense, possibly in the same spirit in which they attacked the idea of designing a supercar. They talked about methods of killing their parents.

But gradually the discussions became more serious. What may have started as another intellectual game for them, discussing ways to kill people, became more specific. At first Elizabeth took the initiative in these discussions, but she soon discovered what she later would describe as Jens's exceptional affinity for violence.

In the beginning the discussions progressed on basically separate levels: One was an abstract debate on how to murder someone; the other was a bitter examination about the abuse her parents were heaping upon her and how they were trying to separate the lovers. But soon the subjects began to merge. By the time they left the Charlottesville Grounds for the Christmas holidays, Elizabeth had built a good foundation for her claims.

She made the short trip home to Boonsboro; Jens joined his family in Detroit, where his father had been reassigned. They kept in touch by telephone.

From Loose Chippings, Elizabeth began a "journal," which she would later mail to Jens. Half diary, half letter, the document ran for nine pages and included a full-page drawing entitled "Still Life." It depicted Elizabeth as an amorphous being, a ghost-like figure remarkable mainly for her huge eyes and squared-off nose. However, her parents were clearly defined. Derek was shown in profile wearing a British gamekeeper's hat and a V-neck sweater. He looked over his bony right shoulder, away from both Nancy and Elizabeth, seemingly disassociating himself from the scene. He had long clawlike hands, one of which was draped over Nancy's shoulder while the other caressed her arm. Nancy wore a dress or sweater with a plunging neckline, and her hair was arranged in a braid curled on top of her head. Her face was long and narrow with oversize eyes and brows that arched almost vertically. In the drawing her nose was broad and flat, and her ears were sharply pointed, like *Star Trek*'s Spock. With a cold expression on her face, Nancy gazed downward without apparent feeling at the Elizabeth-image.

The drawing was dated December 21, 1984, the day after she began the document. The final entry was dated Christmas Eve.

Rather than mailing these scribblings to Jens as she wrote them, she saved them and posted the entire document on December 28, when she left for a ski trip to Yugoslavia. Later she would deny the document was a letter to Jens, claiming it was only a diary intended for her personal perusal.

Elizabeth's document must have been exquisite torture for Jens. If he had received no letter, it would have broken his heart. But the one he did receive took him hours to decipher. Elizabeth's penmanship was, to be charitable, idiosyncratic. She did a funny thing with her *s*'s, frequently forming them in a loop and continuing the line into the next letter. This made them look like @'s or *8*'s without a connecting bar in the middle. She also ran her *t*'s and *h*'s together when they fell in the same word with the result that the first two letters looked like a capital *"h."* Her eccentric hand is a matter of personal pride.

Her December 20 entry was short and cryptic, saying only that she was lonely. But the next day she covered a page and a half, excluding the drawing, complaining about her parents' drinking, particularly her mother's. But Derek was her special target for the day. She noted that Nancy was beginning her sixth drink and Elizabeth hoped it would give her mother courage to kill her father. Seemingly off the cuff, between statements about her parents smothering her with affection and the news that she was painting a mural, she commented that her neighborhood had been subjected to a rash of burglaries.

The December 22 entry began chattily, briefly chronicling their preparations for Christmas. Before long, though, Elizabeth began writing about how much she wished she could be rid of her parents, speculating that supernatural means might be preferable.

Before ending that day's writing with a sonnet, she noted that her focus on bad things that could happen to them seemed to be having some results because of a series of near-cataphoric accidents, which she later claimed were largely imagined.

The December 23 message, except for noting that her mother nagged at her incessantly and refused to do anything about cleaning the house, was devoted largely to poetry, her own and T. S. Eliot's. On a more ominous note, she made two more references to the deaths of her parents. In one, she said she wished her parents would die. Later, she hinted that murder might be necessary.

For the most part, though, her Christmas writings were mainly nonsense with none-too-clear references to David Bowie and Jens's psychological state. After teasing him with references to the rock idol and her possible inherent lesbianism, she swore her undying love. Investigators would also later find an undated letter, probably written during the Christmas break, in which she devoted considerable space to her previous sexual experiences with both men and women. But that was in the past, she added. Since she had met Jens, he was her only interest.

As Elizabeth had done, Jens couched his response in "journal" form. His letter was thirty-nine pages long and, unlike Elizabeth's, it was virtually all typewritten. He didn't want to make Elizabeth have to strain to read his scrawl. His handwriting, while better than Elizabeth's, was not a model of readability. But even with that, he took pains to please her. Propped up in his bed at his parents' home in suburban Detroit, Jens worked through the night drafting his thoughts in longhand before typing the finished letter.

Jens's letters were centered much more on himself and his feelings than on those around him. At this stage the idea of actually killing Elizabeth's parents apparently was not something he took as seriously as Elizabeth did, although he made several veiled references to the possibility. His letters, on the whole, were more general but exceedingly egocentric.

Primarily they reflected two themes: self-doubt and sexual awakening. But in contrast to Elizabeth, whose prose exhibited a certain coherence and a definite direction, Jens's correspondence was totally undisciplined. It wandered all over the place with obtuse references to literature, self-indulgence, intellectualism, insecurity, science, and a dozen other topics.

Although it would later be argued that it was coincidental that both Elizabeth and Jens seemed to be writing more or less simultaneously about the deaths of her parents, there was an apparent pattern to Jens's words. He seemed to be responding to what Elizabeth had written about her parents rather than advancing ideas on his own.

Elizabeth's mention of burglaries in her Boonsboro neighborhood elicited a response from Jens that seemed to hint that something worse than theft could result from a break in. After she referred to voodoo, Jens replied that it was possible.

JENS AND ELIZABETH WERE HARDLY BACK AT SCHOOL BEFORE THEY WERE separated again. Early in March Elizabeth took a week-long break to go skiing in Colorado with her half-brother, Howard. By then the discussion of killing her parents had moved from the general to the specific: They were now talking about Derek and Nancy. Still, Elizabeth must have felt Jens needed some final nudge. Her ski trip gave her that opportunity.

In an eight-page letter dated March 8, 1985, written on stationery from the Ramada Inn at 3737 Quebec Street in Denver, Elizabeth penned an intricate but largely fictional account of her situation.

She said her cousin, Lady Astor, had given her a house in London as a christening present. (This is not impossible, but it is improbable. Lady Astor died seventeen days after Elizabeth was born.) The gift, Elizabeth said, was contingent upon her attending Cambridge or Oxford. In the story she told Jens, she had decided for herself to be an engineer (rather than Derek's having demanded it of her as she claimed in other versions), but her math was inadequate so she had switched to history.

Also in this version she said she had been given a scholarship to Cambridge and had actually enrolled. During a school holiday, she continued, she went to the Continent with Melinda. But, she said, this decision did not sit well with the trustees of Lady Astor's estate, who were anxious to see that she committed no unseemly acts. The trustees' reaction caused her to pause and reconsider her situation, she said. On the one hand were her parents, who wanted her to continue at Cambridge because they wanted the house in London that had been bequeathed to Elizabeth.

On the other hand, she wrote Jens, she wanted her freedom more than the house. So she went off to the Continent for a second time. As a result she lost everything because the trustees removed the bequest.

When she returned from that jaunt, she said, her parents agreed to forgive her if she would enroll at the University of Virginia. In return, she would remain in their wills. In the end, she said, after they died, she would be wealthy. In the meantime her fees at UVA were being paid out of her own money, a $25,000 book contract she had negotiated. But she was tired of being manipulated by her parents. Besides, she said, they could not remove her from their wills.

Then she dangled a carrot in front of Jens. Because she loved him, she said, she would pay for his brother's college education out of what remained of her book contract money. If that was not enough, she said, she would sell her jewelry and steal her mother's to sell as well. Also, she added, she would go to Europe with him that summer, as he had been begging her to do although she had been putting him off by saying her parents were unalterably opposed. But there was a caveat. If she did that, she said, she would forfeit her inheritance.

Then she hit him with the hard one: The decision would be up to him.

What a decision. Elizabeth was telling Jens that she wanted him, but that her parents were in the way. She said she wanted their money, not for herself but for Jens and his brother. Jens did not have to be an Echols Scholar and the holder of a Jefferson Scholarship to understand what she was saying: The only road to their happiness, she claimed, was over her parents' dead bodies.

17

ELIZABETH WAS WRONG ABOUT ONE THING: DEREK AND NANCY CAME VERY close to writing her out of their wills, certainly as far as any ready cash was concerned.

The documents were promulgated in probate court in Lunenburg County, Nova Scotia, on May 7, 1985. Although they were drawn up at different times—Nancy's on October 27, 1978, and Derek's on July 4, 1984—the provisions were virtually the same. According to the wills, if they died within thirty days of each other, a previously created trust fund would be used to pay for Elizabeth's education and to help her get started in her career. After that obligation was taken care of the money was to be divided equally among the six children.

The amount of the money in the trust fund was never disclosed, but the Haysoms had surprisingly little in the way of personal assets. According to documents filed with the Bedford County Clerk of Court on November 8, 1985, Nancy's estate consisted of $10,000 in jewelry, $7,000 in household furniture, and $821 in the bank. Derek's assets were even less. He had the Bronze Belle and the twelve-year-old BMW, each of which was valued at $1,000; almost $3,000 worth of unspecified personal property, and $3,000 in the bank. The house, which they had paid for in cash, was valued at $150,000. Their total assets were estimated at only $175,000, which was far from the wealth Elizabeth had hinted at so broadly.

A year after the murders the house was sold at auction to the man Derek and Nancy had bought it from originally. He got a very good deal. The Haysoms had purchased it in 1983 for $150,000. Three years later, the original owner, Ranny Ferry, bought it back, along with five acres of land, for $101,000.

18

IF RICKY GARDNER AND CHUCK REID HAD KNOWN ABOUT ELIZABETH'S AND Jens's letters, especially their references to voodoo and black magic, they would have gone straight up the wall.

In Boonsboro Reid and Gardner were so frustrated they could cry. Gradually, sheriffs in surrounding counties had begun pulling their personnel out of the task force because there was no appreciable progress and they didn't have enough people to spare for an extended period.

By June the investigation was down to Reid and Gardner and whatever help they could pick up from the Lynchburg PD. The regional homicide squad had set a record for longevity, but the results had been disappointing. No matter which way the investigators turned, it seemed, they ran into dead ends. They were ready to try almost anything.

It was, therefore, an indication of their desperation when Reid and Gardner turned onto Court Street and pulled up in front of LPD's brick building one hot afternoon early in the summer. Clambering down the stairs, they walked into into PD headquarters and buttonholed the first cop that walked by.

"Where's Sergeant Carroll Baker?" Gardner asked.

The cop pointed down the hall.

Reid and Gardner found Baker sitting at a desk in a small office off the main corridor, up to his ears in paperwork.

"Come on," Reid waved. "You've been selected to come with us."

"The Haysom case again, huh?" Baker sighed.

"You got it," Reid replied.

"Oh, well," Baker said, stuffing his papers in the drawer. "Where we going?"

Gardner told him they were going to see a psychic.

"A *what?*" asked an amazed Baker.

"A psychic," Garner repeated. "You know, one of those guys that sees things."

"Have you guys gone nuts?"

"What the hell?" Reid shrugged. "We don't have anything to lose."

They drove for thirty minutes, finally pulling up in front of a house in a small town just outside Lynchburg. Before they got out of the car, Gardner turned to Baker.

"We asked you to come for a special reason," he said.

"Oh?" Baker replied, raising an eyebrow.

"We know you're on the SWAT team and you're good with weapons and all that stuff," Gardner explained. "So what we want you to do is cover our backs. While we're sitting there with our eyes closed, we want you to keep yours open. We want you to be looking around to make sure there's nothing funny going on."

"I don't believe this," Baker mumbled, searching Gardner's face for some sign that he was joking. He wasn't. "Okay. Let's go."

Instead of entering the house itself, they walked around the side and knocked on the door of a small apartment in the back. A small man in his midthirties, dressed neatly in khaki work pants and an open-necked sport shirt, invited them in and told them to be seated.

All around were Native American artifacts, from hand-woven rugs to hand-thrown vases. The man was only a part-time psychic; the rest of the time he operated a shop that sold Native American crafts.

Gardner had called ahead so the man knew what they wanted. He had asked them to bring along some items of the victims' clothing and, if they had them, pictures of some potential suspects. He specified that the latter should be sealed in heavy envelopes because he didn't want to see the faces; he would work through a more esoteric sense.

When Reid handed over the parcel, the man got up and turned on a tape of sitar music. The detectives sat stiffly in their chairs as the music blared at them from speakers around the room.

"It helps me concentrate," the man yelled. Reid rolled his eyes.

The three cops sat silently as the man unwrapped the package and drew out an item. It was Derek's shirt. "Close your eyes and think about the crime," he ordered the officers. "It will help bring the scene into my mind."

Gardner flashed Baker an I-told-you-so look. Reid bit the inside of his jaw to keep from laughing.

Holding the blood-stained shirt, the psychic rocked back and forth. With his eyes tightly closed, he began humming, shaking, and occasionally jerking. Baker looked at Reid, who was turning red in the face as he labored to smother a guffaw. Simultaneously, they looked at Gardner, who looked as if he were asleep. As they stared at him, he opened one eye and stared back. Reid clamped his hand over his mouth and Baker looked away.

"I see a man in dark clothing," the psychic wailed. "He's looking in the windows!"

Three sets of eyes swung to the windows. They seemed surprised when there was no one there.

The psychic let out a sharp squeal. "I feel a knife!" he screamed. "Oh! Oh! Oh! Oh! I'm feeling pain," he moaned. "Oooohhhhh, I'm feeling so much pain."

Baker, Reid, and Gardner shifted uncomfortably.

Unexpectedly, the man's energy gave out, and he collapsed upon himself. "I've lost it," he said weakly. "That's all I can tell you."

Actually, he had told them nothing.

But then again, neither had anyone else.

BACK IN THE CAR, THE THREE POLICEMEN LOOKED AT EACH OTHER disconcertedly.

"Boy, that was something," Baker said.

"Better than television," added Reid.

"Well, what did we learn?"

"Not a damn thing."

"We learned that the killer, as he sees him, is a man who wore dark clothing and that he looked in the windows of the house before he went in."

"What a surprise."

"As I said, not a damn thing."

"Damn," said Reid dejectedly, "we just wasted most of an afternoon."

"I need to get back to my work," Baker said, still not sure he had not dreamed the whole sequence.

"Yeah," agreed Gardner, turning the ignition key. "We do, too."

SOME INVESTIGATORS WHO WORKED ON THE CASE WOULD HAVE BEEN willing to offer sworn statements saying that in their considered opinions even a totally befuddled psychic would give better evidence than Margaret Louise Simmons. Chuck Reid was not one of them. While she drove most of the detectives to distraction, Reid maintained a quiet confidence in her capabilities.

"If you just take the time and listen to her real carefully," a patient Reid explained to Gardner, "she makes good sense."

Gardner shot him a look that said, "Right, and I'm the king of Bavaria."

"No kidding," Reid persisted, "the trick to understanding Margaret Louise is just not to rush her. Let her work things through for herself."

By now, the two investigators had developed their good cop–bad cop routine. Reid was the good cop, the quiet helpful one who said soothing things and always offered to fetch the coffee. Gardner was the bad cop, the one who asked all the pointed questions and kept poking his nose where a lot of people felt it should not be.

Whenever the two talked to Margaret Louise, Gardner's patience ran out quickly. Before very long he would go find something else to do while Reid sat down to chat with her.

One morning Reid and Margaret Louise were having a cup of coffee and shooting the breeze.

"Do you think I did it?" Margaret Louise asked.

The question caught Reid by surprise. He thought about it for a minute, then answered very slowly, "No, Margaret Louise, I don't. But somebody had to do it."

"Yeah, that's for sure."

Reid sensed that she had something she wanted to tell him but wasn't sure how to begin. Feigning casualness, he stretched and looked into his coffee cup. It was empty.

"Would you like some more coffee?" he asked her.

"I don't think so," she said, looking preoccupied.

"You know," Reid said carefully, ""we hear one thing about how so-and-so must have done it, and then we hear another thing about how somebody else must have done it. It's downright confusing. But you're pretty sharp about these things, Margaret Louise. Who do *you* think did it?"

At first he thought she hadn't heard him. She started talking softly about her and Elizabeth and how they used to just sit down and talk but these days they hardly ever did that any more.

Ho-hum, Reid thought, here we go again. Am I ever going to learn?

Margaret Louise was saying how just the other day it was almost like old times because she and Elizabeth were able to have a few quiet minutes with each other. They were drinking orange juice and Elizabeth was playing the hostess.

Reid twirled his empty cup and was debating about a refill.

"I think Elizabeth did it," Margaret Louise said suddenly.

Reid dropped his styrofoam cup. "What was that?" he said, leaning closer.

"I said," she repeated, talking to him as if he were a five-year-old, "that I think Elizabeth did it."

"Is that right?" Reid said, trying to act nonchalant. "Why do you think that?"

"I was just telling you," Margaret Louise explained patiently. "Elizabeth was pouring a glass of juice for me, and she stopped right in the middle and she said, 'You know, Margaret Louise, I'm the devil, and you're the sacrificial lamb.' "

Later, when he and Gardner had a chance to talk about what Margaret Louise had said, they agreed that Elizabeth's remark was a very interesting bit of information, but they had to put it into context. That is, they had to consider the source. Finally, they decided that it was something they should keep in mind, but it was hardly strong enough to allow them to charge Elizabeth Haysom with murdering her parents.

"I mean," Reid told Gardner, "who's going to believe that Margaret Louise has enough wits about her to make that kind of connection?"

A few weeks later some of the lab reports came back. One of them formally eliminated Margaret Louise as a suspect on grounds that her foot impressions did not match any of those taken at the scene. A second report said the same about Elizabeth.

19

SINCE REID AND GARDNER DID NOT AS YET UNDERSTAND THE DYNAMICS of the relationship that existed between Jens and Elizabeth before the murders, there was no way they could gauge the changes that were taking place in the romance. Before the murders Elizabeth was the dominant figure, manipulating Jens through judicious deployment of sex and the promise of money. After the murders, however, Jens began taking an increasingly commanding position.

Once his sexual capabilities were awakened, Jens began making new demands on his lover. Previously content mainly to talk about his sexual fantasies, he now began putting them into play. He became a porn freak, toting home stacks of magazines with wild sexual themes, many of which included some sort of violence.

The relationship was changing in other ways, too. For all practical purposes Jens had moved out of his room in Watson Hall and into a house Elizabeth had rented with her dormitory roommate, Charlene Song. This put Elizabeth effectively under his thumb, and she didn't like it. They argued frequently, struggling mightily for control of the relationship. Threats were hurled; demands were levelled; promises were made and broken. Eventually, an uneasy truce was reached. They would not discuss the murders except in a very elliptical fashion. In the future, they agreed, they would refer to the killings euphemistically as their "little nasty."

Not many weeks after they reached this agreement, the two of them, at Jens's insistence, took off for Europe for a holiday. Klaus had been after him for a year to do this, telling Jens that he wanted him to spend some time in Germany that summer. Jens had been reluctant because he thought Elizabeth would be unable to go because of her parents. Now that they were dead, however, there was no one to put up a fuss.

One of the first cities they visited was Berlin. While there, Elizabeth telephoned Colonel Herrington, saying that she and a friend were in town and they would like to say hello. Herrington invited them to dinner.

"I had a call from Elizabeth," Herrington told his wife. "She and a 'friend' are in town and I've invited them to dinner tomorrow."

"Is the 'friend' a boy or a girl?"

"I don't know," Herrington replied. "I guess we'll just have to wait and see."

Later, Herrington's wife asked him how he was going to bring up the issue of Derek's and Nancy's murders.

"I'm not," he replied. "I'm going to play it by ear and see what happens."

The next night, when Elizabeth showed up with Jens, Herrington caught his wife's eye and winked. It's a boy, the look said. That's good news. The last time Elizabeth had visited their home she had been in love with Melinda Duncan.

Neither Jens nor Elizabeth mentioned the murders, so neither did the Herringtons. It was, in all, Herrington recalled later, a pleasant, relaxed evening. However, he was somewhat taken aback by Elizabeth's and Jens's carefree attitude, considering her parents had been killed less than three months previously. The only word he had had from Elizabeth since the murders had been a brief, bitter note she had written after her interview with Gardner and Debbie Kirkland. He also was mildly shocked by the apparent depth of Elizabeth's and Jens's relationship.

"It was good to see Elizabeth so happy," he told his wife after they had gone. "They're just like a couple of newlyweds."

"Don't you think it's strange that they never mentioned her parents?" his wife asked.

"Yeah, I do. But I guess that's the way she has found to cope with the tragedy. It sure seemed strange, though, for them to be so nonchalant."

He was sufficiently disturbed by their behavior that he wrote Nancy's old friend, Annie Massie, telling her about Elizabeth's and Jens's visit, commenting that they seemed "indecently happy."

ANNIE WAS WORRIED ABOUT ELIZABETH'S ATTITUDE AS WELL. SHE HAD, IN fact, been troubled for a long time, ever since Elizabeth had run off to Europe with Melinda. She could see firsthand what that had done to Nancy, and she couldn't help resenting Elizabeth for treating her mother so cruelly. Then, she had been puzzled by Elizabeth's persistence in going to Yugoslavia the previous Christmas when Nancy clearly wanted her to stay home and spend the holidays with her and Derek.

The strangest thing of all, though, had been Elizabeth's reaction in April, when she learned of her parents' murders. As soon as Annie had explained to police how she had come to discover the bodies, she drove to Charlottesville and went straight to Elizabeth's room to tell her face to face about the tragedy.

Annie was amazed, first of all, by Elizabeth's response when she heard the news. Far from being grief-stricken, she took it all matter-of-factly. Then Annie was shocked again when Elizabeth insisted on bringing two people along on the trip back to Boonsboro—Jens Soering and her roommate, Charlene Song. Annie felt that Jens and Charlene were relative strangers and that at a time like that Elizabeth would be anxious to spend as much time as possible with her family members who had gathered for the funeral.

Annie, who thought she knew Elizabeth pretty well, could

find no explanation for what she considered Elizabeth's peculiar behavior. Unfortunately, she did not share her concerns with Gardner and Reid.

IN BOONSBORO THAT SUMMER OF 1985, WHILE ELIZABETH AND JENS WERE touring Germany, the two investigators were staggering under the pressure of the unsolved murders. For a while, they continued to be haunted by the notion that somehow the killings were cult-related. They made one more visit to the psychic, but when it turned out to be as unproductive as the first, they abandoned that avenue altogether. But the more they looked at the situation, the less they were convinced that satanism or any other form of cult activity had played any role in the deaths. Of course, if they had known about Elizabeth's letters mentioning voodoo and Jens's enigmatic response, they may have focused more clearly on the two of them rather than chasing a lot of useless leads. As it was, they were primarily following their instincts.

Those instincts kept leading them back to Elizabeth.

"Look," Gardner said to Reid one hot afternoon in late June, "we know Elizabeth's lying about the rental car thing. There's no way she simply 'got lost' and drove around for more than 400 miles."

"Especially when that mileage equals almost exactly what it would be if they had driven to Boonsboro," Reid added.

"But how are we going to prove she's lying?"

"I don't know," Reid answered thoughtfully. "I don't know about you, but this case is running my whole life. My wife's patience is running out. These murders are all I can think about. I can't even sleep. Every time I lie down, I start dreaming about the way those people were butchered, and then I start blaming myself for not being smart enough to find whoever did it."

"You can't start feeling like that," Gardner said.

"Don't you? Isn't it affecting you the same way?"

"Yeah," Gardner admitted grudgingly. "I'm waking up in the middle of the night, too. It's driving me crazy. Sometimes I just lie there and keep running over the facts again and again. What I keep coming back to is that without Elizabeth it just doesn't make any sense. I know down here," he said, hitting himself in the stomach, "that she had something to do with it."

"Have you heard from her lately?"

"No, she's off in Europe somewhere. She and that creepy boyfriend of hers."

"When are they coming back?"

"I don't know, but I think we'd better find out."

On July 2 Reid and Gardner were handed a report from the state crime lab saying two fingerprints found on a vodka bottle at Loose Chippings had been identified as those of Elizabeth Haysom.

"So what?" Gardner grumbled. "It would be strange if her prints were *not* there."

On August 29 there was a report on the technician's examination of Julian Haysom's footprints. "Based on some similar physical characteristics noted between the known and questioned foot impression specimens, Julian Haysom cannot be eliminated as a suspect in this matter," it said.

"But we know Julian was in Canada," Reid said when he read the report.

"Yeah," agreed Gardner. "That's one of the problems with lab reports. The guy studying the footprints doesn't know what we know."

On September 12 two reports came in. One said some of the previously unidentified fingerprints found in the Haysom house had been identified as belonging to one of the first officers on the scene. The other confirmed that the attempt to use a laser to pick up prints from an envelope believed related to the case was unsuccessful.

It would not be until November 8 that a report came in saying that Elizabeth's footprints did not match any of those found at the scene.

As far as Reid and Gardner were concerned, that report was irrelevant. Elizabeth and Jens were long gone.

20

When Jens and Elizabeth got back from Germany, they moved into a house near the Grounds and enrolled in summer school. They shared the house with two other students, but they kept to themselves. Except for an occasional disturbance resulting from one of Jens's rather frequent temper tantrums, the others hardly knew they were there. At the beginning of the fall semester, Jens and Elizabeth moved again and became even more reclusive.

A couple of weeks after classes started, Gardner and Reid decided to renew their efforts to question Jens. They hadn't noticed it before, but he was proving extremely elusive. Whenever they wanted to talk to him, he always seemed to have to be somewhere else. The investigators had not attached much significance to this until they realized that he was the only major player left who had not submitted his fingerprints, footprints, or blood samples. At first, he seemed to be too far on the periphery to have been directly involved, but as physical tests eliminated one potential suspect after another, the circle grew wider.

When Margaret Louise's test results ruled her out, Reid was smug. "Like I told you," he told Gardner with a grin, "I didn't figure she did it. She's out of it now."

"So is Julian, for all practical purposes," added Gardner. "And I think we can forget about satanism for a while."

"That leaves us with two other possibilities," Reid said.

"Yeah. I guess its time to go find Elizabeth and Jens. Especially Jens. Let's put some pressure on them and see what happens."

Late in September they tracked Jens down and made arrangements to interview him the first week of October. When he arrived in Bedford, Reid and Gardner fell into their good cop–bad cop routine almost as if it were second nature. Reid was very solicitous and served Jens coffee like a waiter at a private club. Gardner, by nature a garrulous person, played the abrupt, probing inquisitor. Before Jens left, Gardner pressed him for a date so they could take his fingerprints and footprints and draw some blood to compare with the "alien" blood found at Loose Chippings.

Jens stalled, claiming he had exams coming up, and he was going to be too busy.

"We can make it after exams," Reid offered graciously. "Whatever's convenient for you."

Jens suggested the middle of the month.

"The middle of the month is fine," Reid agreed amicably. "We'll see you here on the 15th or the 16th. We'll give you a call first to set a firm time."

By the time he got back to Charlottesville, Jens was in a foul temper. They tricked him, he said, by offering him a cup of coffee. Now he was worried they could get his fingerprints off the coffee cup. He jumped up and stomped around the room. "Why didn't I think of that?"

"Well, it's too late now. There isn't much you can do about it," Elizabeth said.

Jens slammed his fist into his palm. "I can get them. Especially Gardner. God, I'd love to do him. I could catch him at home and get rid of him."

Before they had gone to Europe, Jens also had announced his intentions to kill Howard Haysom, but Elizabeth had talked him out of it. Now she feared she was going to have to talk him out of attacking an investigator. "You can't just go around killing people you don't like, Jens," she said patiently. "Let's see what our alternatives are."

A couple of days later, Howard Haysom called Elizabeth and told her he would be in Charlottesville the following Wednesday,

October 16, and he would like to see her. He said Gardner and Reid had told him they had good news: that they might soon be able to make an arrest for her parents' murders. When Elizabeth told Jens that, he panicked. The next morning, he made arrangements to fly to Europe.

On Saturday, Jens methodically went through the apartment and wiped his fingerprints from every surface he could remember touching. Then he jumped into the red Scirocco his father had given him the previous summer and drove to Washington, parking the car in a back lot at National Airport. The irony of Jens driving a red car was not lost on Reid, who remembered the detective the previous spring who had been obsessed with the thought that he was being followed by a killer driving a red car. Wiping the car as methodically as he had the apartment, Jens abandoned the vehicle.

Twenty-four hours later, Elizabeth followed.

BACK IN BEDFORD ON THAT WEDNESDAY GARDNER AND REID WERE considering driving to Charlottesville to see why Jens had not contacted them about their planned meeting when the telephone rang. It was Howard Haysom calling from Lynchburg. "They've gone," he told Gardner.

"What do you mean, 'They've gone'?" asked Gardner.

"They've left. I just tried to telephone Elizabeth, and her roommate said they've gone. They packed their bags and left. They've run away, probably back to Europe."

"Stay where you are," Gardner said. "We'll be there as soon as we can."

Howard had sounded agitated, but not altogether surprised. "He's not dumb," Reid told Gardner on the drive to Lynchburg. "He wasn't fooled. I suspect he's figured long before now that Elizabeth may have been involved, but he's in the same boat we are: He can't prove it."

"This still doesn't prove anything," Gardner pointed out. "Even if they were here, we couldn't arrest them. Not without some physical evidence."

"I know," Reid agreed glumly. "How well do I know."

ON THE DRIVE BETWEEN LYNCHBURG AND CHARLOTTESVILLE, HOWARD Haysom was calmer than the two detectives expected him to be. It was ironic, Howard said as they raced northward on U.S. 29, shattering the speed limit, how much Derek had professed to dislike Jens, but how trusting he had felt toward Elizabeth. Not long before he was murdered, Derek had written and told Howard that if anything happened to him, Howard should be sure to take care of Elizabeth because she was a "very loving and responsive child."

When they arrived in Charlottesville, having knocked thirty minutes off the hour and a half drive, they went straight to the house Elizabeth and Jens had shared with Charlene Song. The Korean, looking smug, was waiting for them with two envelopes in her hand. One she handed to Howard. It was from Elizabeth. The other she gave to Gardner. It was from Jens.

Howard ripped open his envelope. Inside were two sheets of plain white paper covered with Elizabeth's distinctive uphill scrawl. It was an undated, rather unfocused letter addressed simply, "Dearest All." In it she said she was leaving for an unspecified destination with Jens. She urged the family not to try to find her.

Howard sighed when he read the note. He gave the two detectives a resigned look and tightened his jaw.

Reid and Gardner, who had been reading over Howard's shoulder, then opened their own envelope. It, too, contained a two-page letter and was dated "10/85." Jens did not show the same consideration for the investigators that he had for Elizabeth; his letter to them was handwritten rather than typed. He was giving them the finger every way he could.

He suggested sarcastically that they not make too much of a mess going through his belongings because his parents might want them. Then he arrogantly advised them to "keep investigating as before." He said he was "incapable" of committing murders like those of Derek and Nancy because of his ingrained "pacifism." He implied he was leaving not because of the crime but rather because he was unhappy at UVA. He added he was sorry that Elizabeth had allowed them to take her prints and a blood sample.

After looking through her room, Howard told the detectives that he thought Elizabeth had taken some of Nancy's jewelry, which she probably planned to sell, but other than that, he didn't see anything missing. Even though she was his sister, Howard explained, he hoped that if it could be proved they had anything to do with Derek's and Nancy's deaths, they would be arrested and tried. It was significant, Reid thought, that Howard was not advocating leniency for Elizabeth.

GARDNER AND REID CURSED TO THEMSELVES ALL THE WAY BACK TO Bedford. Their birds had flown, and there was little they could do. They did not have enough evidence to charge them, or they would have arrested them earlier. And without any charges they couldn't launch a spirited international search. The only thing they could do was wait and see what happened.

"You gotta have faith," Gardner told Reid just before they got back to Bedford.

"Right," Reid said disgustedly.

"No, I mean it," Gardner said. "Things work out. I believe that. What goes around, comes around. I think we're going to see them again."

Reid grunted and slumped lower in the seat. His faith ran out some eight months later when he quit the sheriff's office to take a higher paying job with a trucking firm. He left three weeks too soon.

21

MRS. SELFTON WELDON SENSED SOMETHING WAS WRONG AS SOON AS THE young couple walked in. The detective in the Marks & Spencer store in Richmond, England, picked them out as they strolled through the glass door. It wasn't the way they looked, which was ordinary enough. The man had short auburn hair and a skinny mustache and was wearing dress slacks and an unwrinkled new windbreaker. The woman was stylishly clad in a dressed-for-success suit with an expensive silk scarf wrapped around her neck and draped over her right shoulder. Her dark brown hair fell neatly to her shoulders. What Weldon found odd was that the two seemed to be together yet were trying very hard to act as if they weren't. That and the fact that each was carrying one of the store's distinctive green shopping bags. That is, they came *into* the store with Marks & Spencer totes.

Marks & Spencer is a well-known British department store chain, sort of a cross between a K-Mart and a J. C. Penney's. It is popular among British shoppers for its consistency and convenience. At the time, it also had two policies that made it stand out: one was the company's willingness to exchange merchandise for cash as long as the shopper had a receipt; the other was its readiness to accept payment by check.

The company has forty outlets spread throughout greater London, which vary in size and range of products. The store in Richmond, an upper-middle-class bedroom community southwest of the city, covered two floors. On the ground level was food, wine, and notions, while the upper floor was devoted to clothing, men's at the front, women's to the rear. Behind the women's section was a small customer service area. As Weldon watched, the couple made straight for that section, where they emptied their bags and asked for cash refunds. Their receipts were in order, so the clerk smiled and handed over the money.

Then they separated, the man peeling off into the women's section and the woman heading for the men's department. As they wandered, they picked out items for purchase: the man chose slips, panties, and blouses; the woman selected jockey shorts, socks, and a blue blazer. Weldon noted that each time they passed in the narrow aisles, which was frequently because the store is not large, they deliberately looked away from each other. She found that particularly curious. After about thirty minutes of shopping, they went to separate checkout counters and whipped out checkbooks and wallet-sized cards.

In Britain, as in the United States, when someone opens a checking account, the bank provides blank checks the new customer can use until the personalized printed documents arrive. In Britain, it is usually two books with fifty checks in each. Since no names are printed on these checks, British banks also issue an identification card with each new account. With that card a customer usually has little trouble cashing a check for up to fifty pounds. Depending on the fluctuating rate of exchange, £1 equals about $1.65; £50 would be about $82.

Standing a discreet distance away, Weldon watched as the man and woman each wrote checks for the amount of purchase, which was just shy of the £50 limit. Still ignoring each other, they took the escalator downstairs and walked out the door. Each was carrying approximately £50 worth of newly purchased merchandise and £50 in cash, which they had received when they returned the merchandise purchased at another Marks & Spencer store.

Still curious, Weldon followed the couple out onto the busy main thoroughfare, which the British call the "high street." They walked four blocks down the road and turned into an electronics store called Dixon's, an upscale version of a Radio Shack. As

Weldon watched from outside, the two suddenly became a couple again, walking through the store hand in hand, jointly examining an expensive-looking sound system.

They left that store without buying anything and walked a few more blocks to the subway station. Since Richmond is at the western end of London's District Line, there are always trains sitting in the station. Riders may enter the trains at any time, but the trains will not leave until another one pulls in. It is not unusual to sit on a train for ten minutes or more waiting for it to depart.

By then, Weldon was sure some sort of fraud was going on, but she felt powerless to act. She did not have the authority to arrest the young couple. By chance, also waiting at the station was a policeman she knew. Although he was off duty and wearing civilian clothes, she told him what she had observed and pointed out the man and woman, who were sitting on the train chatting and laughing, their green Marks & Spencer bags at their feet. The policeman jumped aboard just as the train was about to leave. Approaching the couple, he introduced himself and said there were a few questions he would like to ask them if they wouldn't mind. They agreed and all three got off at the next stop, Kew Gardens. He hustled them off to the Richmond stationhouse so they could be questioned further. He turned them over to Detective Sergeant Kenneth Beever and Detective Constable Terry Wright.

The forty-two-year-old Beever, who had joined the Metropolitan Police twenty-two years before as a beat-walker in Acton, was a little surprised. A jolly-looking, round-faced man with dark hair and quick, dark eyes, Beever was friendly and easy-going on the surface, stubborn and tough underneath. Beever's accent was sharp—he obviously had not gone to Oxford—and he peppered his speech with street slang. But he was a shrewd judge of people, and his experience with some of London's toughest criminals, from Chinese gang members to international drug smugglers, had left him somewhat jaded. When he first set eyes on the man and woman the constable had brought in, he was surprised; they weren't the type he expected to see in his line of work.

His first impression of the woman was that she was a Sloane Ranger, the London version of the female yuppie, so named because they normally prowled the expensive boutiques on the streets that radiate outward from Sloane Square, in Chelsea, a considerable distance from Richmond. Beever glanced at the man. Medium-sized, solidly built, he was wearing dark, heavy-framed glasses with thick lenses that magnified his dark eyes and gave him a studious, owlish look. Beever looked at him and thought "boffin," which is roughly the equivalent of the American nerd.

When they spoke, his impressions were confirmed. Distinctive public school English flowed out of her mouth; she had just a hint of an American twang. The man sounded like an American or a Canadian.

She told Beever she was Tara Lucy Noe, a twenty-three-year-old Canadian who had come to England to write a book for a New York publisher. The man claimed he was her husband, Christopher Platt Noe, who would be enrolling at a university in Bath for the fall term. In the meantime, they said, they were spending a few days sightseeing and doing some shopping.

While in the city, they were staying in a furnished one-bedroom apartment, the kind of lodgings the British call "holiday lets," on Glouster Place near Marleybone Road, almost out the back door of Westminster City Hall. A hop and skip away was 221B Baker Street, the address of Sherlock Holmes; Madame Tussaud's wax museum and the London Planetarium were also nearby. The flat, however, was far from Richmond, and Beever wondered how two tourists ended up at a Marks & Spencer in a rather ordinary London suburb.

The detective flipped through their identification and asked if he could see their bank books. Thumbing through the documents, he was surprised to see that every check they had written had been made out to a single store. "Rather fond of Marks & Spencer, aren't you?" he asked drily.

Pulling Wright into another room, Beever quickly laid it out. "There's something strange going on here, Terry. I'm not sure what it is, but it just doesn't feel right."

"I get the same impression," replied Wright, tall and slim with a dark beard and a hooked nose, an extremely intense man with none of Beever's underlying humor.

"They could be perfectly legitimate. They're well-dressed, well-spoken, and they look like they come from good homes. But where's all the shopping money coming from? And why do they patronize exclusively Marks & Spencer? Why Richmond?"

"I agree with you," Wright said. "Something's fishy. Do you want to take it a little farther?"

"We don't have anything to lose."

Rejoining the couple, Beever began asking them more detailed questions about their visit to England. The man was affable, but the woman was cold. She was behaving, Beever felt, just like someone from a snooty British prep school, pretending to be outraged, tossing her hair, reaching for a cigarette, then pointedly waiting for someone to light it for her. She's an actress, he decided, and a bloody good one.

The more he talked to them, the more suspicious he became. Before being assigned to duty at Richmond, Beever had been a member of the city's central drug squad and headed the police detachment at Heathrow Airport. He was particularly sensitive to potential drug smugglers, and he was becoming increasing concerned that the man and woman may be involved in the drug trade.

"Do you mind if we take a quick look through your flat?" he asked.

"It would just be a waste of time," the woman answered haughtily.

"Probably," agreed Beever, slipping into the bad cop role Ricky Gardner had occupied in Virginia. "But we don't have much else to do this afternoon."

"Don't you need a warrant for that sort of thing?" she asked.

"Not with your permission," he replied.

"I don't think so," she said.

"Why not?" Beever persisted. "We're asking you very politely. Do I have to remind you that you're a visitor in this country? We don't know when you arrived or where from. You could be a drug smuggler for all we know."

She and the man exchanged glances.

"We wouldn't have any trouble getting a magistrate to sign a paper if you want to force us to do that," Beever pressed. He probably was bluffing but he was gambling on their lack of knowledge of British court procedures and their desire to erase his suspicions that they might be involved in drug smuggling. "It would be a lot easier if you'd just say yes," he urged. "We could pop around, take a quick look to satisfy ourselves, and you could be on your way."

"I think we ought to do it," the man said after a pregnant pause.

The woman nodded her agreement.

THE FLAT WAS A TYPICAL LONDON LODGING, A SMALL APARTMENT IN THE basement of a four-story building. At the basement and ground level, the brick had been faced over with stone, which had been freshly painted white. A wrought-iron fence running along the front was also freshly painted. There was a gate in the fence opening onto a short flight of stairs that angled downward from the sidewalk. They ended at a blue door with a brass knocker, the entrance to the apartment.

At that time, Beever did not know enough about the two inhabitants to appreciate the ironies of the location. Diagonally across from the flat was a narrow street which dead-ended into Glouster Place. It was called Salisbury Place. Salisbury, Rhodesia, is where Elizabeth Haysom had been born. A five-minute walk away was Marleybone Station, a terminus for trains to the Chilterns, including the town of High Wycombe. A person making the journey between High Wycombe and London with any frequency undoubtedly would be familiar with that section of the city.

Standing in front of the flat on Glouster Place, Marleybone Station was to the left. Also to the left, a short walk away, was the Edgware Road underground station, which also is on the District Line. Someone so inclined could get on a train at the Edgware station, ride two stops to High Street Kensington, where there is a Marks & Spencer, get back on the train and ride to the end of the line at Richmond.

"How long've you been here?" Beever asked as the man fumbled with his key.

"About a week," he said. "We were staying in a B&B, but the place was infested with crabs. We got the hell out of there and gave away our clothes."

Opening the door, he waved them in. Beever and Wright took one step into the apartment and stopped cold. Spread around the room, covering most of the floor space, were green shopping bags.

Wright whistled. "I guess you do favor Marks & Spencer," he laughed, starting to count. There were thirty-two bags, each containing almost exactly £50 worth of clothing. Each bag also was labeled with a neatly printed card identifying the merchandise inside the bag, when it was purchased, and from which store. In addition, the labels noted what the two had been wearing when they shopped at that particular store.

"Hey, Terry," Beever called from across the room, "come have a look at this." He was standing over the bed. On the coverlet was a hat, a wig, and a document that looked like a diary. Wright looked at the wig, then at the man. Then he strode angrily across the room. "Take that damn thing off," he said, reaching up and grabbing the man's mustache. With a flick of his wrist, he ripped it off. The man's eyes watered, but he said nothing.

"Here's some more goodies," Beever called, peering into a drawer in chest. Inside was a stack of bankbooks, mostly from rural branch banks. Each book had a different name. There was also a pile of identification cards with names matching those on the bankbooks. In the back of the drawer was a thick leather wallet, which Beever lifted out and opened. Inside was a West German passport with the man's picture inside the front cover. The name on the document was Jens Soering. Also in the wallet was a stack of British currency. Carefully, Beever counted it out. Now it was his turn to whistle. "Almost £800," he said. "That's a lot of money. Where did it come from?"

"I don't think I want to say any more," the man said angrily.

"I don't blame you," Beever said. "Your situation doesn't look exactly promising. Terry," he said, turning to Wright, "would you call for a van? Let's take all this back to Richmond, where we can go over it at our leisure."

While waiting for the vehicle to arrive, Wright opened the bedroom closet. Resting on the floor, under a rack of new clothes that included several smart dresses and three blue blazers, were four large suitcases. Curious, he opened one and saw it was filled with papers. Now, why would they carry a whole suitcase full of papers with them? he asked himself.

22

BACK AT THE RICHMOND POLICE STATION BEEVER PUT IN A CALL TO THE manager of the bank on which the most recent checks had been written. While he held on the line, he spread some of the material they had collected in the flat across his desk. Staring back at him were pictures of the two in various poses with different hairstyles. For Elizabeth alone, there was a whole handful of IDs. There was a University of Virginia student card from 1985 with a photo of a remarkably young-looking Elizabeth Haysom. A similar card dated the next year showed a markedly more mature Elizabeth. There was a Canadian government card that showed Elizabeth with close-cropped hair and a sour expression on her face. And there was a Virginia driver's license in Elizabeth's name. There were also Canadian government cards with Elizabeth's picture, but the names weren't Elizabeth Haysom. They were Caroline Jane Ferrell, Christina May Clarke, Catherine Lynne Peake, Melissa Anne Taylor, Sarah Elizabeth McKensie, Julia Alexandra Holte, and Tara Lucy Noe. Each identification card was accompanied by a driver's license with a name to match. One of the licenses had a Quebec City address on it; the others listed her residence on different streets in Montreal. Each also had a different date of birth, ranging from March 1962 to July 1964, which would have made her either twenty-four or twenty-one at the time. In actuality, she had celebrated her twenty-second birthday two weeks previously.

When the banker came on the line, Beever identified himself and asked him if he could tell him about the account whose number he read off the bankbook. The manager went off to check his records, and when he came back, he sounded excited.

"That account is overdrawn," he said. "Please don't let those people go."

That was enough for Beever to recommend they be held for suspicion of check fraud. In the meantime Wright was plowing through the stack of papers. Included among the documents was a pile of letters held together with a rubber band. Some of the letters were signed "Elizabeth" and some were signed "Jens." This helped them cut through the identification question and pinpoint the two as Elizabeth Haysom and Jens Soering. But at that stage the names meant nothing to either detective.

Separate from the letters was a student's exercise book, which was filled, diary-style, with dated entries in chronological order. The first entry, dated Saturday, October 5, brought Wright to attention. In handwriting he would soon come to recognize as Elizabeth's, it said that Jens had gone to "Bedford" to see "Officers Reid and Gardner." It further noted that the officers were insisting on some type of tests and an answer was being demanded in four days.

Wright began reading faster. Under an October 12 date, he discovered an entry asserting that Jens had methodically gone through his room and car with a rag obliterating his fingerprints. Apparently this was of great concern to Jens, who was worried that he had already inadvertently left copies of his fingerprints on a coffee mug he had used during an earlier interview with the two officers. Very interesting, Wright thought, moving down the page.

Not all the entries made sense to the detective. At one place, Elizabeth made reference to a telephone call from someone named "Howard," who told her that the "case" was all but "solved." What case? Wright wondered. And how was it going to be solved?

Following that, there was reference to another telephone call, that one from someone named "Rover." Then he read three initials which really caught his eye: "IRA." He was puzzled. The initials had to stand for "Irish Republican Army," the dreaded terrorist group that had been virtually at war with the British for decades in Northern Ireland and, in later years, in Britain itself. But how was this woman involved with the IRA?

The next sentence removed any doubt he had about what the initials meant. The writer noted that the IRA felt its position in London had been threatened by "E." That confirmed for him that the writer was talking about the terrorist group and that the person identified as "E" (has to be Elizabeth, he told himself) must be connected. But what was the tie-in with the United States, specifically with a place called "Bedford" and with "Howard" and with a "case" that was nearing resolution?

Confounded, he read on.

The next entry was datelined Paris. There, Elizabeth and Jens explored the possibility of emigrating to Zimbabwe, which was the country of Elizabeth's birth. But officials at the Zimbabwean Embassy turned them away, saying there was no work for them there.

Undaunted, they took a train to Brussels where they tried to get work visas to Botswana. That was unsuccessful as well. Next they went to Luxembourg, where they subsisted primarily on hamburgers. Restless, they began focusing on Thailand, which was where Jens had been born. But Thailand was halfway around the world and air fare to Asia was expensive. So they decided to try to drive at least as far as India.

On October 22 they left Luxembourg in a rented Fiat, first stop Bern, where Elizabeth got an international driver's license. They also dropped in at the Iranian and Turkish embassies to apply for visas.

At that point, the journal entries began appearing in a different hand, one which Wright later would identify as Jens's. The detective welcomed the change; Jens's writing was easier to read. At that point, too, the document changed in style. Up until then the entries had been primarily in note form—short, terse phrases like those a student would take during a lecture. But with the change in writer, the prose took on a narrative cast. The sentences became longer, the phrases more descriptive and the detail more complete. Datelines jumped from Switzerland to Bulgaria to Yugoslavia. It was there, Wright read, that the trip all but ended in disaster. On a narrow thoroughfare outside Pirot, with Elizabeth at the wheel, they narrowly avoided a head-on collision. Their car ran off the road, rolled over, swerved back onto the highway and smashed into another car. Both Jens and Elizabeth suffered head injuries.

After much confusion due primarily to the language barrier, Jens and Elizabeth were taken to a hospital where Jens had several stitches taken in his scalp. The damage to the car, however, was much worse than it was to its occupants. Abandoning the vehicle, they took a train to Belgrade, and from there they headed for Vienna via Trieste.

By that time, they had run out of money so they began making cash withdrawals on a VISA card. It was unclear from the document whether the card belonged to Jens's father or to Julian Haysom, but in any case they succeeded in getting cash.

From Vienna they took a train to Salzburg and stocked up on supplies, buying a guitar, a fancy camera, a tape recorder-radio, and shoes for Jens; shoes, stockings, a purse and a bottle of blonde hair dye for Elizabeth. Hoarding their cash, they paid the bill with the credit card.

The next day, November 5, they negotiated another cash withdrawal. They also made their first apparent serious effort to cover their trail. They left a "delayed" letter at the hotel, one which would be mailed long after they were gone so they could not be traced by the postmark. To further confuse anyone who might be trying to find them, they sent another letter to a re-mailing location in Frankfurt, an address they had taken from *Soldier of Fortune* magazine. In the letters, they specified they would be continuing their travels throughout Europe. In reality, they took a plane to Bangkok.

Thailand, however, turned out to be considerably less than what they had expected it to be. For the first few days they played tourist, taking in the local sites while making a half-hearted attempt to find jobs. In that effort, they were spectacularly unsuccessful.

Although they could find no jobs by which to raise new income they continued to spend. Soon, they were all but out of money. In an effort to find a way to survive, they mailed a flurry of letters to banks around the world applying for credit cards. Their applications were denied. As a result, by early December, they were desperate for cash. It was then, Wright read, that they hit upon the idea of traveler's check fraud.

The idea was quite simple. They would buy traveler's checks with their available cash, report them stolen or lost to get refunds, then hurriedly cash the checks they had reported missing. That way, they would have the cash from the checks as well as the cash from the refunds, in effect doubling their investment.

To accomplish this successfully, however, they needed a supply of fake identification. This problem they solved easily enough. For several days they bounced around from printers to photographers to typists to laminators, carrying forged documents which could be copied to give them a look of authenticity. As a result, they ended up with several sets of credible IDs.

About this time, too, they discovered a book about computer crime which exposed them to even more adventurous avenues for fraud. But most of the schemes listed in the book required time, and time was playing against Jens and Elizabeth. They were running short of cash.

In desperation, they put their traveler's check scheme into effect. Their first try was successful. After reporting the checks stolen, they were immediately refunded $500. But their jubilation died quickly. When they tried to cash the checks they had already been reimbursed for they ran into the impenetrable Thai bureaucracy. They panicked. Certain their attempt at fraud was going to be discovered they returned to the office where they had been given the refund and said they had "found" the checks. They gave back the money and left, vowing to try the idea again in a different country where currency exchange laws were not so dogmatic.

In the meantime, they made an effort to milk Klaus Soering's card one more time, only to find out that it had been cancelled. Elizabeth tried Julian's card, but they discovered that it, too, was no longer valid.

Determined to make something work, they decided to try the traveler's check scheme once again. Jens invested the bulk of their

Derek Haysom in his days as a
Canadian steel executive. (Abbass
Studios, Ltd.)

Nancy Haysom in a playful mood
during a tour of her husband's
steel plant. (Abbass Studios, Ltd.)

Wycombe Abbey in Britain, where Elizabeth attended prep school. (Ken Englade)

Jens Soering during his rock and roll phase in high school. (Margaret Haverstein)

Elizabeth Haysom (Bill Hoy, *The Bedford Bulletin*)

Jens in his University of Virginia freshman yearbook photo. (Lynchburg *News and Daily Advance*)

Derek Haysom (Abbass Studios, Ltd.)

Nancy Haysom (*The Halifax Herald*)

Loose Chippings, Derek and Nancy's Virginia country home, on the day after their bodies were discovered. (Mark Bailey, Lynchburg *News and Daily Advance*)

The London flat in which Jens and Elizabeth were staying at the time of their arrest for fraud. (Ken Englade)

Ricky Gardner (Bill Hoy)

Chuck Reid (Bill Hoy)

Jim Updike (Bill Hoy)

The Haysom brothers listen to first-day testimony in Elizabeth's sentencing hearing. Front row, left to right: Richard Haysom, Howard Haysom. Seated behind them, Veryan Haysom. (Dan Doughtie, *Roanoke Times & World News*)

Elizabeth Walton, an old friend of the Haysom's, who testified on Elizabeth's behalf at the sentencing hearing. (Bill Hoy)

Updike presents Elizabeth with one of her diary entries during their battle of wits at the sentencing hearing. (Lynn Hoy)

Judge William Sweeney sentenced Elizabeth to two consecutive forty-five year prison terms for her role in her parents' murder. (Bill Hoy)

remaining cash, $900, in traveler's checks. But instead of trying to cash them in Thailand they left almost immediately, on Christmas night, for Singapore. Their transportation was by the cheapest and most uncomfortable mode available; they made the trip by bus.

IN SINGAPORE, JENS WENT INTO A CHECK-CASHING FURY. IN THAT COUNTRY, the problem was exactly the opposite of the one they had faced in Bangkok. While the Thai bureaucracy was incredibly ponderous and slow, the apparatus in Singapore was extremely efficient and rapid, so much so, in fact, that Jens panicked again. That time, he feared the Singaporeans would process the checks too quickly and their fraud would be determined before they could get out of the country. While he cashed the checks there, he decided not to report them stolen there. Instead, he decided that he and Elizabeth should take the first plane to Europe and file their claim there. Minutes after cashing the last check, they boarded a flight for Zurich via Moscow.

The plan worked, but only after they got a fright. When they reported the checks stolen, they discovered they could get an immediate refund of only $500. They were told that they would have to come back later to get the $400 balance. Jens imagined that the clerk eyed him suspiciously and was worried that the police would be waiting for them when they returned. Despite their fears, they went back that night and collected the additional cash.

According to the journal, the tingle of risk-taking did wonders for their libidos. They celebrated with a huge feast and a marathon sex session. Perhaps they over celebrated, because Jens was ill for days afterwards.

Physically and psychologically exhausted, but with a new infusion of cash and renewed spirits, they left Zurich for England on January 8. Destination: Canterbury. There they planned to put into effect still another scheme.

Using the alias M. T. Holte, Jens opened a bank account but quickly discovered they would not be able to draw on the account for two weeks. In the meantime, they raised subsistence money by selling the camera and guitar they had bought earlier. They deposited some of the money they got from that sale in a second bank and used the rest to live on. On January 18 they sold Elizabeth's jewelry and deposited part of that money in still another bank. The rest they invested in their favorite fraud: the traveler's check scheme.

READING THROUGH THE DOCUMENT, WRIGHT SMILED TO HIMSELF; HE WAS beginning to see the pattern. Jens and Elizabeth planned to open a number of bank accounts under different names. While waiting for the accounts to become active they could survive via the traveller's check scam. However, once they could use the bank accounts, they could overdraw them outrageously and then disappear before they could be found. They couldn't be traced through normal means because they were using different fake IDs on each account. And once an ID was used, i.e., once they had written as many bad checks against it as they dared or until they ran out of blank checks, that "personality" was removed from their repertoire.

Damned clever, he mumbled.

Wright flipped through the next dozen pages quickly. They were basically detailed listings of where Elizabeth and Jens bought and cashed traveler's checks. But he paused when he hit the mid-February entries. At that point, he saw, they had hit upon a new scam: They would be fake collectors for charity. Jens talked a clerk at the Royal Society for the Prevention of Cruelty to Animals into giving him a collection can, and Elizabeth got one from the Red Cross. Working separate ends of a large subdivision, they went door-to-door asking for money.

In three hours Elizabeth collected £35. But Jens's efforts were not nearly as successful. In an hour and a half, he collected only £5. More important, he almost got busted. While walking from one house to another he was stopped by two bobbies who demanded to see his credentials. Jens proffered the can, but they said that was not enough, that he also needed a badge. Feigning ignorance, he talked his way out of being hauled in, but he was so unnerved by the experience that he abandoned his collections and went back to the room to wait for Elizabeth to return. The journal entry for the next day noted that they had decided to abandon the collection because it was too "dangerous."

Wright noted that there were only a couple of entries left in the journal and they had not yet described how they developed the idea to defraud Marks & Spencer. Unhappily, the document that started so interestingly ended on a whine. On February 18, Jens wrote that he was worried that Elizabeth was pregnant. On February 21 he seemed close to panic. Then, on February 23, he wrote with obvious relief that it had all been a false alarm.

Wright leaned back in his chair. "Kenny," he said to Beever, "I think we've got enough here to sew them up for fraud."

Putting the diary aside, he began wading through the stack of letters they had found in a suitcase in their flat. When he began reading them, his eyes really popped. Spellbound, he pored over Elizabeth's and Jens's "Christmas letters," reading with growing fascination their dialogue about possible ways of "getting rid" of Elizabeth's parents.

"You know what, Kenny?" Wright said, turning to his colleague. "I think they've murdered them. I think they've done them in. Look," he said excitedly, shoving Elizabeth's "Colorado letter" in front of him, "read this."

Beever squinted at the penmanship. Wright had been at the letters for four days and he was getting good at deciphering Elizabeth's scrawl. It took several minutes for Beever to interpret the scribbling, but then he, too, got excited. "Hey," he said to Wright, "listen to this." Aloud, he read the passage in which Elizabeth said they could be rich if only her parents were dead. Then he enunciated the tag line in which she claimed her parents could not entirely disinherit her.

Wright grinned. "I know," he said. "I know. Isn't that great stuff?"

Beever enthusiastically agreed that it was. But then he threw a bucket of cold water on his partner's ebullience.

"We don't know for sure *who* was murdered," he reminded

Wright. "Not even for certain that they *were* murdered. We don't know *when,* and we don't know *where.''*

"We could always ask them."

"No," Beever shot back, "that might be the worst thing we could do. We need to get as many details as we can before we let them know that we're onto 'em. Otherwise they'll clam up so tight we'll never get anything."

"You're right," Wright agreed. "You have any suggestions on where to start?"

"Well, we can begin with the assumption that the murdered party or parties are her parents, so they probably will be named Haysom. We know it happened sometime after early March 1985 because they were still writing about it at that stage. We can assume it happened in a place called Bedford, which is probably in the United States or Canada, more likely the United States. And there appear to be a couple of policemen involved named— what was that?—Reid and Gardner."

"Well," Wright sighed, "it's not like we didn't have anything at all to go on."

23

It was Friday, May 30, almost lunchtime. Ricky Gardner was plodding through a pile of paperwork, trying his best to concentrate, when the phone buzzed. He jumped as though he had been poked with a cattle prod. Before it could ring again, the investigator snaked out his left hand and lifted it off the cradle.

"Ricky Gardner."

"Ricky," said the department operator, "there's some guy on here with a funny accent who says he wants to talk to you."

Just what I need, Gardner thought, stabbing at the blinking button.

"Is this Detective Gardner?" asked a voice in an accent so thick it had to be fake.

"Yeah," Gardner answered unenthusiastically.

"This is Detective Constable Terry Wright in Richmond, England."

"Sure it is," Gardner drawled. To himself he mumbled, I've been to Richmond, and it sure as hell ain't in England.

"I beg your pardon," the voice said.

"C'mon, Chuck, I'm busy," Gardner said, thinking this was a hell of a joke for his ex-partner to be pulling. Now that Chuck Reid was no longer with the sheriff's department, he could see the more humorous side of life, at least more humorous as he defined it from a civilian's point of view.

"Are you the Mr. Gardner who's looking for a Jens Soering and an Elizabeth Haysom?" the voice persisted.

"Who is this?" Gardner asked sharply. "Is that you, Chuck?"

"This is Detective Constable Wright in England," Wright said patiently, "and I have two questions for you."

"Okay," Gardner mumbled. "I'll humor you. Shoot."

"Are Elizabeth Haysom's parents dead?"

Gardner rolled his eyes. "They sure are."

"Were they murdered?"

Gardner pulled the receiver from his ear and stared at it. Listen to this guy, he said to himself. He's really wound up today. "How long does this game go on?"

"This isn't a game," the voice announced. "I'm a detective in England, and I think we have your murderers incarcerated."

Suddenly, it clicked. The police chief in Charlottesville had contacted Sheriff Wells two days before and said he had heard that Jens and Elizabeth had been arrested in London for shoplifting. Wells had gone immediately to Interpol, who told him to sit tight for a few days while the bureaucracy did its work. Wells felt no sense of urgency because they had no more evidence then than they did when Elizabeth and Jens fled—they still had nothing to tie them directly to the killings. But how did this guy in England know about *murder?*

"What makes you think there were murdered?" Gardner asked carefully.

"Because of the letters," Wright answered.

Gardner was dumbfounded. "Letters?" he stammered. "What letters?"

"Their letters to each other," Wright said. "The ones we found in their flat."

Gardner's heart began to pound as if he'd just run up four flights of stairs.

"Where did you say you were at?" he asked excitedly, jumping to his feet.

"I'm in Richmond, just outside London. I think you should get over here right away."

Sure, thought Gardner. I'm on my way. Give me directions. "Look," he said, trying to keep calm, "I can't just drop everything and come to England. I have to talk to my boss."

"That sounds reasonable," Wright replied.

"What's your number there?" he asked, reaching for a pencil. "Okay," he said, writing hurriedly. "I've got it. What time is it over there?"

Wright told him it was almost five in the afternoon.

"Don't leave," Gardner yelled excitedly. "Don't go away. I'll call you right back. Don't leave that phone. Okay? Don't leave."

Hanging up, he punched the number for Commonwealth Attorney Jim Updike.

"Jim," he screamed, "this is Ricky. What are you doing?"

"I'm going through a brief," Updike answered, mildly perturbed at the interruption.

"Throw it on the floor," Gardner said. "I'm coming right over and you aren't going to *believe* what I have to tell you."

Three minutes later, an out-of-breath Gardner burst into Updike's office, slamming the door so hard the glass threatened to collapse.

"They've got Elizabeth and Jens," he shouted. "They've tied 'em to the murders. They want us to come over."

"Slow down," Updike said. "Take it easy. Who has Elizabeth and Jens? What about murder?"

"The police in England."

"Where in England?"

"Some place called Richmond. They have a Richmond, too. I think it's near London. They want us to come right over. They've connected them with the murders. They have letters they say implicate them in the killings. God, I can't believe it. Not after all these months."

Updike's blond eyebrows went up an inch and a half.

"What kind of letters?"

"I don't know what kind of letters. He just said 'letters.' But they know about murder so the letters must say something about that."

Updike felt the blood rushing to his face. "Are you serious?"

"Dead serious."

The lawyer leaned back in his chair and put his hands behind his head. For longer than Gardner could hold his breath, Updike sat there, staring off into space. From past experience Gardner knew it was better not to disturb him when he was thinking. But then he couldn't take the silence any longer.

"Look," he said, thrusting his note at Updike. "Here's the number. They're waiting for a call back. They want us to come right over."

Updike reached for the phone, lifted the receiver, then put it back. "Let's call from your office," Updike said, jerking to his feet. "That way if they have any questions, your files will be right there."

"Good idea," Gardner said.

Both of them ran for the door.

WHILE UPDIKE TALKED TO WRIGHT, PULLING OUT AS MANY DETAILS AS HE could, Gardner paced nervously around the tiny investigator's office. It wasn't easy, pacing, considering the room had almost filled with nosy detectives.

"Uh huh," Updike said. "Okay. Is that right? Uh huh. No kidding?"

Gardner thought he was going to pop.

Finally Updike hung up. "Old man," he said, looking Gardner in the eye, "are you ready to go to England?"

"You mean it?" Gardner asked. "You think they've really got something we can nail them with?"

"Sounds like it," Updike answered. "I can't wait to see those letters."

"When are we gonna see 'em?"

"That's one of the problems. They want you to come over as soon as possible."

"Me?" Gardner said. "I've never been out of the country. I'm not going over there by myself. You come with me."

"Whoa," Updike urged. "First off, I don't know if I can. I have to check my schedule. Then there's the money. I don't have any funds in my budget for a trip to England."

"Money hell," Gardner roared. "We can't let a few bucks hold us back now."

"Maybe I can ask the Board of Supervisors to hold a special meeting to see if we can dig up some funds . . ."

"Maybe the sheriff can pay for it."

"The sheriff's out of town," one of the detectives reminded Gardner, "at the national convention in Las Vegas."

"Damn, that's right. Where's Ronnie Lockland?"

"He's off today."

"Well, let's find him. Time is really important here."

A deputy found the chief deputy working in a pasture on his farm, explained the situation to him, and asked him if he had any suggestions. "Tell 'em hell, yeah, they can go," Lockland said, scraping the remains of a cow patty off his boot. "We'll find the money somewhere."

The decision sent Updike and Gardner into a whirl. Since neither had ever been abroad, neither had passports. That was the top priority. Calling a local photographer and swearing him to secrecy, they arranged to have their pictures taken. Swearing the clerk of court to secrecy, they began a search for the documentation they would need to clear the hurdles at the passport office. Secrecy was vital, Gardner and Updike agreed, because they didn't want the news media getting wind of the project. They figured if they could show up in London unannounced and confront Jens and Elizabeth, the shock of seeing Updike and Gardner there might help to loosen their tongues. It was a good plan, but it never got a chance to be put into operation.

Almost immediately they ran into a problem. Gardner sped home and returned immediately with his birth certificate. Updike raced to his safety deposit box and came back with what he thought was his birth certificate. In fact, it was a registration of birth, a notification from the hospital to his parents that Mrs. Updike had delivered a child. It was not official; it wouldn't satisfy the passport office.

Frustrated, Updike called the local congressman and asked for his help in snipping some of the red tape. He would help every way he could, he promised, but first Updike had to be able to prove he was an American. Updike scraped up every document he could find: his marriage license, affidavits from his parents, copies of his oaths of office, school diplomas . . . Finally he had it all together. "This is going to have to do it," he told Gardner. "Keep your fingers crossed."

They left Bedford on Sunday, June 1, and spent the night in Washington so they could be at the door when the passport office opened Monday morning. Lockland had made them reservations on a flight leaving from Dulles late that afternoon. They were cutting it close.

While they waited for their documents, they smoked one small cigar after another, enough, they joked, to substantially raise the city's pollution level. And they laughed nervously about the prospect of going to London.

"We can make a movie out of this," Updike quipped.

"How's that?"

"Call it 'Goober and Gomer go to England.' "

"I'll be Goober."

"And I can jump off the plane, look around and say, 'Gaaaawwwdd Daaaaammmnnn."

"But first," Gardner reminded him soberly, "we need to get the passports."

Much to their relief, the documents were ready shortly after noon. Since they still had a few hours to kill until their flight, Updike did some last-minute shopping.

"You know what I've always heard about London?"

"What's that?"

"I've heard it rains all the time. I'd better get an umbrella." He bought a travel iron, too. And a hair drier. And then he was ready.

BUCKLED SECURELY INTO HIS SEAT IN THE SMOKING SECTION OF THE BRITISH Airways jumbo jet, Updike reached for his usual cigar, then remembered cigar smoking was prohibited on airplanes.

"You know," he confessed to Gardner, "until you got that phone call, I was really beginning to believe we'd never see 'em again. Did you feel that too?"

Gardner thought about it. "No," he said slowly. "I guess I just always figured they'd stub their toes somehow. I just kept telling myself that someday this case was going to be solved, but it wouldn't happen until the good Lord was ready. It was going to be at his leisure."

Updike nodded. "I wish I'd had your faith. Right now I have to believe that this is going to result in some type of conclusion."

"Tell me again," Gardner said. "How are we going to handle this?"

"I'm not going to question them. I can't. I'm just there as your legal adviser. We need to take a look at those letters and work out a plan of attack."

"Sounds good to me. Right now I'm going to get some sleep."

"Before you doze off," Updike said, "let me bum a cigarette."

Gardner handed over his pack, then slumped in his seat. In a matter of minutes, he was snoring softly. But Updike sat wide-eyed, lighting one cigarette from the end of another. While *Young Sherlock Holmes* flickered on the screen, Updike ran over in his mind yet again the legal steps he thought would be necessary to bring Elizabeth and Jens back to Virginia for trial. As it turned out, he thoroughly underestimated the machinations of the extradition process, especially when one side started playing power politics.

24

GARDNER AND UPDIKE DEPLANED AT HEATHROW AIRPORT RED-EYED, dry-mouthed, fuzzy-headed, and pumped up with enough adrenalin and caffeine to power the British Airways jet back to Washington.

"Let us take a quick shower, put on some fresh clothes, and then we can go talk to Jens and Elizabeth," Updike said as soon as they were in the car with Beever and Wright.

"You can't," Beever said.

"What do you mean?" Updike asked, surprised.

"British law. You can't question them until they've been remanded."

"When will that be?"

"Thursday."

"Today's only Tuesday."

"I know. I feel badly about it, especially after you've traveled all this way on such short notice. But there's nothing I can do. It's the law."

"Exactly what do you mean by 'remanded'?" Gardner asked.

Beever explained that under British law, suspects in criminal cases may be held indefinitely as long as they are brought into court regularly for their cases to be reviewed. The process is called *remand,* and it must be performed at least once a week. Beever said he planned to ask for a seventy-two-hour remand for Elizabeth and Jens, although the time would actually be 96 hours because the legal clock did not run on Sundays. The plan was to have them remanded on Thursday so investigators would have until Monday to question them.

In their case, particularly, location was as important as time. Normally, Beever said, suspects are remanded to whatever prison has space. At that time, Elizabeth was being held at Holloway Prison, the main institution for women, and Jens was across the city in the Ashford Remand Centre. It would be easier for investigators to conduct their interrogations if both were in the same place, so Beever intended to ask the court to order them to the Richmond jail.

Updike, who was warming quickly to the capable British detective, asked if a judge had been selected to hear the request. Beever chuckled. In a British court a remand decision in a case such as the one involving Elizabeth and Jens was not handled by a judge but by a panel of three magistrates. He added that the magistrates were not trained in the law but were community leaders who volunteered their time.

Updike was aghast. If they were not legal experts, he wanted to know, who interpreted the law?

That was the job of the clerk of court, Beever explained.

Updike slumped back in the seat. In many ways, he was discovering, the British legal system, which was the foundation of the American system, was as different from what he was accustomed to as baseball was from cricket.

"Do they have any idea what's coming?" asked Gardner.

"Not the foggiest," said Beever. "They still think we're interested only in the fraud case. They haven't a clue that we're onto them for murder."

Gardner and Updike exchanged grins. "I hope we can keep it that way," Updike said.

Until the hearing, there was not much Updike and Gardner could do except go through the documents that had been found in Jens and Elizabeth's apartment and work out strategy with their British counterparts.

In the thirty-six hours they had to kill until the remand hearing, the two Americans discovered that the infamous British reserve was a myth, at least as it applied to law enforcement officers. On the first night they were there, jetlag and emotional exhaustion forced Updike and Gardner to curtail their celebrations. On their second night, however, they buried their inhibitions; they wound up in a policemen's pub, and Updike found himself defending the United States' honor in a drinking bout with a burly British imbiber. No one remembered who won.

DESPITE THEIR WELL-LAID PLANS TO KEEP THEIR PRESENCE IN LONDON A secret, the story leaked to the press. On the morning of the remand hearing the tabloid *Daily Mail* published a story about how Updike and Gardner had come to London to question the pair about a grisly "voodoo killing." Up to then, Jens and Elizabeth had escaped public attention, but that shattered their anonymity. It also ruined Gardner and Updike's planned surprise.

When the couple's lawyer met with Jens minutes before he was to be taken to the Richmond magistrate's court, he thrust a copy of the *Mail* into his hand. "You'd better take a look at this," he said.

Jens scanned it, then hurriedly scribbled a note to Elizabeth that she should get rid of all evidence. He slipped it to her when they met minutes later in the hallway of the police station. She read it quickly, then handed it back. He tore it into little pieces and threw it on the floor. A few minutes later, a police officer picked up the tatters and spent hours piecing them back together. It would be another link in the evidence chain.

THE MAGISTRATE'S COURT IN RICHMOND IS HOUSED IN A MODERN, two-story building, a cold-looking, soulless edifice painted a stark white with black ironwork trim. At midmorning Thursday a white van with a red stripe carrying Elizabeth and Jens in the back pulled up to the massive iron gate that guards the entrance to the basement garage. Once the vehicle was inside and the gate had been slammed closed, they were led through a blue steel door and put in separate holding cells, effectively unable to communicate with each other. Designed for utility rather than comfort, the cells contain only a wooden bench built into the back wall and a bell-push to summon a warder.

A few minutes after they arrived, they were led up two flights of steel stairs into the courtroom itself. Like the cells, the courtrooms are small and conspicuously spartan, furnished with about fifty pull-down chairs for spectators and permanent benches with tables for the lawyers. In Britain prisoners are relegated to the dock, a small box with chest-high walls. Elizabeth and Jens filed into the box and stood, according to British custom, while Detective Inspector Peter Shepperdson outlined a case for holding the two for investigation of the murders of Derek and Nancy Haysom. Elizabeth, looking pale and much thinner than when she had been arrested five weeks previously, kept her eyes focused on the floor the entire time. Jens glanced up once, focusing briefly on Gardner. He looked away without acknowledging his presence. He had never seen Updike before.

The court consisted of one woman who served as chief magistrate and two men. After Shepperdson's speech, the solicitor representing Jens and Elizabeth argued against the proposal for half an hour. When he finished, the three magistrates consulted in a backroom for ten minutes and returned with their verdict: Elizabeth and Jens could be held at the Richmond police station for seventy-two hours, at which time another hearing would be held.

Gardner sighed in relief. Leaning over to Beever he whispered, "When can I talk to her?"

Up until then, Jens and Elizabeth had felt secure about their ability to escape the past. They had hardly talked about their "little nasty" since they left Virginia, and, from all indications, they never expected to hear again about the deaths of Elizabeth's parents. Even while they were being held in British prisons they apparently gave little thought to the possibility that Ricky Gardner was going to catch up with them.

In retrospect, the month of May had not been an unduly uncomfortable one for the two. Prison was not a pleasant place, by any means, but during that period they still had hope that they would soon be freed. In a six-page letter to Jens, Elizabeth poured out her frustrations and fears, chronicling her ups and downs and complaining about one thing and another. She never mentioned the possibility of facing murder charges.

Although the letter was undated, she did write in the days of the week. And, as she had done in her letter from Loose Chippings over the Christmas holidays in 1984, she strung several days' worth of thoughts into a single document. Beginning with a two-page paean to sex with Jens which rivaled letters printed in *Penthouse,* she slid into the more practical side of their situation—namely, how, when, and where they were going to get out.

Since they were both foreign nationals, they had the option of appealing to their embassies for aid. Elizabeth, with no political influence, made very little headway in her pleas to the Canadians. In her notes on "Friday" she said the embassy was not able to do very much and that no one was particularly interested anyway.

Jens, on the other hand, being the son of a career diplomat, had considerable influence at the German Embassy and was offered ample aid, which he shared with Elizabeth. At this stage of their relationship, Elizabeth was content to have these details arranged by Jens; she said she had confidence in his judgment.

On Tuesday, she wrote about the possibility of being deported, maybe to Canada but, better yet, to Germany with Jens. Undoubtedly she was aware of the difference between deportation and extradition, that deportation meant that she would no longer be able to stay in Britain and would have to go to another country. It did not mean that she would face charges there. Extradition, on the other hand, was a proceeding under which she could be expelled from Britain to face specific charges somewhere else. There were no criminal charges pending against her in Canada, and she apparently did not even consider the possibility of any being filed against her in the United States. Her main concern seemed to be what she would do and where she would live in Canada. It is curious that she made no mention of the fact that she had three half-brothers and a half-sister in Canada. As a last straw, she wondered if the German government would recognize her as Jens's fiancée.

The next day, Wednesday, Canada was still on her mind. In a more depressed mood, she pondered if it might not be better to volunteer to be sent there. At least, she moaned, she would be free.

In the meantime, she wrote, Jens should continue to fight to be released on bail because he had a much better shot at it, what with his enviable governmental connections. In the next breath, however, she cursed those same connections, angrily attacking the representative from the West German Embassy who had brought her some clothes as a "stupid woman" who was so thoughtless she included a white sweater when she should have known how quickly white would get dirty in a prison cell. The rest of the clothes, she groused, consisted of a pair of Jens's trousers and a pink tee shirt.

For his part, Jens was having his own problems. While he continued to profess his love and devotion in letters to Elizabeth, he apparently was having second thoughts about their relationship. On May 18, maybe during the same period that Elizabeth was writing him about her rampant sexual desires, he began an eleven-page letter to Neil Woodall, a friend who, Elizabeth would testify, Jens had made earlier when the two spent a week together in a cell.

In typical Jens fashion the letter was introspective, pseudo-philosophical, and self-centered. It did, however, give some valuable insight into how his relationship with Elizabeth was evolving.

The fact that he was in jail and separated from his lover had made him take a closer look at their situation. What he was discovering was that each had come to depend on the other to an unhealthy degree. For different reasons both were looking for love, he because his mother had always loved him unselfishly and he feared losing that attachment, Elizabeth because she felt she had never really been loved. In the long run, he wondered, had he and Elizabeth—while they gave lip-service to the notion that they were in love—simply been embarking on a course of mutual destruction?

Even the pleasure they received from sex was suspect. In fact, he said, he was forced to admit that their sessions of self-proclaimed marathon sex might not have been as satisfying as he had once thought. He admitted that, in retrospect, he did not enjoy making love to her as much as he thought he had. But maybe, he equivocated, that was because she was the only one he had ever made love to and he was without a basis for comparison.

Before he ended the letter, he threw out one more intriguing thought: a hint that he was examining, perhaps at a level he did not yet want to admit, his own potential for violence. He decided that he was going to have to examine his inner feelings more closely to see where this wellspring of possible violence lay and how it manifested itself, that is, whether it came out in actions, thoughts, or attitudes.

Curiously, the letter did not mention the status of the proceedings against him or Elizabeth, what he might be doing to prepare his defense, or if he was worried that police had by then read the letters that he knew they had recovered from the flat he had been sharing with Elizabeth. Elizabeth would say later that she did not know the letters still existed, that she thought they had long ago been destroyed. Jens, however, had to know they were there and what the results would be once the police read them. Perhaps in his arrogance he had convinced himself that the police would not find the letters, would not take the time to read them, or would not recognize their significance even if they did. Why he kept them at all is a mystery.

Instead of giving some hints to his thoughts on these issues, Jens's letter to Woodall focused almost entirely on his "philosophy," his "separateness," and his need to think of himself first. More than a year later Elizabeth would see a copy of the Woodall letter and would be so outraged that it would have tremendous repercussions on her own legal proceedings and ultimately on Jens's as well.

25

RICKY GARDNER AND KEN BEEVER WANTED VERY BADLY TO TALK TO Elizabeth Haysom.

Just as badly, Elizabeth Haysom did *not* want to talk to them.

But, instead of immediately summoning her for an interview, the investigators went first to Jens. It was not until late the next afternoon that they brought Elizabeth in. She was not at all happy to see them.

The day before officers had searched her cell and confiscated letters Jens had written her since they had been arrested. She was angry about that. She also was still off balance from the unexpected appearance of Gardner and what brought him: the fact that police had found the journal of their travels through Europe and Asia *and* the letters they had written each other while they were at UVA.

In Virginia she had been cooperative and voluble, willing to expound to Gardner at any time on practically any subject. When he met with her on Friday afternoon she was surly and tight-lipped, determined to say as little as possible. When she came in the room, Gardner stood and offered her a chair. She refused. He read her rights and asked her to sign a paper confirming that he had complied with U.S. law. She refused that too. He shrugged and nodded at Beever, who explained her rights under British law. "You're not obliged to say anything unless you wish to do so," he said kindly enough. "Anything you do say will be taken down in writing and later given in evidence. Do you understand that?"

"Yes, I do," Elizabeth answered churlishly.

Beever asked her if she would tell him about her parents, where they were and where she was in early 1985. She snapped that she had already been through that with the Virginia investigators. Beever ignored her rudeness, reminding her firmly that she was not in Virginia but in England.

Elizabeth said she wanted to talk to her solicitor. Beever ignored her, pointing out that she had just met with him for thirty minutes. "You had an idea before we came in what we wanted to talk to you about. I think it's fair to say that we should be getting on with it."

Reluctantly, like a chastened child, Elizabeth confirmed facts about her family as Beever read them out from a transcript of the interview she had with Gardner and Debbie Kirkland on the day after the memorial service for her parents.

"Would you just care to discuss with me briefly how well you got on with members of your family?" Beever asked.

"No," she shot back.

He managed to look looked surprised. "Do you think it's anything sinister in me asking that?" he asked innocently, mindful that he was trying to lull her into a confession.

"No," she replied in a tone that let him know she knew what he was trying to do. The cat and mouse game was underway.

"Do you remember discussing how you got along with your brothers and sister in the previous interview?" he continued.

She looked at him blankly and said she couldn't recall.

THROUGH A SERIES OF QUESTIONS, WHICH ELIZABETH ANSWERED TERSELY, Beever and Gardner established for the record that she had lived at home with her parents for approximately nine months before leaving for UVA.

"During that period of time was your relationship okay?" Beever wanted to know.

"I—" she started, then clamped her mouth shut.

"Did you have any arguments with them?"

"No reply," she said emphatically. The investigators would soon come to hate those two words.

"Do you remember telling me," Gardner interjected, "about your very, very loving relationship with your parents, how much in love you were with the two of them?"

"I'm trying, but that's been a long, long time ago," she said caustically.

Beever tried a softer approach. "Perhaps that's what I was trying to get at as opposed to arguments with your parents," he said. "You loved your parents, didn't you?"

"I loved my parents," she said emphatically.

"We've all got parents," he said soothingly. "We've all had tiffs with them, and we've fallen out with them for a couple of days and everything is fine again. That's what I was trying to get at."

She was not to be mollified. "I have always loved my parents," she repeated.

"Always?" Beever pressed.

"Always!"

Seeing they were running up a dead-end street, the investigators went at the issue from a different angle.

"Did you intend to get married to Jens?" Beever asked abruptly.

Elizabeth was not surprised. "When?"

"At any time. If you would like to give me a date, I'd accept it."

"We discussed the possibility, yes."

"Just you and Jens?"

"How many are getting married?" she asked sarcastically.

"I'm sorry," Beever apologized. "When you said 'we,' perhaps I was reading more into it. Did you discuss it with Mom and Dad?"

"No, we hadn't discussed marriage at all at that stage."

"Were your parents aware of your association with Jens?"

"Yes."

"Do you know what they thought of your association with Jens?"

"I know what they said. I don't know what they felt."

"What did they say to you then?"

"I don't think it's relevant."

"Well, it might not seem relevant to you," Beever said in exasperation, "but it could be fairly relevant to me. Would you like to answer the question?"

"No."

In fact, Derek and Nancy had been increasingly anxious about the relationship. Elizabeth's half-brother Howard told investigators that Derek had particularly disliked Jens and that he and Nancy were trying to find a way to separate the two young lovers, even if it meant sending Elizabeth away again. Almost certainly, Derek and Nancy would not have told Howard anything they would not have told Elizabeth, so she undoubtedly was aware of their attitude.

Since she and Jens had fled to Europe, Elizabeth had had no contact with her siblings. They, in turn, had informally designated Howard to be the family contact with the Virginia authorities, and the Houston physician took a deep interest in the case, frequently calling District Attorney Updike two or three times a week to discuss the progress of the investigation.

Beever and Gardner continued prodding Elizabeth, not always gently. She remained brusque and evasive. When they began asking her about the weekend her parents were killed, Elizabeth became particularly uncooperative. Beever got more abrupt as well.

"At one stage I was going to interview you purely about your background," Beever said. "Well, I've finished asking you questions about your background, and I'm now going to mainly ask you questions about why you're here. You're here on suspicion of being concerned in the death of your parents. I'm merely asking you your whereabouts for that weekend. If you choose to make no replies, that's entirely up to you. Can I ask you if you stayed in Washington all weekend?"

"No reply," she snapped.

"Were you with Jens all weekend?"

"No reply."

Beever paused. "I can stop this interview," he said patiently, "and read the one you made in April 1985. Have you already answered these questions to officers from Virginia?"

"Yes."

"And you told the officers the truth?"

"Yes."

"About that weekend?"

"Yes."

"So without reiterating too much, you've accounted for your movements from Friday the 29th until your return to UVA?"

"No reply."

"Would you care to tell me how you traveled to Washington?"

"No reply."

"Are you finding it distressing to answer these questions?"

"No reply."

"Can I take it that you are going to choose to make 'no reply' to any questions about that weekend?"

"No reply."

"Have you anything to say at this stage?"

"No, sir."

Beever and Gardner looked at each other. "May as well terminate it," Beever suggested. Gardner agreed. He saw it was 5:37 P.M. The first phase of the interview had lasted a mere forty-two minutes.

AFTER MEETING WITH HER SOLICITOR FOR ALMOST A HALF-HOUR, ELIZABETH agreed to resume the session. But she was no more cooperative than before. She had sensed from the beginning that Beever was going to be tougher than Gardner had been, but she had not known how much tougher.

Gardner was a relatively inexperienced interrogator. Beever was not. Gardner had always worked in a rural, relatively unsophisticated setting, but Beever had come up the ranks in a different world. It was the difference between urban and rural; Beever was a city cop with wide exposure to a plethora of crimes and criminals. In the process he had become more cynical, but he also had learned to judge suspects shrewdly and to estimate correctly how far he could push them. Elizabeth was playing tough, but Beever knew it was only an act; given time and the right nudges, she would tell them what they wanted to know. There was one other factor to consider, too: Beever had the tremendous advantage of having read Jens's and Elizabeth's letters—both those written in Virginia as well as those written after they were jailed in London—before he interviewed either of them, a privilege Gardner and Reid had not had when Elizabeth was within their grasp in Virginia. Beever intended to take full advantage of that.

At that point the only crime Elizabeth and Jens could be charged with in Britain was fraud, which was picayune compared to murder. They could not be tried for Derek's and Nancy's murders in the United Kingdom, but British investigators felt that if the two knew that more serious charges were forthcoming, they might be more willing to talk about their activities in London. British police were not convinced that Elizabeth and Jens were not involved in some type of drug smuggling operation or were not connected with IRA terrorism.

With such issues at stake, Beever was in no mood to play games. When he and Gardner began the interview, they hoped that when they asked Elizabeth about her background, she might be open with them about the things she had written to Jens in Virginia, things that would tie her to the deaths of her parents. But by then it was apparent she was not yet ready to cooperate, so they were going to have to do things the hard way.

Taking the issues step by step, they showed her copies of the documents and got her to admit that the handwriting was hers. Then Beever read her the excerpts where she talked about doing voodoo on her parents, willing them to death, taking up black magic, wishing they would lie down and die, and getting rid of them.

"See what I'm getting at?" Beever asked. "You told me earlier on today that you've always loved your parents. But here we have you writing about how much you despise them, how much you want them dead. Which one are you lying about now?"

"No reply."

Beever pushed on. "Let's go to other extracts. All the letters that you've admitted to writing. There's one here about your parents' deaths. Dated April 18, 1985, about two and a half weeks after the death of your parents—and you write Jens criticizing him for threatening to surrender, for threatening suicide. What does that mean?"

"No reply."

"You then go on to say that the deaths of your parents made it easier for you to select your own lover." He looked at her, waiting for a response. When there was none, he added, "That sounds to me as though they didn't really want you to associate with Jens. Is that true?"

"No reply."

Beever kept at it. What did she mean when she wrote Jens angrily accusing him of being unfairly jealous of her? Why did she say that their deaths made her free? "What did he do then?" Beever asked. "Would you like to offer me an explanation now?"

"No reply."

"He killed your parents, didn't he?" Beever said loudly.

Elizabeth looked up, surprised by the detectives's tone. "No reply," she said firmly.

"And you knew that, didn't you?"

"No reply."

"And then you almost made a threat to Jens, I believe. Did you mean that?"

"No reply."

"And lastly, what did you mean when you said you didn't want his 'sacrifice' to be a burden? Do you mean that also?"

"No reply."

There was a long silence, then Beever began asking her again in detail about the entries in the journal. She responded with "no reply" to each question. He slammed down the papers, feigning disgust, and told her he was through talking to her. "If you don't want to answer me now, I would ask you to go downstairs and consider your position," he said. Rising, he, Gardner, and Wright walked out. It was 6:20 P.M., only eighteen minutes after the interview had resumed. Total time elapsed with Elizabeth that afternoon was one hour and twenty-five minutes.

26

WHILE ELIZABETH HAD BEEN SURLY WITH INVESTIGATORS AND SEEMED uncomfortable in their presence, Jens reacted differently.

At the beginning Jens was Jens: arrogant, argumentative, and egotistical. As soon as he walked into the interview room and sat down, he looked defiantly at Beever and asked him to turn off the tape recorder. He let them know immediately that he was more concerned with getting information than giving it. "What's going to happen to me?" he asked.

"Are you worried about it?" Beever responded with a chill in his voice.

"Yes," said Jens.

"Why?"

"Because I murdered two people," he said matter-of-factly. "You know that, don't you?"

That said, he appeared to relax, to view the interview from then on as a game or an intellectual exercise. Pushing his glasses up on his nose, he seemed to say, Okay, let's see you top that.

Beever was inwardly pleased, but his face showed no emotion. Leaning over, he opened a dialogue, trying to establish a rapport with the owlish-looking young man on the other side of the desk.

Jens was circumspect and evasive, but in a different way than Elizabeth. Her area of expertise was obfuscation; her tactic had been to retreat into silence. But Jens was verbally aggressive; he wanted to toy with the investigators, to challenge them to a rousing argument.

One of the first things Beever noticed was Jens's irritating habit of answering a question with a question, which was quite disconcerting until investigators began to expect it. Where Elizabeth's tactic was to lead investigators down paths that twisted and turned, dipped and ran into each other, Jens's was to attack. He could be quite voluble, but only if he thought he was controlling the interview.

Jens had overlooked one thing: In his disdain for investigators, he had woefully underestimated them. For their part investigators had to get a feel for Jens; they had to work out a formula for drawing him out. It was a learning experience on both sides.

Not long after Beever began chatting with Jens, the detective maneuvered the conversation to Derek's and Nancy's murders. Soon, what had been a discussion turned into a question-and-answer session. Jens seemed to be reacting well to Beever's questions, and the detective thought he was cleverly leading Jens into his trap. Finally, the detective got to the big question: "You murdered the Haysoms, didn't you?" he asked for the record, expecting Jens to reply in the affirmative.

Jens responded with a huge grin. "You handled that very nicely," he said with apparent sincerity. "But you know I'm not going to answer that."

27

FOR TWO DAYS THE INVESTIGATORS LEFT ELIZABETH ALONE IN HER CELL while they concentrated on questioning Jens. Then late Sunday morning, Wright and Beever brought her in for another session. Gardner was absent because the British detectives planned to question her only about journal references regarding their fraud schemes and about the possibility that Jens and Elizabeth had smuggled drugs into England. Beever and Wright also were curious about the reference to "Rover" and the IRA. In Britain police take talk about the IRA very seriously indeed.

As soon as Elizabeth was seated, Beever pointed to an entry in the journal. "It states here, 'Walk to Faulkner to pick up stuff,' then an arrow points eastward and the number *803.* What does *stuff* mean?"

Elizabeth shrugged, replying that "stuff" referred to cake mix and chocolate that she and her roommate, Charlene Song, had left behind in a friend's apartment. They went back to pick it up, then returned to their dwelling at 803 Rugby Road. She shook her head vigorously when Beever wanted to know if Jens had been with her at the time. Jens had already left for Europe by then, she asserted.

Beever was disbelieving. "The word *stuff* could mean drugs, couldn't it?" he asked.

"Yes," she agreed. "It could mean anything."

"The problem I have is that Jens has offered me an entirely

different explanation about the entry 'stuff,' " he said, giving her her first indication that Jens was talking freely to investigators.

It was Elizabeth's turn to look disbelieving. "I don't know why he would say that," she said. "He wasn't even there. He doesn't know anything about it."

For the moment Beever let it drop. Instead, he asked her about the notes mentioning Rover.

Elizabeth smiled tightly. Rover, she said, was a product of her imagination.

When Beever asked her why she had made up material to insert in the diary, Elizabeth said she and Jens planned to use the document as the basis for a book they wanted to write later and they were trying to spice it up as much as possible.

"Are you saying that all these entries would form part of a book?" Beever asked incredulously.

"No, I'm *not* saying all of these entries would form part of a book," Elizabeth said petulantly. "What I *am* saying is that I was interested or amused by the possibility of writing an adventure book and the entries would be the basis for that."

She told him that she fantasized a lot, that she often said or wrote things that were not true. She added that the diary was actually written several weeks after the events took place and that she and Jens had both contributed information. They even took turns writing the entries. Some of the details she inserted about what happened after Jens had left for Europe were fiction, but Jens did not know that.

"Do you suffer from a lot of fantasies like this?" Beever asked.

"Yes," she said. "I've always let my imagination run away with me."

Beever still was skeptical and asked her again about her use of the word *stuff,* trying to get her to admit it was a euphemism for drugs.

She shook her head. "In America, they use that awful expression to encompass anything," she insisted. "For instance, 'I'll go pick up your stuff' can mean anything like books or clothes or bicycle. It could be lecture notes or a car. Whatever."

Beever asked her why, since they had been intent on running away together, they had traveled separately.

Smiling tightly, she replied that they had decided it would look odd if they disappeared at the same time.

Reading from the journal, Beever asked her if she had, as she had written, flown from the United States to Paris or if she had gone to London first. The implication, which she recognized immediately, was that she had stopped in England and left a package, perhaps containing drugs, for the IRA.

Elizabeth's eyes flashed. "Look at my passport," she said. "You'll notice that I did not enter London or England before 1986."

Beever, undiscouraged, pressed on. If she and Jens had nothing to do with drugs, he asked, why did they write in the journal that they had discovered in Thailand that the only way to make money there appeared to involve drugs.

That was more fantasy, she replied nonchalantly.

ALTHOUGH THE INTERVIEW CONTINUED FOR ANOTHER TWENTY MINUTES, Beever and Wright were unable to get her to admit to any other significant contradictions in anything she or Jens had written in the diary. Outside of her admissions that she lied indiscriminately and often, both in words and on paper, Beever had not pulled much of value out of her. In fact, he may have given more than he got. When she went back to her cell, Elizabeth must have been thinking, correctly, that Jens was spilling his guts while she, so far, had said nothing. Now *that* was something to ponder.

28

ELIZABETH MAY HAVE BEEN REFUSING TO COOPERATE, BUT JENS SOON abandoned his misgivings. Indeed, he got almost chummy with his old enemy, Ricky Gardner. When Gardner asked the youth if he had suffered any wounds during his struggle with Derek, Jens's eyes lit up. "Oh, yeah," he said, lifting his left hand. "Look here," he directed, pointing to two thin scars. "I got those at Loose Chippings."

After a few sessions with the investigators, Jens overcame his aversion to the tape recorder as well as his unwillingness to discuss his role in Derek's and Nancy's deaths. Before Sunday rolled around Jens had told the detectives practically everything they wanted to know about what had happened at the Haysom house on March 30, 1985. Exactly what he said has not been disclosed because, for a variety of legal reasons, his transcripts were ordered sealed. There is no doubt, however, that he admitted to the killings. At length and in detail. Although prohibited from discussing *what* he said about the murders, investigators readily confirmed that he *had* been very forthcoming.

There was, however, one thing he would not talk about, and that was Elizabeth's role.

"She knew why you were going to see her parents though, didn't she?" Gardner asked.

Jens was silent for a long time. Finally, he said slowly, "I would have to say that we discussed it, obviously, but I don't think that either of us was truly clear about what was going to happen at all."

He asked Jens to elaborate.

"Well," he said after another pause, "we knew that sooner or later I was going to have to speak to Mr. and Mrs. Haysom about their feelings about me. But I don't know how Elizabeth felt about me driving down there or what she thought my motives were. I don't know what she thought."

When Gardner asked him why he did it, Jens said the answer was simple. "I fell in love with the girl," he said, as though he were explaining long division to an eleven-year-old. "We talked about killing her parents. I didn't want to do it, but I drove to their house to kill them, and I got caught."

To Elizabeth the explanation was not clearly so clear-cut.

29

ELIZABETH SPENT ALL THAT SUNDAY AFTERNOON AND MOST OF THE EVENING thinking about what Jens may have told the detectives. The more she thought about it, the more she was convinced that she had been betrayed—that she had maintained her silence while Jens was jabbering his head off. At five minutes before ten o'clock she pushed the call button in her cell. When the duty officer appeared, she told him she would like to see Beever.

Beever had been waiting for her call. Shrewdly, he had judged that she would change her mind. But when he appeared at her cell door, she asked only to see Jens. He refused. "I can't let you do that," he said. "I'm still conducting a murder inquiry, and it would be highly irregular for you to see him at this point."

Elizabeth thought about that for a few moments. "Has he admitted the murders to you?" she asked softly.

"I'm not going to tell you that," Beever replied, inwardly jubilant. "But I can say I'm perfectly happy with the way the investigation is going."

Having said that, he turned on his heel and walked away, noting with content the worried look that flickered across her face. Back in his office, he looked at the clock. She will call me back, he told himself. He was right. Fifteen minutes later she summoned him again. "I'd like to speak to you alone," she said.

That time there was no mention of Jens. She had apparently decided—correctly it turned out—that Jens had told his side of the story. Now she wanted to tell hers. "I want to get this off my chest once and for all," she began.

Beever let her talk for about ten minutes before he stopped her. Her statement was useless, he said, unless he had a witness and a recording. She said she had no objection, but she did have one request: For reasons she did not share with Beever, she asked that the witness *not* be Gardner. Beever nodded and called Wright, who also was waiting in the wings. After ordering steaming cups of coffee for everyone, Beever propped a recorder on the desk, punched the "record" button, and noted for the record that the date was June 8, 1986, the time 11:15 P.M. Elizabeth swallowed hard and began Version 1 of the story of her parents' deaths.

Actually, Gardner and Reid had pretty well deduced the basic outline months before, but for Beever and Wright she began filling in the details. Some of them anyway.

She and Jens had gone to Washington, she said, just as she had told the Bedford investigators. But they didn't get lost, and they didn't spend all their time together in movie theaters. They arrived on Friday night, March 29, 1985, and checked into the Marriott Hotel, where she had made reservations. The next morning, Saturday, she and Jens went shopping for a birthday present for Jens's younger brother. Jens wanted to give him a knife, she said, a specific kind of knife that could be purchased only in a martial arts store. It was called a butterfly knife.

They went to a store in Washington, where they were told that District law prohibited the sale of butterfly knives. But the clerk was helpful, and he recommended a store in nearby Maryland. So they drove over there. They quickly found the kind of knife they were looking for, Elizabeth said, and, since she was carrying the cash, she paid for it.

By then, it was lunchtime, so they went to eat. Over lunch, she said, Jens told her he wanted to get together with some friends of his from Atlanta who were coming to Washington for a basketball game. This surprised her, she explained to Beever, because they had driven from Charlottesville specifically so they could have some time to themselves. Without putting up much of an argument, she agreed and told him to take the car. While he was gone, she would pass the time by going to a movie.

They left the restaurant, she said, and Jens dropped her at the cinema. On the way, he told her that if he wasn't back by the time she got out of the movie to go back to the hotel and order meals for both of them from room service. If he still wasn't back, she should go see the midnight showing of *The Rocky Horror Picture Show,* and he would pick her up there afterward. As she got out of the car and walked toward the ticket booth, he called after her: "Get *two* tickets," he said. She wondered why he had said that, but she got them anyway. She went inside, pocketing the extra ticket.

When she got out of the movie, she stood on the sidewalk hoping that Jens was waiting for her or that he might return. After a few minutes she gave up and got in line for a second movie. The name of it, she brightly told Beever, was *Witness.* She bought two tickets for that movie as well.

"Why did you do that?" Beever interrupted.

"I just went and did it," she said, shrugging. "I was in a fluster. I half thought Jens was going to come up, to tell you the truth."

"There is one small point," Beever added. "He didn't know you were going to see *Witness,* did he?"

"No," she agreed.

Beever motioned for her to continue.

After she saw the second movie, Jens still had not returned, so, Elizabeth said, she walked back to the hotel. She took a shower, changed clothes, and ordered two meals and a bottle of liquor from room service. While waiting for Jens to return, she sampled freely from the bottle and picked at the food. By 11:30, when he still was not back, she left the hotel and took a taxi to the Georgetown cinema where *The Rocky Horror Picture Show* was playing continuously.

Afterward, she stood at the curb waiting for Jens, certain he would appear at any minute. Just when she was about to give up and return to the hotel, he drove up. The problem was, he was traveling against the traffic. Thankfully, the street was all but empty.

"I shouted at him, 'You're on the wrong side of the road,'" she said, but by then he had stopped beside her and she was reaching for the handle. When she opened the door, the car's overhead light went on, and she saw that Jens had a sheet draped across his waist. It was covered in blood.

Elizabeth got excited in the telling. "I screamed at him, 'Are you all right? Are you okay? What happened?' "

By way of an answer, he gave her a wild look and yelled, "Shut up!" Then he yelled twice more: "Shut up! Shut up!"

"I shut up," she said.

She got in the car, closed the door, and they drove in silence to the hotel. When they got to the parking garage, he halted out of the light and ordered her to walk to the window and get a ticket so they could drive through the gate without him having to stop. He drove through the barricade quickly, then waited for her on the other side. She got back in the car, and Jens drove to a particularly dark area of the garage and pulled into a parking slot.

Beever and Wright were following her story intently, the coffee forgotten and growing cold on the desk. Except for that one time, they had not interrupted her.

Jens turned off the ignition, Elizabeth said, and swiveled to face her. "He told me, 'I killed your parents.' "

Before she could respond, he ordered her out of the car. Go to the room, he commanded, and fetch a change of clothes. Instead, Elizabeth slipped out of the raincoat she had been wearing and offered it to Jens. It was long enough to cover him from his shoulders to his knees. Together, they walked through the garage and took an elevator to their floor.

At that point Beever interrupted her again.

"Did you believe him?" he asked, meaning did she believe that he had indeed killed her parents.

Elizabeth pondered the question. "There was blood everywhere," she said, swallowing a lump in her throat. "I had never seen so much blood. I didn't know what was going on." Shaking her head, she added, "I didn't know whether I believed him or not."

She paused, remembering. Some of the blood was his, she added, telling the detectives that Jens had suffered cuts on his left hand. As well as she could remember, they were on his thumb and little finger. In the room, without further explanation, Jens stripped and climbed into the shower, calling out instructions to her as he lathered up. Go down and clean up the car, he told her.

She did. When she came back upstairs, he was asleep.

"DID HE TELL YOU WHAT HAPPENED AT LOOSE CHIPPINGS?" BEEVER ASKED.

"He said a few things. He said things like 'My God, your father put up a hell of a struggle.' And he said something about seeing just masses of blood."

"What did you think of him then?"

"I was terrified."

"Terrified of him?"

"I think it crossed my mind that he might roll over and kill me, too."

With Beever questioning her closely about the details, Elizabeth finished her tale. She said the next morning they gathered up his bloody clothing and stuffed it in a bag to be disposed of later. Most of it was dropped down the garbage chute in their dorm when they got back to UVA. She said she never again saw the knife that she had paid for that morning, but Jens had told her that he had thrown it away.

Beever wanted to be extra sure about the knife. "Did he tell you that he used the butterfly knife to kill your parents?" he asked.

"No, he never said that," Elizabeth replied. "He just said he'd thrown it away."

Beever considered what she had told him for a few moments. Then he asked about something that had been bothering him from the first. "I'd like to know why, after Jens had told you that he had murdered your parents, why you stayed with him? Why you traveled with him to Europe and stayed with him without telling any authority?"

Elizabeth seemed to consider those fair questions, ones she had asked herself numerous times. One reason, she said, was guilt, that she felt responsible for what happened. A second reason was that she felt loyal to Jens. "I loved him very dearly, and I needed him so much, especially since I didn't have my parents." Additionally, she said, she didn't want to see Jens executed for the murders. And, finally, she was afraid that if she reported the crime, police would blame her for it, at least in part.

Beever asked her if it was true, as she had written in one of her letters, that Jens had threatened to surrender to police or commit suicide if she ever tried to leave him.

She said it was, that Jens had become very upset when he saw how much she had actually loved her parents. Jens had told her, she added, that if he were ever arrested and accused of the crime that she would be equally responsible and would be as liable to be executed as he because she had been an accessory.

Beever asked her about the entries in the journal in which she said that she and Jens had both gone over their apartments with a dust cloth in an attempt to wipe away all their fingerprints.

She brushed that aside, saying that Jens indeed had done that, but that she had not. After all, she had already voluntarily submitted her fingerprints, footprints, and blood samples to the police. What would wiping her prints in her apartment accomplish?

Then why did she write that she had? And why did she tell Jens that she had? Beever asked.

She shrugged. It made him feel better, she said.

Beever had a crucial question for her: "You're maintaining to me now that you weren't at the scene of your parents' deaths?"

"No," she said, meaning that she wasn't there.

Beever wanted to make sure. "That's what you're saying? That you weren't there?"

"Yes," she replied.

Still not sure of the extent of her involvement, Beever asked if the two of them had ever discussed a plan to kill her parents.

"No, we never discussed it in terms of, you know, why don't we go knock them off, that sort of thing. We did a couple of times talk about the difference in life without parents, and we talked about it concerning his parents and if his parents divorced, and we talked about it concerning my parents, but never in a sort of conspire-to-sit-down-and-murder-somebody type thing."

Beever wasn't satisfied with her answers regarding her role in her parents' deaths. The more specific he wanted to get, the more evasive she became. Finally, he asked Wright to fetch the letters they had taken from Jens and Elizabeth's apartment. While

Wright was gone, Beever asked her why she had written such things if she wasn't talking about killing her parents.

Elizabeth said she used many of the same phrases in notes to herself about wanting herself dead. But she had never attempted suicide, she pointed out, so why should she have been trying to convince Jens to kill her parents?

On the other hand, she confessed, she was very sorry she had ever written the letters. "I hate myself for having thought those things, and I will always feel the guilt of that."

Beever wanted to know what her parents thought of Jens. Did they dislike him?

It wasn't a question of disliking him, Elizabeth said. They thought he was too young for her. They thought he was too possessive. They thought he took up too much of her time. And they thought that she should have more than one boyfriend. At the same time, she added, they liked some of his qualities. They respected his intelligence, and they realized that he, as a German, was probably a better companion for her than an American would have been because they knew she had trouble adjusting to Americans.

By then Wright had returned with the letters. What, he wanted to know, had Jens told her about killing her parents? Be as specific as possible, he urged.

"I don't know very much because I couldn't stomach talking about it," Elizabeth said. "I mean, it was hard enough to walk around, and sit in classes, and sleep in the same bed, and say to myself, 'That person over there that you're spending your life with, he killed your parents.'"

Wright wasn't satisfied. He asked if he had told to her in detail some of the things he had done to them.

Elizabeth lit a fresh cigarette, stalling for time. "One of the first things he said was, 'My God, your father put up a hell of a struggle.' And then he said that Dad had said, 'My God, what do you think you're doing?' He said that he killed my mother first. They had been talking for about forty minutes, and then he stood up and slit her throat."

Beever asked if he had said what room they were in when the events occurred.

They were in the dining room, she said. Jens told her that after he slashed her mother's throat, she staggered into the kitchen and he continued fighting with her father. "He said to me that my father was very strong and that—that he just—he said over and over again, 'He just wouldn't lie down and die.' "

She sighed. "He said that my father was struggling right to the very end and calling out and had enormous strength." Her shoulders slumped, and she looked exhausted. "I don't know any other details than that," she added.

Beever looked incredulous. "And you stayed with him after hearing all that?" he asked.

Elizabeth paused a long time before answering. Then, in a meek voice, she said, "I was very scared."

BEEVER STUDIED HER. SHE'S A GOOD ACTRESS, HE THOUGHT—NOT FOR THE first time. He felt some relief because she had finally opened up. But he had deep misgivings as well. What she had told him, he was certain, was only part of the truth. She had been honest about some things, he suspected, and dishonest about others. While she had been very candid about Jens's participation, she had been much less so about her own. Now, while she was in a talkative mood, it was no time to stop. He decided to put additional pressure on her. As he expected, she gave ground, but listening was like sinking one's hand into a barrel of water: one keeps going deeper and deeper but with no way of knowing when one is almost at the bottom. Without skipping a beat, she flowed into Version 2 of the story about her parents' murders.

30

"WERE YOU SCARED," BEEVER ASKED, "OR DID YOU KNOW IT WAS GOING to happen anyway?"

Elizabeth was surprised. "I beg your pardon?"

"Did you know it was going to happen anyway?" Beever repeated.

"What? The murder of my parents?"

"Yes."

"No."

"Not when he goes and buys a butterfly knife that morning?"

"No," Elizabeth said indignantly. "I mean it never crossed my mind that he was going to go off and murder my parents."

Elizabeth spun her story, knowing that she was liberally and deliberately mixing fact and fiction, telling the two detectives things that she wanted them to believe. Things that *she* wanted to believe. Maybe she thought they were going to swallow every word she said. Or maybe she was just testing the waters to see how gullible the detectives actually were. In any case, Beever didn't want to play. It was murder they were talking about—cold-blooded murder—and Beever was through with being Mr. Good Cop.

"Let's make a start with point number one," he said coldly. "When is Jens's brother's birthday?"

Elizabeth admitted she had no idea. He nodded, letting her know that demolished her claim that they had been shopping for a gift for Jens's brother, Kai. Next he turned to the issue of the cinema tickets. Whatever possessed her to buy two tickets to each movie?

Elizabeth had no answer.

Beever kept hammering at her, pointing out that the things she said were not logical. "You know what I'm getting at, don't you? You knew what was going to happen. You knew what you were doing all day, didn't you?"

She remained silent, so he asked again: "Didn't you?"

"No," she said slowly, "I did not."

"You were creating an alibi."

"That is not true."

"Why isn't it true?" he pressed.

"Because that's not an alibi that sticks," she said, letting him know that she could use logic, too. "That's not an alibi at all. You know that. I know that. It's nothing. So you said you went to the movie. Yeah! You bought two tickets. Wow! Yeah! Nobody believes that."

"So why did you buy the two tickets then?"

"I don't know," she said more calmly. "Because he asked me to."

Beever was not impressed. "Why did you buy two meals when he wasn't there?"

"I was expecting him to walk in the door."

"You weren't expecting him to walk in and see *Witness* with you. You weren't expecting that. I caught you out on that one. Now you're wrong. Now what's going on? You knew when he bought the knife that morning. You knew in buying those tickets. You knew that he was going for a confrontation with your parents."

"I did not know that," she insisted.

He was insistent, too. "And your parents were probably going to die as a result of that confrontation," he said accusingly. "You knew that, Elizabeth."

"I did not," she said stubbornly.

"After writing all those letters to him?"

"Look," Elizabeth said angrily, "I have enough guilt about egging him on, so to speak, with those wretched letters."

"You egged him on, all right," Beever shot back. "And not only with the letters. You egged him on in private, didn't you, Elizabeth? You knew it was going to happen, and you were creating the alibi while he was committing the crime. That's true, isn't it? Tell me the truth, Elizabeth."

She remained silent.

"Are you going to answer me?"

Silence.

"Well, are you going to answer me? You've written letters to him willing your parents to death. You've led him to it most probably. Or are you both guilty?"

"All right," Elizabeth spat. "I led him into it. I did everything."

"You knew he was going to do it, didn't you?"

"I did it myself."

"Don't be silly."

"I got off on it."

The Americanism threw him. "You did what? What does that mean?"

"I was being facetious."

Beever looked disappointed in her. "Okay," he said. "Now tell me the truth, please, without being facetious. You did hate your parents."

Elizabeth was insulted by that. She insisted she did *not* hate her parents.

Beever went on. If she did not hate her parents, why did she allow Jens to kill them? And why did she create the alibi, knowing that it was going to happen? "Come on, answer me," he urged her. "Just give me an answer."

Elizabeth stared at him.

How stupid did she believe he was? he asked. Did she really expect him to believe that she bought two tickets to each movie just because Jens had yelled that to her as he was driving away? Did she think he was going to believe that she did not have something else in mind when she ordered two meals from room service, then charged the meals so there would be a record of their having been ordered? "What do you want me to believe?" he demanded.

She was silent.

"And an alleged birthday present of a butterfly knife that morning? Come on, now. Are you going to tell me the truth or not?"

No answer.

"Well, are you? I can't sit here all night, not getting an answer."

"Yes," she said softly.

"Yes what?"

"Yes, I'll tell you the truth."

Beever relaxed a little. "Okay, then," he said. "Tell me now. In your own words."

Elizabeth said nothing.

Beever feigned exasperation. "Come on, Elizabeth," he coaxed. "Come on. You told me you were going to tell me the truth. Tell my why you created the alibi in the first place."

"Because he was going to confront my parents."

"Yes," he said encouragingly. "About what?"

Again she was silent.

"What was he going to confront your parents about?"

"Their attitude towards me."

"Yes?" he said brightly.

"And Jens."

He took a deep breath. "Yes," he said slowly. "It's got a ring of truth to it now. I've already spoken to Jens. Carry on."

"He went down there with the knife with the possibility of killing them."

"And you knew that, didn't you?"

Silence.

"Didn't you?"

"Yes, I did."

How long had they been plotting it? A long time? A short time? Many months? A few days?

She shook her head. "It wasn't too long, really," she said. "About a month."

Beever looked puzzled. He wanted to know *why* it had occurred. Why had she felt it necessary to take such drastic steps?

Elizabeth paused a long time, formulating her answer. "My

father was violently jealous of anybody, really, who I associated with," she began. "He disliked anybody I knew. He was hugely possessive of me. If they were invited to a function which wasn't even appropriate for me to go to, they would insist that I come along. They very rarely gave me any space or privacy. If I went upstairs to my room, they were always inquiring what I was doing, telling me not to do it and to come down. My father wouldn't even let me work. He wanted me to be with them all the time."

Beever was skeptical. "You built up so much resentment for all these things that you thought murder was the answer?"

"There were things that had been building up for a very long time," Elizabeth said, citing the decision to send her away to boarding school and how they had tried to manipulate her college plans by signing her up for advanced science and math courses without consulting with her, causing her to have to spend an extra year at Wycombe Abbey.

"So you're saying it was a multitude of events throughout your life that caused you and Jens Soering to put your heads together between about Christmas 1984 up until the end of March 1985 to devise a plan kill your parents. Is that right?"

No, Elizabeth said quickly. It wasn't that long a time. "We discussed it in a sort of grotesque way earlier, but we didn't start seriously discussing it until March."

Beever wanted to explore the motive some more. Did she think she was going to inherit a lot of money? he asked.

She shook her head. That was never an issue, she said. She knew that she would not inherit anything except enough money to pay for her college education.

Beever accepted that. But there was still the question of the knife. Unaware of Washington-area geography, he wanted to know why they had driven all the way to Maryland to buy it.

Elizabeth smiled tightly, explaining that it was not very far.

"But why did you choose a weapon like that?" Beever asked. "I can understand why you didn't choose a gun because it would make a noise and attract attention. But why this particular butterfly knife?"

"I have no idea," Elizabeth said. "It was Jens's choice."

"Did you see others?"

"I'd never seen one before."

"I see," Beever said. "What does it look like?"

Elizabeth began to describe it, but Beever interrupted her. "Take that slip of paper from the top of that pile there and draw it for us." Elizabeth drew.

IT WAS 12:36 A.M. on Monday, June 9. They had been going for an hour and a quarter, but it seemed much longer. Still, there was some ground Beever wanted to cover, some points he wanted to clarify. In answer to his questions Elizabeth admitted that she conceived the idea of going to Washington and that they originally planned to go twice, the first time to set a precedent so it wouldn't seem strange when they went again. But they didn't have enough money to make two trips, so they had to make the first trip do.

Why, he asked, was she surprised when Jens returned covered with blood?

"I didn't think he was going to do it," she said. "I knew that he *might* do it, okay, but a large part of me didn't honestly believe he was going to do it. I thought he was going to come back and say that he had spoken to them, and then just come back, and that would be it. I just simply didn't think that he would do it."

"But the reason you stayed with him and continued to love him, the real reason is because he has carried out your wishes, because you both wanted your parents dead," said Beever.

"That's not why I love him."

That may be true, Beever conceded. But it was why she didn't hate him. How could she hate him when all he did was carry out her wishes?

Elizabeth took offense at that. "I don't think that's completely fair," she snapped.

"Okay," Beever said agreeably. "It's a suggestion by me. It wasn't really a question. The truth of the matter is that your parents are now dead and you are part and parcel of their death, aren't you?"

"Yes," she admitted.

Beever, looking sad and weary, reached over and pushed the stop button on the recorder. "I don't think I want to say any more at this stage," he said, rising and walking out of the room.

IT MAY HAVE BEEN THE END OF THE INTERVIEW AS FAR AS BEEVER WAS concerned, but it was not for Elizabeth. She went back to her cell, thought about it for an hour, then pressed the bell-push again. "Would you call Detectives Beever and Wright again, please?" she asked the duty officer. "And," she added, "Investigator Gardner, too."

At 2:06 A.M. on Monday, only a few hours before she was scheduled to reappear in magistrate's court, Elizabeth met with Gardner, Beever, and Wright so she could make one more point. Far from being defiant, she looked lost and lonely, almost on the verge of tears.

"I requested further statement to be given," she said meekly when they invited her to sit, "because I felt that I had betrayed my love for Jens—my loyalty to him—and that I had done him a disservice. I don't know if the charge against me—what it will be—but as I said in one of my letters, we did it together and in some ways I'm more guilty than he is. He loved me beyond reason," she said haltingly. "I love him beyond reason, too."

Taking a deep breath, she added softly, "I suppose I used that love. Because of my own weakness of character, many times I have tried to wriggle out of that responsibility and the guilt of putting him in this position. I can't do that any longer. I can't bear leaving my last statement as it stands. I believe Mr. Beever referred to Jens as 'that poor boy.' I suppose that's accurate, for it was my will that made him kill my parents. He wouldn't have done it, I am sure, if he hadn't loved me so much and I, him."

For a long moment there was silence in the room. Then Gardner spoke up. "You don't have anything else to say?" he asked.

"I don't think so," she replied.

Wright, however, had one more question. He asked her to expand on her assertion that they "did it together."

Elizabeth thought for a moment, then said she had best articulated that feeling in the letter to Jens in which she seemed to criticize him for threatening to surrender or commit suicide. It was written, she said, after an argument that stemmed from her feelings about her parents' deaths. "He had seen how upset I actually was, and he felt that in some way I was turning on him and accusing him of doing something that I hadn't wanted. So in the letter I was trying to reassure him that in my mind we did it together. Although I wasn't physically present, I suppose I was spiritually there."

Seven hours later Elizabeth was roused from her cell and told to prepare for the short ride back to magistrate's court for another remand hearing. She was told to take everything she had with her because she probably would not be returning to the Richmond police station. As she filed out of the cell area on her way to the van, she paused by the duty desk and dug in her pockets. She didn't have much money, but she gathered all she had in her fist and dropped it through a slot on the desk. It was a collection box for the Metropolitan Police Widows and Orphans Fund.

31

ELIZABETH STEADFASTLY MAINTAINED THAT SHE HAD NOT BEEN INSIDE Loose Chippings when her parents were killed so she could not chronicle what happened. But Jens was there. Although his statements to investigators of what occurred inside the house that night were locked up for an indefinite period, a recounting he presented to a psychiatrist was not.

Jens met with Dr. John Hamilton, the medical director and consulting forensic psychiatrist at London's Broadmoor Hospital, six months after he made his admissions to police and gave him a version of events. How it compared with what he told Gardner, Beever, and Wright and later a German lawyer is not known. But what he told Hamilton is this:

He said that the Haysoms were not glad to see him when he showed up on their doorstep, but they invited him in nonetheless. Nancy offered him dinner while she and Derek had dessert. They all had something alcoholic to drink. While they were still at the table, Derek and Nancy began telling him about plans they had made for Elizabeth. They wanted her to break up with him. Although Nancy said she felt the two could still be friends, Derek took a harder line. He said he didn't want Elizabeth to see Jens again. Derek told Jens he was not "their kind of people" and that if he persisted in trying to see Elizabeth, he would remove her from the university and try to get Jens dismissed.

When Derek said that, Jens said, Jens himself sprang to his

feet. He said Derek also jumped up. Derek pushed him and yelled, "Sit down, young man." Derek caught him off balance, Jens said, and when shoved, he staggered backwards. His head and shoulders slammed against the wall. The next thing he knew, he told the psychiatrist, he flew at Derek, who had turned away from him. Jens had a knife in his hand and he slashed at Derek, cutting him deeply on the left side of his throat. Without uttering a word, Derek slumped into a chair.

Frozen by the sight of blood, Jens stood motionless, staring at Derek. Suddenly he looked up. Nancy was charging at him with a knife in *her* hand. He wrestled with her and took the knife away. But while he was occupied with her, Derek recovered. Rising from the chair, he attacked Jens screaming, "Are you crazy?" Again and again he yelled, "Are you crazy?"

The two began to fight. During the struggle, Jens lost his glasses and couldn't see too well what was happening. By then, the floor was covered with blood, and he and Derek were having trouble keeping on their feet because they kept slipping in the gore. During the struggle, Jens cut himself at least twice on the hand, and his blood added to that already on the floor.

At some point, Jens said, Nancy rejoined the battle. But he maneuvered behind her and cut her throat. She then staggered off and collapsed on the floor.

Finally, the fight with Derek ended. Elizabeth's father dropped in a heap on the floor, and he did not rise. Jens looked down and saw that he himself was covered with blood. Some of it was his own but mostly it came from Derek and Nancy.

Because he was leaving footprints, he took off his shoes and padded around in his white socks. He bandaged his hand and tried to wipe away some of the shoe prints so they could not be used in identification. He assumed Derek and Nancy were dead, but he did not check to make sure. The last time he saw them, he asserted, they were lying close together at right angles to each other. He denied making any voodoo symbols.

When police found the Haysoms, they were in separate rooms, and both were stretched out on a north-south axis with their heads pointed north.

After wiping up his shoe prints as best he could, Jens climbed into his car and drove off toward Lynchburg. Not far away, he ran over a dog. That upset him terribly, he told Hamilton. He also stopped soon afterwards and disposed of his bloody clothes in a dumpster.

After Lynchburg, as he was speeding down the highway heading toward Washington, he turned on the car radio and tuned in a rock station. Blasting back at him was a song by the Talking Heads entitled "Psycho Killer."

Less than a month after meeting with the psychiatrist, Jens had a session with a prosecutor sent in from Bonn. As a German citizen, Jens claimed the right to talk to a German official.

The tale Jens told then put him in a much more favorable light than anything he had said previously. According to the prosecutor, Jens told him that "he had never had any intention of killing Mr. and Mrs. Haysom and . . . he could only remember having inflicted wounds at the neck on Mr. and Mrs. Haysom, which must have had something to do with their dying later." He also claimed "there had been no talk whatsoever [between him and Elizabeth] about killing Elizabeth's parents."

32

As soon as he got back to Virginia, suffering from jet lag and a cigarette cough, Jim Updike, whose only lasting souvenir from his first and maybe final trip to Britain was the addition of cigarettes to his repertoire of addictions to tobacco products, asked that a special grand jury be convened as soon as possible to hear the accusations against Jens Soering and Elizabeth Haysom. The five-member group met before the week was over, on Friday the 13th, and listened to Ricky Gardner for an hour. Soon afterwards they handed up indictments charging Jens and Elizabeth with first degree murder for the deaths of Derek and Nancy. Since Jens had allegedly committed the crimes, he was charged additionally with capital murder, which meant Updike could seek the death penalty.

Despite the speedy action by the grand jury, there was not much Updike or anyone in Bedford County could do about bringing the case to a speedy conclusion. Both Jens and Elizabeth first had to answer for the fraud in Britain. And then there were the complicated extradition hurdles to be cleared. These would be made even more difficult because of Jens's governmental connections and the breadth of legal representation available to him.

For Ricky Gardner, who had lived, eaten, and breathed details of the Haysom murders for fourteen months, the long fight was all but over. For Jim Updike it was just beginning. His struggle to bring the two former lovers into court would drag on for three times as long as the original investigation.

Even if he had known what an arduous task it was going to be, Updike would have plunged ahead anyway. He may speak slowly, softly and courteously with a pronounced drawl, but buried in that county boy persona is a sharp legal mind and a sense of determination that would make Margaret Thatcher look wishy-washy.

JAMES WILSON UPDIKE, JR.'S FAMILY HAS BEEN IN VIRGINIA FOR generations, possibly as long as Elizabeth's. While her ancestors, however, were in the upper social strata, Updike's were firmly in the middle; mostly they were farmers and construction workers. His father was an electrician, and his mother managed a grocery store.

When he was a teenager, the family lived in Pittsburgh for two years. Before then, in high school in Bedford, Updike played keyboard in a band. The drummer in the group was Chuck Reid.

Updike, who began by playing his grandmother's organ when he was ten, was seriously interested in music. When he was a senior in high school, he auditioned for the Cincinnati Conservatory of Music but was not accepted. A year later he was told there would be a spot for him at the Conservatory as a music theory major, but by then he had already decided on law.

After two years at the University of Cincinnati, Updike transferred to UVA and was graduated "with distinction" in 1975 with a major in English. The next fall, he was accepted into the law school at William and Mary. During his law school summers he clerked for the prosecutor in Roanoke County. After he graduated, he was offered a job with the commonwealth attorney in Bedford County.

As recently as the late 1970s, Bedford was such a sleepy county that the prosecutor spent more time on his private practice than he did working for the government. With population growth and a concomitant increase in crime, however, that began to change. In 1980, when Updike was twenty-four and only two years out of law school, the board of supervisors decided to make the commonwealth attorney's job a full-time one. Since the man who held the title was too entwined in his private practice to seriously consider switching to a county job, he resigned and recommended his assistant as his successor. Updike took the job on an acting basis until an election could be held. He won that in a snap, just as he has won reelection every four years since then, always without opposition. When he and Gardner went to London in June 1986, he had been a prosecutor for six years but had never tried a capital murder case. In the next year, though, he tried two and won them both.

A slim man of medium height with thinning blond hair, blue eyes, and a ginger-colored Fu Manchu mustache, Updike faintly resembles Robert Redford. Put astride a horse, he could be a Marlborough Man, except he prefers Merits and he has a curious attachment to small, dark cigars, which he keeps in a brass container large enough to serve as a beer cooler. With the cigar box within reach to his left and a bright red thermos filled with strong coffee to his right, Updike feels he can get through almost any crisis.

His office on the second (and top) floor of the county courthouse is both large and spartan, with the latter accentuating the former. The furniture is strictly government issue: a battered wooden desk probably taken from another bureaucrat's office when he died or retired, two institutional-style visitors' chairs covered in green plastic, an ashtray on a pedestal, a formica sideboard and a second, smaller desk. Wall decorations consist of the traditional diplomas, citations, and plaques. The floor is cracked linoleum the color of milk chocolate, marked here and there with cigarette burns and stains from mysterious liquids, perhaps Updike's corrosive coffee. The office, like its occupant, is plain and unpretentious.

He is non-assuming enough to dress in off-the-rack suits, short-sleeve shirts, conservative ties, and scuffed white bucks, but vain enough to wear contact lenses rather than spectacles. He has a quiet sense of humor and likes to tell self-deprecating stories. One of his favorites is about his trip to London and how he was never able to master the British currency system. "There was a cigarette stand I used to go to, and whenever I did, I always went through the same routine. Since I never could figure out the money, I'd just point to a pack of cigarettes and hold out my hand which was full of coins. The attendant would take a few out, put a few back, and I'd go on my way. I never did know how much I was paying for them, but it didn't matter. I had my cigarettes, and I was happy."

Another story he likes to tell is how he and Jens Soering celebrate the same birthday: August 1.

THAT IS ANOTHER OF THE SMALL IRONIES OF THE CASE, ONE OF THE FEW things he can chuckle about in what otherwise has been a grim, numbing experience. For Updike the prosecution of Elizabeth Haysom and Jens Soering was to become an all-absorbing passion; since April 1985, the case has never been out of his thoughts. This has changed him considerably, his wife, Marilyn, said, turned him from a gregarious, fun-loving spouse, who enjoyed his evenings and weekends away from the office, to a man obsessed with bringing the two of them to trial.

When Elizabeth and Jens were arrested in England, Updike had no interest in or knowledge of international law. His world consisted virtually exclusively of Bedford County and Bedford City, an orderly community of six thousand people with shady streets and magnificent old houses built on gently rolling hills in the shadow of the Blue Ridge Mountains, a town of neat, spotless streets lined with stately homes and ancient hardwoods, of old churches, new schools, friendly people, good neighbors. The power politics of the British Parliament and the Council of Europe were as far removed from Updike's world before 1986 world as it was possible to be.

He proved to be a quick learner, but while he was immersing himself in the intricacies of extradition, the case was proceeding at its own pace on the other side of the Atlantic.

33

IN THE OLD DAYS, THERE WAS ONLY ONE FORM OF "RECREATIONAL" exercise in Her Majesty's prisons: walking. It was compulsory. Every prison had an oval, like a miniature horse-racing track, where on certain days large numbers of prisoners would be taken. Masked and chained together, they would be marched around the oval in opposite directions, one group going clockwise, the other counter-clockwise. Typically, the space inside the oval was filled with mulberry bushes. This exercise regimen was the origin of what later would become a children's game, an activity in which tiny tykes formed two groups, joined hands and raced in opposite directions in a circle chanting, "Here we go 'round the mulberry bush . . ."

British prisons still have exercise ovals. And the guards in the prisons are still called *screws*. The derogatory nickname came about because they controlled a piece of machinery called a *crank*, which was dreamed up by someone concerned that prisoners had too much idle time. It consisted of a gearbox on a pedestal with a protruding handle or crank. Each prisoner had to turn the crank ten thousand times a day. If the guard wanted to make it tougher for them, he could increase the resistance against the handle by tightening a screw on the back of the box.

AFTER THEIR JUNE 9 REMAND HEARING IN THE RICHMOND MAGISTRATE'S court, Jens and Elizabeth were split up to await legal developments. They faced check fraud charges in England, and Updike was anxious to get them back to Virginia to stand trial for Derek's and Nancy's murders. Also, Beever and Wright were still working to see if they could develop drug or IRA connections, both of which they still considered possible.

In the meantime Elizabeth was sent to the newly built Prison, a structure completed only in 1985. It was, all things considered, not a bad place to be. Built on the same site as the original prison, which is well out of tourist London to the North, almost in Camden Town, the new Holloway consists of a series of rambling, modern, brick buildings set in the middle of a quasi-residential neighborhood. It has an indoor swimming pool, a gymnasium, and spacious exercise yards as well as the traditional oval. There is a color TV on every floor, and, in addition to three meals a day, every afternoon at four o'clock the 350 inmates take tea.

Upon arrival, Elizabeth was assigned to a private cell on an upper level in D Block, one of four such facilities that radiate outward from the central structure. It was comfortable by prison standards: large enough to hold a steel-framed bed, a small desk, a metal clothes locker, and a lavatory. In an alcove off in a corner was a private toilet. Elizabeth's most prized piece of furniture, of course, was the desk. Sitting in her cell, Elizabeth scribbled and scratched, filling page after page with notes, explanations, and excuses.

JENS WAS NOT AS LUCKY IN HIS PRISON ASSIGNMENT. IT IS APPARENTLY ONE of the vagaries of the British prison system that male prisoners are moved more frequently than women. At least Jens was. While Elizabeth went straight to Holloway, Jens was moved about from prison to prison for several months before he finally settled at Her Majesty's Prison at Brixton, a once-fashionable suburb south of London.

Built in 1819 as a county house of correction, it was designed loosely to resemble a "model prison" that had recently been completed at Milbank. In 1852 the county sold the facility to the national government. The plans at that time were to use it to house the mentally ill, but that never came about, and the facility was put on the auction block. An architect named Sir William Tite bought it for £8,400, intending to demolish it and sell the material. Before he could do that, however, the government bought it back to use as a woman's prison. Tite made a nifty 50 percent profit on the deal.

It served that purpose from 1853 until 1892, when the original Holloway was built. When the women were transferred, Brixton was converted to a military prison. Then, around the turn of the century, it was enlarged and converted to *the* trial and remand prison for the London area. That's what it still is today, with most of its 1,000 or so male prisoners being held there only temporarily.

Temporary, however, is a broad term. Jens Soering became one of the "temporary" prisoners.

Brixton Prison has a central building constructed in a polygonal shape, originally so the chief administrator, called a *warden* in the United States and a *governor* in Britain, could walk around inside and look out in all directions to make sure the prisoners were working. The cellblocks where the prisoners lived were built in a semicircle around the main building. The original cellblocks at Brixton, which are still in use, are two-story affairs containing a total of 149 single cells and twelve double cells. By modern standards, these are cubicles. Each single cell is only 369 cubic feet, which translates into a space large enough for a prisoner to stand up and lie down and wide enough for him to stretch his arms from wall to wall. But barely. By contrast, death row cells at the Mecklenberg Correctional Center, Virginia's maximum security institution, are ten feet long and seven and a half feet wide.

Jens was assigned to one of Brixton's original cells. As a Category A, or high security, prisoner he was shuffled into a suffocatingly small cubicle with a tiny window that provided some light but not much in the way of a view. Since the prison predated modern sanitary facilities, there was no indoor plumbing in Brixton cells when the facility was built. There still isn't. If Jens has to answer the call of nature between lockdown time in the evening, about eight o'clock, until the next morning, again about eight o'clock, there is only a slop jar. And if he wants to wash, he has to use a pitcher and bowl. He can use the exercise oval or other facilities, but Jens was never the athletic type. Because of the lack of activity and the starchy prison food that comes four times a day—the usual three meals plus tea (and a pint of ale a day if he wanted it)—Jens rapidly gained weight. When he was arrested in Richmond in June 1986, he weighed about 145 pounds, which he carried well on his five-foot-eight frame. But in no time at all, on prison fare, he ballooned to 180. He became a German dumpling, pale and soft and vulnerable looking.

But his physical condition had nothing to do with his mind. Like Elizabeth, he is a prodigious letter writer. Together, their demand for writing paper is such that something like an entire forest has probably been decimated to cater to their needs.

The volume of material they exchanged just among themselves is impressive. Add family, friends, and lawyers to the list, and the amount of correspondence flying back and forth is really stupendous. The only way to have kept up with it accurately would have been with a computer. Unfortunately, there was no computer, so the details about who wrote what to whom and when are a little fuzzy. Letters were lost, destroyed, stolen—whatever. But one thing is certain. As time went on, their relationship quickly unraveled. It was not strong enough to survive the strains and pressures of separation, imprisonment, and the conflicts inherent in preparing their cases for trial. They were backed into opposite corners, and their positions would become increasingly adversarial as the days and weeks flew by.

Occasionally they saw each other, such as at joint court appearances or when they met together with the lawyer handling the fraud case. But it was not enough. They began arguing and exchanging accusations. Keeping track of what was said at those sessions is even more confusing than trying to piece together the history of the correspondence. Each had his or her own version of what the other said, suggested, or proposed. Rarely did these versions correspond. Still, the pattern quickly becomes clear: Elizabeth's and Jens's great love was falling apart by the day.

Basically, the problem was that each had totally different ideas about what they should do next. Elizabeth, burdened with guilt, wanted to go back to the United States and be punished. The harsher the punishment, the better it would be. She had adopted a martyr complex: She acted as if she wanted to scream *mea culpa* on prime time and put it on page one of the *New York Times* and the *Washington Post.*

On the other hand, the United States was the very last place Jens wanted to go. The thought of being electrocuted gave him nightmares even in the daytime. All of Elizabeth's instincts said "surrender"; all of Jens's said "fight"—fight at all costs either to stay in Britain or be extradited to Germany, neither of which had a death penalty.

Jens started laying the groundwork for this strategy barely a month after their weekend in the Richmond police station. He began his campaign subtly, mentioning matter-of-factly in his letters to Elizabeth that he thought he would be tried in a German court, where, he figured, he probably would get a six-year sentence. That wouldn't be hard to serve, he added, because German prisons are very "cushy."

A couple of weeks later, though, he realized that he could be in for a fight. In a communication to Elizabeth he asked her to contact everyone she knew who might have influence. He hinted at another time that his parents were willing to back him all the way.

After his arrest, Jens's parents were very supportive. Elizabeth's family, on the other hand, ignored her. Except for a few letters to a maternal uncle in California, she was without contact with her siblings.

┌─────────┐
│   *34*   │
└─────────┘

THIS MANEUVERING WAS COMPLICATED BY THE FACT THAT NEITHER WAS operating in a vacuum. If Elizabeth had been acting alone and she wanted to go back to the United States, that was one thing. If Jens had been acting alone and he wanted to direct his efforts toward getting to Germany, that was another. But they were irrevocably bound together; neither was free to act independently. They were tied inseparably by the murders of Derek and Nancy as well as their emotional involvement.

Jens was afraid Elizabeth could sabotage his efforts to be extradited to Germany. Then if he were extradited to the United States instead, she could testify against him and help seal his date with the executioner. So he had good reason to worry about what she was saying and doing.

Elizabeth feared that Jens could insure she got as stiff a sentence as possible by putting the blame for the murders squarely on her shoulders. In that case, she would become the Wicked Witch of the West, the older woman who lured a young schoolboy into crime and depravity.

Needless to say, given such conflicting interests, the situation soon got nasty.

It is difficult to determine exactly what happened and when. Elizabeth saved some of Jens's letters. Some, she said, were stolen as part of a plot hatched by Jens, which involved representatives of the German government. And then there were those that were shortstopped by prison officials. She saw enough, though, to make her realize that their relationship was undergoing a metamorphosis.

On August 11, Jens wrote to her saying that his father had seen a clipping from a Virginia newspaper saying Elizabeth had been giggling during one of the court hearings. Jens said he *knew* this didn't happen because he had been there, but Klaus, who had *not* been there, was convinced it had occurred. He warned her to be on her best behavior.

On August 30 Jens wrote encouragingly, saying that the American judicial system treated violent criminals very leniently, and, since she had not been accused of any violent action, she was even better off. Elizabeth took this as a strong hint not to make waves.

In a postscript he asked whether Ricky Gardner had asked her about Annie. Elizabeth interpreted this as a way of reminding her that she could do both of them a favor by suggesting to investigators that Annie Massie may have played a role in the murders as well. He had told Elizabeth before that he believed Annie had been in the house after Nancy and Derek were killed. That is, actually *in* the house and not just to open the door, glimpse Derek's body sprawled on the floor, and summon the police. Jens had sworn to Elizabeth that he had not mutilated Nancy's and Derek's bodies. If he didn't do it, he argued, someone must have come in after him and done it. During one of their fights he had even accused Elizabeth of hiring someone to do it.

This message hit home to Elizabeth because she was still perplexed about one thing Annie had done soon after the murders. The night after she found the bodies Annie and her husband drove to Charlottesville to tell Elizabeth the horrible news. Elizabeth said she noticed that Annie was acting strangely but she attributed that to shock. However, she said Annie also gave her Nancy's old address book. When she got to thinking about it later, Elizabeth said she decided that Annie *had* to have gone into the house at some point because that book was kept on a desk on the far side of the living room from Derek's body.

Then Jens wrote angrily attacking Virginia officials. This may have been a response to the formal extradition request filed with the British government a few weeks previously, a copy of which may have just found its way to Jens. He expected Virginia officials to seek the death penalty. He predicted that regardless of their efforts he would still be extradited to Germany and tried for manslaughter. If that proved to be true, he said, it would be very difficult for the Virginians to try her as an accomplice to murder, which would be a more serious charge than the one he would face.

As far as the extradition battle went, Jens was still certain that the best way to go was for them to direct all their efforts toward getting him sent to Germany. If he could be tried there before she was tried in Virginia, her trial would be anticlimactic and she would get off lightly because he, the "star attraction," would not be making an appearance.

Elizabeth, on the other hand, felt increasingly put upon. All of Jens's energy was focused entirely on his getting extradited to Germany. Granted, he kept telling her how much that was going to help her as well, but the main purpose was to save him.

On October 10 they met face to face during a joint legal visit, and Jens increased his demands on her by suggesting to her that she ask for a meeting with officers from the British Special Branch, which is roughly like the American FBI, to hint about their possible involvement with the IRA. This was part of one of Jens's subplots. If the plan to be sent to Germany ran into problems, he figured they could delay a stepped-up move to extradite them to the United States by making themselves too valuable to the British to be surrendered. In other words, given the emphasis put on antiterrorist activities in the United Kingdom, if Jens and Elizabeth could make the British want to keep them more than they wanted to send them back to Virginia, it would be to Jens's and Elizabeth's advantage. One way they could do this, Jens reasoned, was by claiming dealings with the IRA. They already had hinted at such connections in the journal that was confiscated in their flat when they were arrested.

Twelve days later Jens again wrote encouraging news, saying his government connections were beginning to pay off and his lawyers had lined up some valuable allies in the United States, including a federal judge and a district attorney in Virginia. He did not identify either one.

His mood was not so cheery three weeks later, after he saw a television program on capital punishment in the United States. One of those interviewed was the executioner for the state of Virginia. Jens described to Elizabeth in detail what the man had said, including how witnesses to the execution sometimes had to insert Vaseline into their nostrils to help block the smell of burning flesh. He added that fortunately she had very little to worry about because she, unlike him, would be treated leniently.

That letter had a tremendous effect on her. Jens knew the right buttons to push.

THE MORE SHE THOUGHT ABOUT EXTRADITION, THE MORE SHE REALIZED SHE did not have the will to fight as hard as Jens. She was too overwhelmed by guilt. On December 11 she wrote him a letter of a page and a half saying she had decided not to fight extradition, that she planned to go back to Virginia and plead guilty to the charges against her.

There were a number of other wrongs, she added, that she was guilty of but she would never be officially called to account for. One that was weighing heavily on her mind was something that Jens may not have even stopped to consider, and that was what she had done to him, how she had ruined his life. Since he was so "saintly," she said, he probably had not given that issue any thought, but sooner or later he would and when he did she hoped he would not think too badly of her.

Jens, of course, *did* realize that. He was not "saintly" about it. And he was already beginning to think not very kindly toward her.

35

On December 17 Elizabeth and Jens appeared in Kingston Crown Court to be sentenced on the bank fraud charges. She and Jens each got one year sentences with credit for time served. As soon as the sentences were handed down, Scotland Yard detectives produced warrants for their arrest for the murders of Derek and Nancy.

Months later Elizabeth told Ricky Gardner that while she was in the dock that day, a woman she had never seen before tried to attack her, but a court official stepped in and turned the assailant away. She said she believed the incident was planned by Jens to try to frighten her. Curiously, a story in the next day's London *Times* did not mention an attempted attack. It could have been another of Elizabeth's excursions into fantasy.

Jens's letter in response to Elizabeth's message, however, was no fantasy. Dated December 18, 1986, it began by urging her to stop and think about her actions, to quit acting stupid.

The charges against her, Jens said, could not be made more severe, and despite how grim it might look, the situation was completely under control. It was a puzzling statement, and Elizabeth could only believe that Jens was confused and operating under the impression that she was charged with second degree rather than first degree murder.

As far as his not realizing that she had ruined his life, he said that was ridiculous. He was not so dumb, he said, that he did not realize how he had gotten into such a mess.

It was, however, the death knell for their relationship. When they appeared together in court again in February 1987, Jens growled at her, "You're going to be damned sorry." He must have added something even more threatening because the next time they appeared in court, he was handcuffed to a policeman and was kept well away from her.

That was the last time she saw him, but it was not the last contact.

A couple of weeks later, a woman visited Elizabeth, saying she had news from Jens. He no longer loved her and had not for a long time, she said, but he was worried that she was going to try to get even by putting the blame for the murders on him. Instead, the woman said, Jens had a counter suggestion. If Elizabeth would allow Jens to blame *her* for the killings so he wouldn't get the death sentence, he would compensate her with money when she got out of prison. This could easily be done because Elizabeth planned to plead guilty anyway. Since that would be before Jens was even extradited, she could testify at his trial that it was all her fault. This would make a jury look more favorably upon him.

Elizabeth was too shocked to reply immediately, but on March 19 she wrote Jens an abrupt letter asking what was going on.

Jens responded that he was surprised at her hostility. Personally, he felt no enmity at all. He still loved her, he said, even though she did not understand what was happening.

Whether she understood or not on the day before her twenty-third birthday, April 14, she appeared in court for an extradition hearing. The judge ordered her returned to the United States. She had made up her mind not to fight the decision.

HOLLOWAY PRISON HAD THREE PRIMARY CENTERS FOR SOCIAL ACTIVITY. One was the dining hall. Another was the common area on each floor where inmates could gather to play pool or watch video-tapes. And the third was the window. Each of the cell windows, instead of bars, had barriers, disguised as windows, which were cleverly worked into the framework so there was no "prison" look. More importantly, inmates could open the louvered panes and use the windows as communication ports.

One of the favorite pastimes at Holloway was for the women prisoners to yell greetings to male prisoners who were imported to do the gardening. Frequently, through this hollering back and forth, friendships developed. Names and addresses were often exchanged, and pen-pal relationships blossomed. Elizabeth became quite friendly with a male inmate from Pentonville Prison about halfway through her stay. Cupping her hands to her mouth, she shouted her name and address. He wrote her. She answered. But that was all. The relationship proved short-lived.

On the whole, Elizabeth kept a low profile among the other prisoners, concentrating on her reading and writing rather than on friendships. The prison library had a rule that limited inmates to three check-outs per visit. But Elizabeth convinced the librarian to double her ration, and she went through the stacks voraciously.

As far as writing went, Elizabeth must have been the prison's Letters Division champ. During a 10-week period between early February and late April, she posted 76 letters, an average of almost one a day, and received almost as many as she sent, 65. Her correspondents, in addition to Jens, were a varied group, ranging from her former UVA roommate, Charlene Song, who was then studying at Cambridge, to an old friend in Belgium. Prison regulations restricted inmates' letters to four surfaces—the back and front of two pieces of paper—and this proved confining to the compulsive writer. Frequently, Elizabeth tried to get around this rule by writing very small, an infraction for which she was continually reprimanded. In addition to her letters, Elizabeth also wrote stories, essays, and may even have continued the novel she began at UVA. One of her short stories, entitled "The Sleeper Awakes," won a prison-wide competition.

More poetry than prose, it is largely autobiographical, detailing the thoughts of a female narrator laden with guilt. Written with a ballpoint pen on a lined yellow pad in her characteristic cramped, hard-to-decipher script, it is part fact, part fiction. But that doesn't matter. It is all Elizabeth Haysom, a young woman to whom fact and fiction were consistently intermingled.

The protagonist in the story was suffering from insomnia, unable to sleep because of the memories churning in her brain, haunted by the knowledge that there were many things she had omitted to do.

Grudgingly, it seemed, the protagonist confessed that her biggest sin was that of omission. Normally, that was not a truly terrible sin, but it multiplied in severity because it was one that she habitually committed.

Her protagonist had a physically repulsive lover who also was mentally unbalanced. Although this man loved her "beyond reason" she did not love him, and her reluctance to tell him that was an example of her sinful ways.

Failing to tell her lover that she did *not* love him was one of her sins of omission. Another was her failure to tell her father that she *did* love him.

Still another was her attitude toward her mother. Her protagonist wrote that she was deeply resentful because the woman tried to control her life. Nevertheless, that did not absolve the protagonist from *her* sin, which was to omit to make allowances for her mother's weaknesses and forgive her for them.

Now both her parents were dead and there was nothing she could do to rectify her omissions.

As for herself, her protagonist said, she was just another of her own victims. By neglecting to stand up for her right to self-determination she had allowed her parents to impose their ambitions and desires upon her. That had not been fair to them or to her and she despised herself for it.

By the time her protagonist had written these thoughts, she had purged her conscience; her insomnia was cured.

IN REAL LIFE ELIZABETH'S REMORSE WAS EQUIVOCAL. AT NIGHT, WHEN THE male prisoners had all been driven back to their own institutions, the women of Holloway used their cell windows for their own internal communications system, gathering at their windows and speaking their thoughts into the night air. Communication in this manner was rather limited because a voice can carry only so far, especially when there are competing voices. But it was convenient if an inmate happened to have a good friend in the next cell. Elizabeth *did* have such a friend, one of the very few she cultivated during her stay at Holloway. Her name was *Joan Alexander*, and she was serving a sentence for a drug law violation. She and Elizabeth were of similar backgrounds, and they had similar interests. They spent countless hours at their windows laughing, chatting, and exchanging verities in uninterrupted semiprivacy. Just before she left for the United States, Elizabeth's conversation with her friend turned serious. Speaking of the fate that awaited her, Elizabeth was optimistic. "They have nothing on me," Elizabeth whispered into the dark, referring to Updike and Gardner. "There's no way they can tie me to the murders."

Although she professed at length, particularly to Jens, to be truly contrite over the deaths of her parents, many who have come in contact with her over the years, including some members of her family, have serious doubts. This very lack of remorsefulness, in fact, was the first of three things one of her warders at Holloway remembered most about Elizabeth. The second was that she always hated to shampoo her hair, being content to let it fall in long, greasy strands. The third was that she was utterly convinced she would "walk" on the charges in Virginia. When she left Holloway in May 1986, she told her fellow inmates that she was confident she would be able to return to the United States and convince the judge to give her a sweetheart sentence.

36

Elizabeth was not the only one Jens told about his theory that she was to blame for the murders.

In addition to Dr. Hamilton, Jens also met with another psychiatrist, Dr. Henrietta Bullard from the West Berkshire Health Authority. He told her virtually the same tale he had told Hamilton. However, Jens did not meet with the psychiatrists simply to make additional confessions. He was subtly planting the idea that although he had killed the Haysoms, he was not responsible. The fault, he implied, was Elizabeth's. She had, after all, talked him into it.

Jens told Hamilton that Elizabeth had been "psyching him up" to kill her parents for a long time, but at first, as far as he was concerned, the thought of murder was "pure fantasy." If he had been left to his own devices, Jens said, he would have picked a gun as the murder weapon because he knew how to get one, and he also knew how to construct a silencer, apparently as a result of his avid perusal of military-adventure magazines.

Before he knew it, he said, Elizabeth had convinced him that her parents had to be murdered, and she provided him with the knife to do it.

Jens elaborated on this tale slightly when he talked to Bullard. He told her that when he went to Loose Chippings on March 30, he was "prepared for violence."

As he had done with Hamilton, Jens denied to Bullard that he had left any cult-style symbols in the house. He also said he was at a loss to explain the widespread carnage that investigators found when they discovered Nancy's and Derek's bodies four days after he killed them.

Jens's tactics worked. Both Bullard and Hamilton agreed independently that Jens was suffering from a malady called *folie à deux,* which is characterized by the victim submerging his or her personality into that of another.

"It is by no means rare for the close associate of a psychotic person to share his or her delusions," Hamilton wrote. "It is possible that Jens Soering, by reason of the dependent and immature traits in his personality, believed to be true the pathological lies told to him by Elizabeth Haysom and felt compelled to act upon them."

His opinion, he said, was that Jens was, at least at that time, mentally ill. He was, Hamilton averred, "suffering from an abnormality of mind in which the predominant feature was an impaired appreciation of reality in this circumscribed but crucial area." In other words, he was mentally disturbed to the extent that his judgment was impaired, and he was not responsible for what happened.

Bullard said virtually the same thing. Jens "had the misfortune to meet a very powerful, persuasive and disturbed young woman whom he believed and trusted implicitly," Bullard wrote. "He became tangled in her web of deceit and lies, and began to live with her a life of fantasy and unreality. He seemed devoid of judgment and was not only taken in by her fantastic stories, but came to agree with her as to the ultimate solution. He was flattered by Miss Haysom's apparent emotional and sexual needs for him, and her suffering became his suffering."

The relationship was a sick one, she said, and the most disturbed partner was Elizabeth, whom she described as bordering on the psychotic. "It is easy to see how an immature, sensitive and altruistic young man might become the prey of a woman such as Miss Haysom," Bullard said.

"The strength and importance of this relationship cannot be over-emphasized," she added. "Miss Haysom had a stupefying and mesmeric effect on Soering which led to an abnormal psychological state in which he became unable to think rationally or question the absurdities in Miss Haysom's view of her life and the influence of her parents. They were not the powerful and destructive people she described, and Soering was unable to apply ordinary principles of reasoning and logic."

It was her professional opinion, she concluded, that Jens's mental state was such that his judgment was impaired to the extent that he was not responsible for his acts.

It was exactly what Hamilton had said, and if Jens were being tried in England, it would make a difference. Under British law, the *folie à deux* syndrome was a legally recognized form of mental illness. If Jens was tried in the United Kingdom, he could claim a psychiatric defense, known as *diminished capacity*, based on the diagnoses. If a British jury heard the case and its members agreed that he did indeed suffer from the syndrome, the charge could be reduced from murder to manslaughter.

Unfortunately for Jens, this was not the case in Virginia, where there was no such defense as diminished capacity. A Virginia jury hearing Jens's case would not be able to reduce the charges against him on grounds of insanity, based on those diagnoses, even if his psychiatrists were persuasive. In Virginia he wasn't going to be able to dodge the electric chair on those grounds no matter how many psychiatrists he got to agree that he had been bewitched by Elizabeth Haysom. With Updike refusing to consider any charge other than capital murder, punishable by electrocution upon conviction, Jens flew into a panic. It was imperative, he decided, that he not be extradited to Virginia.

37

RICKY GARDNER FOUND ELIZABETH IN THE HALLWAY OF THE BEDFORD County Jail. She was sitting in a straight-backed chair with one leg tucked under her, looking somewhat disheveled. Her white blouse was wrinkled, her hair was uncombed, and she wore no makeup. But her physical condition was not indicative of her mental one. Despite nineteen-plus hours on the road, she was running hard on adrenalin and was quite alert.

She had left Holloway at dawn that morning, British time, flying to Washington and then to Roanoke, where Sheriff Wells was waiting to pick her up for the final thirty-five-mile leg of the journey. The first thing she told the sheriff when they got to Bedford was that she wanted to talk to Gardner. It was after ten o'clock on May 8, a Friday night. Gardner had gone for the day, but Wells called him back.

Gardner was only slightly surprised and not at all unhappy about the summons. It had been eleven months almost to the day since he had last talked to her. But he had not stopped thinking about the case. He had read the transcripts of her interrogations with Beever and Wright, and he wanted to ask her a number of questions in addition to what he had already queried her about.

After a greeting that was not as cold as he expected, Gardner led her into a small, quiet room and fetched her a cup of black coffee. Settling down with his omnipresent tape recorder on the desk, he invited her to say what was on her mind.

Elizabeth had done a lot of thinking since her last meeting with investigators. Over the months she had had time to consider the things she had said and, more importantly, the things she now *wanted* to say. She still professed a desire to expiate her guilt, but she didn't want to be *too* guilty. She was ready to accept punishment for the role she had played in the murder of her parents, but she didn't want the prosecutors and the public to think that Jens was a saint and she totally evil.

By then she had been given a copy of Bullard's and Hamilton's reports on Jens's psychiatric state, and these made her seethe. If she was going to be called to account for her actions, she was going to try her best to make sure Jens was, too. After all, he had been the one who had done the killing. Also, she now had the benefit of Jens's correspondence, so she knew, at least in rough form, what his strategy was going to be. His first priority was to be extradited to Germany. If that didn't work, his fallback position was to blame it all on her. In actuality the latter served a dual purpose because he also could use claims of her pervasive influence as part of his defense in a German court, where the potential punishment was fifteen years at the maximum as compared with a possible death sentence in Virginia.

Elizabeth had decided that she would accept her punishment, and she wanted Jens to do the same, especially after the way he had treated her following the murders. Or at least the way she *wanted* everyone to think she was treated. One of the possible reasons she asked to talk to Gardner could have been to start laying the groundwork for a story that would mitigate her behavior. She knew she could not excuse it, but if she could explain *why* she ended up in the position she did, she would seem a more sympathetic figure. Sitting stiffly in the tiny office with a cup of lukewarm coffee in her fist, she launched into Version 3 of what happened in March 1985 and in the months that followed.

Since he was not present when she made her admissions to Beever and Wright, Gardner had not heard her stories directly. So he guided her through a reiteration of events leading up to the night her parents were murdered. She told him, as she had the British detectives, that they had planned the murders for a month and then gone to Washington to set up an alibi. On that Saturday morning, they had shopped for a knife.

"Now, for the sake of asking, why did you want to buy a knife?" Gardner inquired.

"To kill my parents," she said.

AT FIRST, HER STORY WAS IDENTICAL TO THE ONE SHE HAD TOLD EARLIER. Then, unexpectedly, it took a sharp turn. When it got to the part where she said she had gone to two movies after Jens dropped her off, she made a major modification. She told Gardner she didn't go to the movies that afternoon at all. In reality, she said, she had gone to a bar.

That caught Gardner by surprise. With a puzzled frown, he asked her why she had done that.

She must have anticipated—hoped for—the question. Elizabeth replied that she had gone looking for drugs.

Oh-oh, Gardner thought, we have a whole new element here. But his curiosity was piqued. What was she looking for? Coke? Pot? Hash?

No, she said, she was after the really hard stuff: heroin. Furthermore, she added, she was successful. At least, she was successful in getting what she was looking for, but it turned out to be so diluted that it failed to transport her on the expected high.

Gardner wasn't sure he was hearing what she was telling him. While her boyfriend was on the way to kill her parents, Elizabeth's only interest had been in getting high: Is that what she was saying? Didn't she even give a minute's worth of thought to trying to warn her parents?

Elizabeth looked slightly contrite. "Oh, yes," she said. "During that afternoon I'd come very close to phoning somebody. I was going to phone my parents, but then the more I drank, especially after my hit, it just seemed silly. How could I call them and say Jens was on his way to Loose Chippings to kill them?"

From there, her story converged temporarily with the one she had told Beever and Wright. But if she were trying to make excuses for herself, she could not have found a better one than drugs. Her mention of her excursion into the Georgetown bar was just a teaser, though. She would later discourse extensively on the subject. By the time she was through, she would paint herself as a full-fledged addict.

It wasn't long, though, before she added another wrinkle to her tale. When she got to the part where Jens picked her up and the two returned to the Marriott, she appended a fascinating detail. Jens had already mentioned it, but she elaborated. When they got to the hotel, she said, Jens jumped in the shower without much more than a few grunts and curses. When he had washed and dried himself, he had added more particulars about what had happened. That's when he told her about something that really seemed to be troubling him: that he had run over and apparently killed a dog. Elizabeth was aghast. He had just finished butchering her parents, but he wasn't worried about them; he was worried about killing a dog.

He also was worried about her doing her part. Before he climbed into bed, he ordered her to return to the parking garage and take care of the car. "Clean the seat," he told her. And while she was at it, she should also clean the pedals, the steering wheel, and all the attachments, the radio, the dashboard, the rearview mirror, and the front of the car where he had hit the dog. He was emphatic, she said, about her making sure that the dog remains were removed from the front of the car.

Gardner was amazed. As well as he thought he knew the case, as well as he thought he knew Elizabeth, her capacity for continually surprising him knew no bounds.

"When you went back upstairs, was Jens asleep or awake?" he asked.

"He was asleep," she said.

And what about her, Gardner wanted to know. Did she climb into the bed next to him and go to sleep as well?

No, she said. She got into the bed, but she couldn't sleep. She lay awake all night. Just before dawn, she got up, went back to the garage, and double-checked her cleaning job on the car. She didn't want to raise Jens's wrath.

"Were you relieved at this point that your parents were dead?" He asked.

"No," she replied. "At no point was I relieved that they were dead. Afterwards, I should have been relieved, but I wasn't. My first thought was that Jens was alive. And my next thought was to save our skins."

GARDNER, WHO HAD HEARD JENS'S VERSION OF THE KILLING, WAS CURIOUS about what Jens had told Elizabeth. When Jens awoke the next morning, he asked, was he more forthcoming about what had happened at Loose Chippings?

Elizabeth chewed her lip. Yes and no, she replied. He told her more, but his description was not very lucid. He told her that he had claimed he was undecided during the entire drive about whether he actually was going to kill them.

"But you and he had purchased a knife," Gardner said.

"Yes, but he didn't know whether he had the—whatever was necessary—to do it."

"Well," Gardner inquired, "what did he tell you?"

Jens told her, she said, that he went into the house and spent about forty-five minutes talking to her parents. Despite his best efforts, he had been unsuccessful in convincing them to give the two of them more freedom. So, during a lull in the conversation, he said he "decided to go for it."

He told her he attacked Nancy first and that he had a "hell of a fight" with her father. As Jens mentioned to Hamilton and Bullard, he had lost his glasses during the fight and everything had gone hazy so he was not able to give precise details on what had happened. He had also temporarily lost control of the knife, but he had wrenched it back and continued to slash and stab at Derek.

"He said that my father just wouldn't die," Elizabeth explained. "He kept saying that over and over again."

When Gardner asked what Jens had said about the attack on Nancy, Elizabeth shrugged. He did not go into a lot of detail about that, she said, except to say that he tried to slit her throat and that it was not as easy as it looked in the movies.

While they were talking about what happened at Loose Chippings, Elizabeth added one more thing. She said Jens told her that he had left, then he had come back. He did not explain why he had done this, she said, except that he had felt compelled to. "He just kept saying that he thought somebody was watching him or he hadn't done something and he went back. I think he said he went back to make sure they were dead."

Up until then Elizabeth had not really had a chance to give her view of Jens's role, to suggest that he was not the innocent he wanted everyone to think he was. She had her chance when Gardner began asking about a story that appeared in a London tabloid.

Elizabeth said the reporter had been a friend of her cousin. When the journalist came to see her, Elizabeth said she naively thought she was speaking friend to friend, not subject to reporter. But the writer betrayed her and published what she had said. When Elizabeth heard about the story, she was furious.

What she had *told* the reporter, in contrast to what had been published, she claimed, was that she thought the public would be quick to accuse her of maneuvering Jens into murdering her parents but that wasn't the whole story. It was natural for people to think badly of her, she said, because she was older and more experienced while Jens appeared so innocent and he could be so charming. He also had an unblemished past, while hers was filled with hints of drug use, parental defiance, and homosexuality. "People see me as the manipulator," she said.

"You don't think you were?" Gardner asked.

Elizabeth nodded. "That was quite possibly true at one stage, but the roles very quickly reversed." After the murders, she said, Jens decided that killing people was "quite a nice occupation." He had, in fact, drawn up a hit-list of people he wanted to get rid of. Among those on the list were her half-brother, Howard, Jens's grandmother, and his parents. Elizabeth looked pensive. "His parents wouldn't be giving me such a hard time if they knew that I prevented him from doing them as he had done my parents," she said.

Why did he want to kill Howard? Gardner asked.

"He just didn't like him," Elizabeth said matter-of-factly.

Why his parents?

"He didn't like them either. I think he found them too difficult."

Jens threatened her at one time, too, she added. Plus, there was one other person on his list: Ricky Gardner.

The investigator was taken aback. "Me?" he asked.

Elizabeth nodded. "This was a drastic change in his personality," Elizabeth said. "I remember saying to him, 'You know, you can't just go around killing people when you don't like them.' I tried once to explain to him that what he had done was really wrong, but he wouldn't have any of that. He had to justify it. So did I. It got worse."

After they had left Virginia, she said, Jens took firm control of their relationship. He became increasingly interested in violence, especially violent pornography. That was particularly intriguing to him, she said, because for most of the early days of their relationship Jens had been impotent. Later, he had found his potency, but only if violence was involved. He could get an erection, she said, by just thinking violent thoughts.

"Did he ever try any violence with you?" Gardner asked.

He had suggested it, she said, but she had refused to go along.

"Do you think he got sexually aroused during the murders?"

"I have no idea," she said. "But I can tell you that he attacked me the night of the funeral. We were staying at the house of some friends of my parents. Jens was sleeping in a different room. He came into my room and said he was really frightened and could I come share his bed with him. And up to that point he had been completely impotent. So I got in bed with him. I was on sedatives at the time, and I kept throwing up. I woke up, and he was all over me."

"Did you have sex that night?"

"Yes."

PERHAPS ELIZABETH'S GREATEST TALENT WAS SOUNDING CREDIBLE. SHE could make the most outrageous statements and still come across as thoroughly believable. By now, Gardner was well aware of her abilities, but he seemed mesmerized by her string of surprises. Having a conversation with her was like opening one unmarked, sealed box after another: There was no telling what was going to be inside. In each interview she would add some new tidbit, throwing it out casually as though she were reporting the time of day. Then she would expand upon it, little by little, until it mushroomed with a life of its own. Gardner had the feeling that he could question her every day for the rest of his life and he would never hear the end of her tales. He was more on target than he knew.

38

IN HER STATEMENT TO BEEVER AND WRIGHT IN RICHMOND, ELIZABETH HAD whined about her father, but she had hardly mentioned Nancy. This time Gardner wanted to steer the conversation in that direction. Gradually he got her talking about her mother.

Over the years, Elizabeth said, she had grown very resentful of her parents. There were times when she couldn't stand them, especially when they had been drinking. "My father would become very, very cold. He would just blank everything around him. He would just be rude." But her mother was different. There were times, she said, when she deeply loved her, but now, when she remembered her, she thought only about the torment that her mother had put her through. She was often hysterical, Elizabeth said, shaking her head, and she taunted her frequently, especially when she had been drinking. At times like that Nancy would deride her because she had run off to Europe with Melinda or because of her perceived character faults.

Remembering the pictures of a nude woman that had been found in Nancy's bureau, pictures he now knew to be of Elizabeth, Gardner asked if there were some significance to them. "Did your mother ever have any lesbian affairs?" he asked as gently as he could.

She didn't know, Elizabeth said, but she frequently commented on how much she hated men. And Elizabeth remembered how, when she was a young girl, her mother often told her about a school she had gone to where she and classmates used to listen to the head mistress and another woman making love.

Gardner caught the words "hated men." She couldn't have meant all men, he thought. "She loved your father, didn't she?" he asked Elizabeth. He was surprised when Elizabeth shot back, "No."

"Did she ever tell you that?" Gardner asked

"Yes," she said. "My mother and father both told me separately many times that the only reason they stayed together was because of me."

"Elizabeth," Gardner said, looking uncomfortable, "we found some photographs of you in the house after the murders. You were nude. Do you know which photographs I'm referring to?"

"Yes."

"Can you tell me how they came to be? Did your mother take them?"

"Yes." She said it was in the summer of 1984. Her father had gone back to Nova Scotia on business, and she and her mother had spent a lot of time together. Toward the end of the summer they had gone to Rochester, New York, so Elizabeth could attend a writer's seminar. When they got back, her mother was upset because it was time for Elizabeth to leave for UVA and she was searching for a way to keep her daughter from breaking loose again. "What she said," Elizabeth recollected unhappily, "was that she wanted to impress upon me how absolutely filthy and disgusting I was."

There was a long silence. Gardner twirled his cigarette lighter, and Elizabeth stared at the wall. Finally, she spoke again. "What she said was that I could prove how filthy and disgusting I was by allowing her to take the photos." She paused. "We were having a very vicious argument," Elizabeth said, then, struck by the incongruity of the statement, she began laughing nervously. "That was strange because I never argued with my mother."

"Do you remember the poses?" Gardner interjected, trying to break the mood.

"I remember her making me kneel."

"That's right," Gardner agreed. "But why was she making

you do that? Was she trying to destroy your sexual esteem or what? Did she sexually—"

Elizabeth interrupted. "She slept with me," she said, looking Gardner in the eye. "Ever since I was a little girl."

Gardner looked uncomfortable. "When was the last time that happened?" he asked.

Elizabeth said it was the Saturday before her parents were murdered, March 23, 1985. She remembered it vividly because it was her father's seventy-second birthday. Her parents had gone out. They had both been drinking. When they got home, Nancy came up to her room, as she always did. Then Nancy got undressed and got in bed with her.

"Was there some sexual activity?" Gardner asked.

"No," Elizabeth said slowly. It wasn't what most people would call sexual activity, she explained. But her mother liked to kiss. She liked to hug. And she liked to touch.

"Was that activity conducted in a mother-daughter way?" Gardner asked.

Elizabeth thought about the question, then gave a typical Elizabeth answer, an answer that wasn't one. "It was just very affectionate," she said. "My mother craved affection. She was aggressively affectionate."

Gardner was eager to drop the subject. But he had one more question. When she and Nancy slept together, he wanted to know, were they clothed or unclothed?

Either way, Elizabeth said. "Sometimes I'd be clothed. Sometimes I'd be wearing nothing. My mother usually was wearing nothing."

GARDNER LOOKED AT HIS WATCH TO COVER HIS EMBARRASSMENT. WHAT Elizabeth had said had shocked him, but the impact was eased because he wasn't sure whether to believe her or not. By then, he was getting to know her. He realized how easily she navigated between truth and untruth, and he had no way of determining when she was speaking one or the other. Only two people knew for sure what occurred on those nights Nancy and Elizabeth slept together, and one of them was dead. But there was one thing he did know: It was getting late, and he was tired. His shoulders ached, and his eyes felt as if he had taken a long swim in a highly chlorinated pool. It was after 2 A.M. Elizabeth had to be tired, too; she had been up for more than twenty-four hours. We've covered a lot of ground, he told himself, and perhaps we ought to call it a night. But there was one other area Gardner wanted to explore. Remembering how investigators had been sidetracked so devastatingly by the possibility that satanism had played a role in the murders, he brought up her Christmas letters, specifically the one in which she wrote Jens saying she was considering invoking voodoo against her parents. "What did you mean by that?" he asked.

Elizabeth laughed. "It was supposed to be a joke, okay? Jens was really into psychology. He was studying psychology at UVA and he had read all these ridiculous things. I used to ridicule him about some of the things that he thought possible." What she had done, she explained, was to tease him by mentioning events that had occurred at widely separated times, except in the telling she condensed them into a much shorter time-frame to make it appear as if they had occurred in rapid succession.

Was that true for other events she mentioned in the letter as well? Gardner asked.

She confessed it was. "I go on to describe more of the things that supposedly happened, but they didn't happen then. I was just projecting some things that weren't there."

How about the part where she referred to black magic? Gardner pressed.

"I don't know anything about black magic," Elizabeth said wearily.

Gardner, Reid and the rest of the investigators had spent too many hours running down deadend streets looking for ties to satanism for him to drop it without exploring the possibilities as far as he could. There were, in fact, some who still believed that it had played a role in the killings, or at the very least, that an attempt had been made to make it look that way. Gardner wanted to know if they had all been wasting their time. "Have you or Jens either one ever been involved in the occult?" he asked.

"No," she said. "Never." She didn't even know anything

about the occult, she added. The closest she had come to it, she swore, was when some of her fellow prisoners at Holloway used a ouija board and that had made her very uncomfortable. "It totally freaked me out," she said. "It scared the shit out of me."

Satisfied, Gardner changed the subject. "Do you realize how many times your father was stabbed?" he asked, anxious to gauge her reaction.

"Yes," Elizabeth said sadly. She had, in fact, seen the pictures of her parents' bodies. They were part of the legal records turned over to her to help her formulate a defense.

"You think Jens was in this by himself?" he asked.

"No," Elizabeth said.

Gardner's head shot up. His fatigue was forgotten. He opened his mouth to speak, but Elizabeth spoke first. "Jens was in it with me," she said.

Gardner relaxed. Did she think, he asked, that anyone else had been in the house when her parents were murdered?

Elizabeth gave him a look that said, what a preposterous question. "No," she said emphatically. She had no reason at all to think anyone else was in the house at the time.

"So to sum it up," Gardner began, "you and Jens Soering talked of killing your parents for several weeks—"

"It was premeditated."

"—prior to March 29, and he went to the house and murdered your parents, and you assisted him in establishing an alibi both before and after the two murders."

"Yes." Elizabeth said.

But she didn't mean it.

39

WHEN GARDNER LEFT ELIZABETH AT 2:30 A.M. ON MAY 9, HE THOUGHT he had participated in his last interview with her. He was wrong. Three days later she asked to see him again. When he met with her, she showed him a stack of letters from Jens that she said she was willing to share with him as long as the session was not recorded. After she had gone over the letters with the investigator and was leaving the room she stopped at the door. "There's something else I want to tell you."

Gardner looked at her quizzically.

"I'm not saying this to lessen my guilt or anything."

"What's that?" he inquired.

"I told you that I was with Jens when he bought the butterfly knife. That isn't true. Afterwards we decided I would say that. Jens wanted me to say that because it would make me more of a participant than I actually was."

Gardner was puzzled. She had already admitted she was up to her eyebrows in the murders. "Why are you telling me that?"

"I just thought you might want to know."

He didn't believe her. She had told Beever and Wright she had bought the knife. She had told him that as well. Jens had verified it. He didn't know why she was changing her story now, but he had a good idea. He thought she was searching desperately for a way to reduce her responsibility, perhaps to get a lighter sentence. He was certain that her first stories about the knife had been true and that she was blowing smoke at him now.

THREE MORE DAYS WENT BY, AND ELIZABETH ASKED FOR ANOTHER "official" session with the investigator. That morning, Thursday, May 14, Elizabeth had appeared before Judge William W. Sweeney to ask for court-appointed counsel. Following the brief session, she sent word to Gardner that she wanted to see him. So, shortly after noon Gardner met her with her again. This time, he had his tape recorder. She had changed her mind and was willing to talk about the letters on the record. But Elizabeth was incapable of operating within a restricted format. As usual, her comments covered a broad range of issues pertaining to the case. Practically all of them were designed to strengthen the case against Jens.

Apparently reading over the letters and then thinking about them for the last few days had made Elizabeth angry all over again. "He was manipulating me," she complained to Gardner. "He knew that I loved him very much and I did a lot for him. I mean I really *had*. I aided and abetted him. I covered up. I lied. I betrayed my family and friends. I left Virginia with him against what I wanted to do. I agreed to go into fraud with him because he thought it was exciting. I allowed him to get hold of my brother's credit card number and he bought stun guns or something—"

Gardner broke in. "Let's get back to the letters," he said. The noose was already around Elizabeth's neck, he figured, but he wanted to nail down the case against Jens. The German was proving exceptionally slippery, and Gardner was sure Jim Updike could use all the evidence he could get.

Elizabeth dug into the pile of correspondence, but a few minutes later she was off again, attacking Jens for his cold-bloodedness. It had been during the previous spring that she had really begun seeing through him, she claimed. That is when she learned that he was lying to just about everybody, not only about things she had said—which she was willing to write off as third-party meddling—but about other things as well. "His whole attitude towards the situation is totally foreign to mine," she grumbled. While he had tried to make her believe that his reasons were altruistic and stemmed from his love for her, she no longer believed that.

Gardner wanted to make sure he was reading her correctly. "You mean you think he's going to do everything humanly possible to get out of it?"

She nodded vigorously. That was correct, she said. Jens was searching for a way to justify the murders. She had felt that way at first, too, she confessed, but she had realized she was wrong. Jens, however, had not changed his attitude. She was remorseful about the murders, but Jens was not. "He *justifies* them," she repeated angrily.

Then she retreated a bit. "To tell you the truth, I don't know how he feels, all right?" But she thought she had a pretty good idea. "All I know is if the door opens for him and the door opens for me, I'm staying where I'm seated, but he would run. He will try everything within his means to get out of what he has done." Scornfully, she criticized him for referring to the murders as an "honest mistake." Her eyes grew cold. "I just don't think that premeditated murder is an honest mistake. Somewhere else in here," she said, waving the stack of letters, "he mentions that it was a silly mishap or something. I don't consider it a silly mishap either. It was horrible."

Gardner was intrigued by the insight she was giving him into Jens. He was curious to know just how far she thought Jens would go to escape his responsibility. "You said if the door opened, you would stay and he would run. Do you feel he would still commit murder if that's what it would take to get him out of this?"

This gave Elizabeth the chance to expound again on how Jens was not the innocent youth that many thought, that deep within his superior intellect brewed very disturbing thoughts. "That I do not know," she admitted. "But I do know that after he murdered my parents, he considered murder a trivial thing."

"Like solving a problem?" Gardner suggested.

"Exactly!" Elizabeth said. "He liked violence. He thought it was an okay means of obtaining money or solving any sort of problem that came up."

It was a perfect opportunity for Gardner to get back to what Elizabeth had said the previous Friday about the people Jens allegedly had contemplated killing because they were obstacles in his path. He invited her to tell him in more detail about Jens's murder plans.

She collected her thoughts. "Take his grandmother," Elizabeth said. "He wanted her money." He had a plan, she said, whereby she and Jens would go to his grandmother's house in Germany and lock themselves inside. "Then he wanted to hook her up to some kind of electric gizmo and torture her until she gave us money. Then afterwards we obviously would kill her."

"But you never went there," Gardner pointed out.

She conceded that was true. But it did not stop Jens from planning. For instance, there was his plot to murder Gardner.

"Tell me about that," Gardner said, curious to see how far Jens had gone in allegedly mapping out his demise.

"He found out where you lived," Elizabeth said.

That surprised the investigator. "What else?" he asked.

Elizabeth hesitated. Jens had told her, she said, that she was going to have to be his alibi again. "He felt we'd definitely need an alibi if we killed you," she said. "I mean, if you were killed, we would be suspects."

That made sense, Gardner agreed, feeling a chill run down his spine. "So what happened?"

Elizabeth said she was able to distract him. She told him a wild tale about being diagnosed as having a brain tumor and how her doctor wanted to try to excise it with a new laser technique rather than surgery. She got him so worried about her alleged illness that he temporarily forgot about Gardner. By that time, Gardner and Reid were putting pressure on him to submit to the blood and print tests, and he was beginning to get panicky. Then they decided to flee, and the investigator was forgotten altogether.

Gardner wondered if he should feel grateful to her for perhaps saving his life, or if she was just weaving another story to make herself look good. That was the thing about Elizabeth: No one ever knew for sure. He shook off his introspective mood. "How do you feel about Jens now?" he asked. "Do you still love him?"

"Yes, I do," she said quickly. "I mean, I'm very angry with

him, but I don't think I could possibly feel so awful about talking about him if I didn't love him. I feel I have betrayed him. I don't think I would have stayed with him all that time if I had not had this blind obsession, this love, for him. But I'm so overwhelmed by what I've done and the horror I've caused, I think that outweighs any affection I could possibly have for him."

Gardner wanted to warn her not too get too carried away with her emotions. "Don't forget that he went hands-up first," he said, reminding her that Jens was confessing to investigators while Elizabeth was still holding out.

"Oh, yeah," she said bitterly. "That was a very nice little set up, that's a fact. I honestly feel he set me up for that. There I was, lying and making a total idiot out of myself, lying away and refusing to make any comment and being as difficult as possible while he was being the good little boy."

There was one other thing she had better consider, too, Gardner felt. How would she feel if Jens received only a short prison sentence?

It didn't take her long to answer that question. Or at least answer it in words she thought Gardner wanted to hear. "That's why I want a life sentence," she claimed. "I don't want to walk the streets again if Jens is going to be on them. I have nightmares about that all the time. I would never feel safe."

DURING THE LONG PERIOD THAT JENS AND ELIZABETH HAD BEEN GONE, Gardner had kept the faith. He was convinced that someday, somehow, they would be caught. He and Chuck Reid had been sure they had been involved in the murders, but they had not been able to prove it. Never in his most imaginative moments had he dreamed that it would happen as it did. It would have been so easy for them to have escaped, he told himself. The fact that they had not still amazed him. He might not have a chance to question Elizabeth again, and there was one thing he was dying to find out, one question he absolutely had to know the answer to. "Tell me something," Gardner asked. "There's something I've been curious about ever since y'all were arrested." He paused. She waited for his question. "Why did he keep those letters?"

Elizabeth smiled. Jens had promised her he had destroyed them, she said, and she didn't doubt him because she loved him. Jens was always shuffling papers, she explained. It was almost an obsession with him. He was continually making files and gluing things and collecting documents. Periodically he would clean out the files and destroy large stacks of papers. One day he tossed out a sizable pile she thought was their letters. Why he had not destroyed them, she could not fathom. "I guess it just seemed natural to me that if you're carrying evidence on you, you destroy it."

Why did she think he kept them? Gardner pressed.

She gave a who-knows shrug. It may have helped his ego, she guessed. He was proud of the murders. "For a long time he said it was the most notable thing he had done. It was like winning a personal kind of freedom. It was something he did on his own."

Gardner shook his head in incomprehension. People do strange things, he told himself.

WHEN ELIZABETH WENT BACK TO HER CELL, GARDNER THOUGHT HE AT LAST had a comprehensive picture of the events surrounding the murders of Derek and Nancy Haysom. Again, he was wrong. Not for the first time—and not by himself—Ricky Gardner yet again had underestimated Elizabeth. So far she had given only three versions of the events leading up to and surrounding the murders. There was more to go.

40

IN VIRGINIA ELIZABETH WAS GIVING THE IMPRESSION OF COOPERATING TO the utmost. In England Jens had taken a contrary stance; he was fighting extradition as energetically as he and his battery of lawyers could.

At that time Elizabeth's legal team consisted of two court-appointed lawyers. Jens's team, however, included one court-appointed lawyer in London, one or more additional London lawyers hired by his father, and a team of German lawyers acting behind the scenes as consultants. His father also had hired a lawyer in Detroit, a well-known prosecutor-turned-defender who eventually would add two Virginia lawyers to the payroll as well. No doubt about it, it was a formidable array of legal talent.

Jens had good reason to want to fight extradition. If he were returned to Virginia, he would be tried for capital murder. If convicted, he could be sentenced to death by electrocution. Alternatively, he could be extradited to Germany, which has no death penalty. As a very long shot he hoped he could remain in the United Kingdom. His main interest, though, was going back to Germany. Even though Jens had not lived there since he was eleven, and then for only three years, he still maintained his German citizenship and was demanding that his case be considered under German law, which guaranteed every German citizen the right to be tried by a German court no matter where the crime was committed. Since he was only eighteen at the time of the murders, he would, if tried in Germany, be recognized as a juvenile, and the penalty upon conviction would be less severe: a maximum of fifteen years in prison. In Virginia, he would be tried as an adult. Furthermore, in Germany he could use a psychiatric defense, a maneuver that would be denied him in Virginia unless he came up with something other than diminished capacity.

In August 1986, two months after Jens confessed to Beever, Wright, and Gardner, the United States formally asked for his return to stand trial in Virginia. But that was only the beginning. One obstacle after another arose. The first revolved around Updike's insistence that Jens be tried on a capital murder charge and that the death penalty be sought. The British chapter of Amnesty International, a well-known civil rights group widely recognized for its opposition to the death penalty, said it would fight the extradition as long as Jens's possible execution was a factor. As a possible solution to the dilemma, the British government asked the United States for assurances that Jens would not face the possibility of being executed even if he were to be convicted. Such assurances could come only from Updike, who refused to give in. Updike wanted the death penalty for Jens Soering.

This impasse was doubly interesting because there were issues simmering in the background that went far beyond Jens's case. While the British government also had qualms about the death penalty, it was at the same time eager to extradite Jens. That was not because of Jens, and it had nothing to do with the death penalty. The Home Office wanted him sent back across the Atlantic because that gave the British the best chance of securing an IRA terrorist who was being held in a U.S. jail. It was a case of tit for tat that both parties understood.

MONTHS AFTER THE DEATH PENALTY DEBATE STARTED, UPDIKE GRUDGINGLY made a minor concession. He reluctantly agreed that if he could bring Jens back and try him for capital murder, he would tell the judge at the time of sentencing—if Jens were convicted on that charge and the jury sentenced him to die—that it was the British wish "that the death penalty should not be imposed or carried out."

That was good enough to break the impasse; it represented a face-saving alternative all around. It satisfied the British because it let them make their point. It satisfied Updike because it did not require any promises on his part; he could still fight for the death penalty, and the judge would be under no obligation to go along with the British request. But while that proposal was being studied, Jens intensified his efforts to be sent to Germany.

By then, though, several dramas were being played out. While the Home Office and U.S. officials were trying to work out a compromise and Jens was fighting to go to Germany, there was another battle being fought in a London appeals court. In June 1987, while Elizabeth was sitting in the Bedford County Jail waiting for her proceedings to start, Jens, who had completed his one-year sentence for check fraud, went into the Bow Street Magistrate's Court to determine if there were grounds for the British to continue holding him pending a decision on the U.S. extradition request. The court took one look at the evidence against him and ordered his incarceration continued. Jens's lawyers appealed that decision on grounds that the court did not take Jens's psychiatric condition into consideration. It was a smokescreen, and a British appeals court, seeing through it, quickly rejected the claim. That, however, did not mean the issue was settled. Not by a long shot.

41

IT WAS ONE OF THOSE COINCIDENCES THAT A PERSON IS NOT LIKELY TO forget. Not ever. The way Lynchburg attorney Hugh Jones recalled it, he was sitting in a Sunday school class several years ago and the group was discussing evil, whether it existed and whether there were truly evil people in the world. Since this was in Lynchburg and the brutal murders of Derek and Nancy Haysom were on everyone's mind—and since everyone present had heard the rumors about the murders being cult-connected—the talk had focused on speculation about the killer. Had the Haysoms been murdered by an "evil" person? Somehow, Jones remembered, probably because there were several lawyers in the group, the talk got around to attorneys and how they were bound by their oaths to work with all kinds of people, evil or not. In the middle of the debate, a thought flashed through Jones' mind: Wouldn't it be something if I got that case?

He did.

A towering man weighing more than two hundred pounds, Jones came south in the early 1960s because he wanted "to try something different." He enrolled at the Virginia Military Institute and signed up for football. He played both offensive and defensive tackle for the Keydets for four years. After he graduated, he went to law school at Washington & Lee and then enlisted in the Army, where he worked exclusively in criminal law. When he got out in 1974, after having spent four years of his five-year tour in Germany, he went back to Virginia and opened a general practice law firm in Lynchburg. As a general practitioner, he did a lot of real estate law, handled bankruptcy cases, and took enough criminal work to keep his hand in. Unlike a lot of lawyers Jones enjoyed criminal cases. They weren't lucrative, but they helped make life interesting.

When Elizabeth asked Judge Sweeney for court-appointed counsel, he picked up the list of available lawyers and the name Jones jumped out at him. But since Sweeney was a cautious man and he did not want to take even the smallest chance that the case could be bounced back on appeal, he decided to name a second lawyer as well. That was not unusual for him; in serious cases he almost always named two defense lawyers. As someone to pair up with Jones, he picked R. Andrew "Drew" Davis, a trim and athletic-looking thirty-one-year-old, who fancied a neatly clipped mustache and short dark hair without sideburns. Davis's father was a circuit court judge in Franklin County, which adjoined Bedford on the southwest, so he had grown up with the law. A graduate of the University of Richmond law school, Davis worked for three years as prosecutor Jim Updike's assistant before going into private practice. He left the commonwealth attorney's office six months before the Haysoms were murdered.

WHEN HE AND DAVIS VISITED ELIZABETH FOR THE FIRST TIME IN LATE MAY 1987, Jones was surprised by how emaciated she looked, how tense and scared she seemed. But her physical appearance had nothing to do with her mental state. From the beginning she let them know that she had made up her mind. Still bitter about the run-around she had received from her lawyer in London, who she felt was kowtowing to Jens and had little interest in her, she told Jones and Davis from the first that she wanted to decide her own fate. "I want to plead guilty" were practically the first words out of her mouth.

Jones and Davis urged her not to make a snap decision. "At least let us investigate other possibilities," Jones urged. But no matter how hard they tried to talk her out of it, she refused to budge.

Whether she could be released on bond was never an issue; no matter how small an amount would have been set by the court, Elizabeth would not have been able to raise it. She was penniless and unable to turn to her well-heeled siblings for help, who had ceased communicating with her. So she stayed in the jail, in a cell by herself, and spent her spare time poring over documents relating to her defense, reading books brought in by a few friends, and, as usual, writing letter after letter.

Over the next two and a half months Jones and Davis met dozens of times with Elizabeth in a tiny eight-foot-square consultation room at the Bedford County Jail. For long into the night, fueled by hot coffee and stale sandwiches, they went over every aspect of the case time and again. Why was she inconsistent with investigators? they wanted to know. Why did she contradict herself so often? What had she said to Jens? What had he said to her? What did they do? Whom did they know?

No matter what avenues they explored, they kept coming back to a guilty plea. It was what Elizabeth wanted. Since she was the client and since she would have to suffer the consequences, the lawyers acquiesced. The best they apparently could do was get her to gain sympathy when she entered her plea.

Elizabeth was charged with two counts of first degree murder, with each charge carrying a potential life sentence. She was ready to plead guilty as charged, but Jones and Davis convinced her to consider admitting instead to being an accessory before the fact. The punishment was the same, but there was a subtle difference. If Updike accepted that plea—which meant exactly what it said, accessory *before* the fact—he was in effect agreeing that Elizabeth was not at Loose Chippings when Nancy and Derek were murdered. This was an important point to the defense lawyers. They knew that members of a certain faction, including Elizabeth's brother Howard and her mother's friend Annie Massie, believed that she had been present when Derek and Nancy were killed.

Davis and Jones kept Elizabeth's intentions secret. One reason for that was that the decision right up to the end would be Elizabeth's, and they could not speak for her. Until a defendant stood before a judge and said "guilty," there was no way of being sure of what would happen. This was especially true with Elizabeth, who was capable of changing her mind in a flash or saying something completely unexpected if she thought it was to her advantage. A couple of days before the hearing at which Elizabeth was to plead, Davis and Jones hinted to Updike that they thought their client was going to plead guilty, but they stressed there was no guarantee. Updike, well aware of Elizabeth's unpredictability, wasn't depending on it. But when she appeared before Judge Sweeney on August 24, 1987, braced on one side by Jones and on the other by Davis, and pleaded guilty to two counts of being an accessory before the fact, Updike was not totally surprised. Just about everyone else was, though, including Judge Sweeney. When the soft-spoken jurist, a not unkindly looking, bony-faced man in his fifties with close-cropped gray hair, asked Updike if he would accept the pleas, he sounded amazed.

Unknown to the defense, Updike had long before rejected any plan to try to prove that Elizabeth had been at Loose Chippings on the night of the murders. As far as he was concerned, none of the evidence really substantiated such a claim, and in the end it made no difference anyway unless he could also prove that she had actually participated in the crime. He felt her presence or absence was irrelevant. When Sweeney asked him if he had any objection to the pleas, Updike replied that he did not since essentially a plea to a charge of accessory before the fact was the same as one to the original charge of first degree murder.

"So you're saying it's a different form of plea which carries the same punishment as the original offenses. Is that your position?" the judge asked Updike, pushing his heavy, dark-rimmed glasses back on his nose.

Updike agreed that it was.

After checking with Davis and Jones to make sure they interpreted the plea the same way, Sweeny turned to Elizabeth and began questioning her to make sure she understood what she was doing.

"Has it been explained to you as to what the range of punishment under Virginia law is for these two offenses?"

"Yes, your Honor," she answered softly.

"Do you realize that by pleading guilty as you have that you waive or give up the right to a jury trial?"

"Yes, your Honor."

"Do you understand that a plea of guilty is a self-supplied conviction which for most purposes would deny or cut off a right of appeal?"

"Yes, your Honor."

"All right," Sweeney nodded. "And finally has it been explained to you that on a plea of guilty that I will be the one fixing your punishment?"

Elizabeth put her chin on her chest and mumbled that, yes, she understood.

Her plea did not end the proceeding. Even though she had admitted her guilt, Judge Sweeney still had to have some idea of the depth of her participation so he could determine her sentence. The way to do that was to let both sides present evidence just as though there were a trial. Witnesses would be called, arguments would be heard, and Elizabeth would take the stand to give her side of the story—and be cross-examined by Updike—just as if the conclusion were not preordained. The difference in this proceeding and a trial was that a jury would not determine her fate; she had waived that right. After all the evidence was presented, Judge Sweeney would pronounce the punishment.

BEFORE UPDIKE BEGAN HIS OPENING STATEMENT, OUTLINING THE EVIDENCE he planned to present during the state's part of the proceeding, there was one thing he wanted to clarify: that there had been no plea bargaining involved in Elizabeth's decision to plead guilty. "There have been no negotiations on the part of me or my office with the defendant or her counsel," he said for the record.

The state's version of the murders was essentially the same as the story that investigators had eventually wrung from Elizabeth with a few elaborations. Updike placed considerable emphasis on the viciousness of the murders, for example, and went into detail describing the wounds inflicted upon Derek and Nancy. Surprisingly, considering that the occult-connection theory eventually had been rejected by investigators, Updike thought it was important enough to give more than passing mention in his opening statement.

"I do not wish to sensationalize this, but on the other hand I do not wish to ignore it," he said, directing his remarks at Judge Sweeney. "There is one photograph taken near Derek's body which shows a vee mark of some sort with a figure drawn in it. The autopsy report reflects that there was an incision on the chin which was of a nature that could be categorized as a vee. There was a mousetrap, a rather commonplace kind of mousetrap, but it was rather odd at the time, that had a vee on it. There is a drawing which we will be introducing, and although I'm no art critic certainly, we think it can be categorized in bizarre fashion if not demonic, and the vee motif is throughout that. We're not," he emphasized, "arguing specifically the exact bearing of this on the murders themselves or stating whether or not that was just something left there for the purpose of leading police on. Again, as I stated, it should not be sensationalized or exaggerated or taken out of context, but based upon evidence we will be getting into, it should not be forgotten as well."

There was one other thing he wanted to bring out that had not been touched upon by Elizabeth herself in her statements: her unusual behavior after the murders. When Annie Massie and her husband drove to Charlottesville to break the news to her, Elizabeth had reacted strangely. "Her response was one of being very quiet," Updike said. "We do not think she displayed any tears or outward displays of emotion."

In addition, he added, when she was interviewed by Gardner and Kirkland on the day after the memorial service, her tone was almost light-hearted, and she laughed at several points in the discussion.

But what he really found unusual, he said, was Elizabeth's insistence on cleaning up the blood at Loose Chippings even though other family members had agreed they would hire a commercial cleaning crew to take care of the gruesome task. Before the cleaners came in, however, Elizabeth went in and began the job.

"We have a witness who has been subpoenaed who would testify that Elizabeth was cleaning in the area of the fireplace, which the photographs show is the area where Mr. Haysom's body was found, when she made some statement to the effect of, 'Here are Pop's brains,' or something of that nature while she was wiping. She also saw one of the footprints that I have described there on the floor and upon removing her shoe, placed her foot in that impression to perform some type of comparison, I suppose. Dr. Howard Haysom would say that he considered that unusual and told her to stop it."

The purpose of such testimony, he said, was to show that there was little if any remorse on Elizabeth's part. "However," he added, "we understand that she is indeed quite theatrical."

He would prove, he promised, that Elizabeth had conspired with Jens to murder her parents and that as part of their plot, they had gone to Washington, D.C., the day before the killings. "Our evidence will establish that the purpose of them going there was that they had previously planned the murder of Derek Haysom and Nancy Haysom, that Miss Haysom was indeed an accessory before the fact in her planning, encouraging and entreating of Jens Soering to murder her parents, and that thereafter she assisted and abetted by providing an alibi."

Elizabeth had rented the car, made reservations at the Washington hotel, and helped set up a series of incidents that made it appear that both she and Jens were in Washington while he, in fact, was in Boonsboro. After the murders she had tried to mislead police, but when she and Jens had felt investigators were closing in, they fled the country and did not indicate they intended to return.

It was a dramatic presentation. When he finished, the courtroom was as quiet as an empty school. When Updike sat down, a low buzz started around the room. Sweeney rapped for silence with his gavel. "It's a good time for a recess," he said. "Let's take ten minutes."

In the excitement of the moment, with the anticipation of titillating revelations to come, no one noticed that there was one thing Updike had *not* promised to produce. That was a motive. Even long after the proceedings were finished, Updike would moan that he had never heard an explanation that satisfied him for Derek's and Nancy's murders. "If I could ask Elizabeth only one question with the assurance that it would be answered absolutely truthfully, that question would be: *'Why* are your parents dead?' "

$\boxed{42}$

THE WOOD AND RED-BRICK TWO-STORY COURTHOUSE IN WHICH THE proceedings were being held dated from 1930. It was the latest in a series of structures in which Bedford County justice was administered since the town became the county seat in 1782. On the building's first floor are the clerk of court's office and various administrative cubbyholes. About one-quarter of the second floor is taken up by offices for the commonwealth attorney and his assistant. But the bulk of the space is reserved for the courtroom and its subsidiaries: the judge's chambers, a jury room, a clerk's room, a room for deputies and court officers, and three witness rooms, all of which branch off the main room. The courtroom itself, since remodeled, was a large, square-looking chamber lit by recessed overhead fixtures and six large windows, three on each side of the judge's bench. The windows, usually covered with translucent, wheat-colored curtains to cut down on the glare, made the room look larger than it actually was. A bureaucratic decorator, trying to give it some warmth, had hung oil portraits of former judges, some of them dating to colonial times, on the beige-colored walls. The attempt was only moderately successful; there was still a palpable museum feel to the space. It was not a comfortable room, but neither was it anywhere near as austere as the magistrate's court in Richmond where Elizabeth first learned that Bedford authorities had caught up with her and Jens.

TRADITIONALLY IN AN AMERICAN CRIMINAL PROCEEDING THE PROSECUTION has the first word. In a trial Updike would begin by listing the reasons he thought the defendant was guilty. In this case, since Elizabeth had already pleaded guilty, Updike's role was restricted to demonstrating her degree of guilt. The difference was subtle: Updike would begin essentially where he would in a trial, by demonstrating to Judge Sweeney that Elizabeth Haysom encouraged Jens Soering to murder her parents, helped him prepare for the murders, and aggressively assisted in the cover-up.

The defense role, in contrast, was to try to minimize her participation by presenting mitigating circumstances. The more convincingly Jones and Davis could draw Elizabeth as a victim, the more sympathetic Judge Sweeney would be. If they could convince him that she was an unwilling pawn of Jens Soering, her punishment would be less than if Updike persuaded the judge that she was the instigator of her parents' murders.

By pleading guilty, Elizabeth removed much of the suspense. But what was still to come would be just as enthralling. The public was going to get its first look at what motivated a young woman, one who seemingly had everything, to systematically encourage her boyfriend to kill her parents ruthlessly, and then lie to protect him.

UPDIKE GLANCED AT ELIZABETH, WHO WAS SITTING EIGHT FEET AWAY, slumped in her chair at the defense end of the long common table that stretched in front of the judge's bench. For her first court session she wore a plain, light-colored, floor-length dress that deemphasized her figure and made her look asexual. As far as Updike was concerned, it was the first of several Joan of Arc costumes she would wear in an attempt to make herself appear more homely and less like a seductress. She wore no makeup, and her hair, which by then had grown quite long and fell well below her shoulders, was combed straight back in a severe schoolmarm-ish style. Yet again, Updike was amazed at her ability to present herself in the most advantageous light possible. He recalled the mood that had prevailed in the region soon after the murders, when people were stopping him on the street and demanding that something be done to bring the killer or killers to justice. And the harsher the justice was, the better they would like it. But that attitude had changed significantly. Now that he had one of the people responsible for the murders in the lockup, Updike could sense an undercurrent of sympathy on her behalf. Mentally shrugging at the incomprehensibility of public opinion, Updike cleared his throat and called his first witness.

Ricky Gardner popped through the narrow wooden door at the end of the room and strode briskly down the central aisle. His footsteps echoed in the half-filled chamber. Judge Sweeny, in anticipation of a trial, had summoned a roomful of Bedford County voters from among whom he had intended to let lawyers begin selecting a jury. When Elizabeth pleaded guilty, thus obviating the need for a jury, Sweeney dismissed the panel but invited any who wanted to stay to remain in the courtroom. A number of them did, and they filled some of the 175 or so available seats on the straight-backed, black, wooden benches. The public, figuring the first couple of days would be taken up by the monotonous questioning of potential jury members, stayed home. They would stay home later as well because the proceedings were broadcast on local cable television as part of an experiment with cameras in the courtroom. At first, though, they decided to wait for the more exciting days when lawyers would be calling witnesses. Even the army of reporters was smaller than expected. Some of them also decided to skip what they thought would be the jury selection phase. As a result, there were plenty of seats.

Gardner passed through the barrier separating spectators from court officials, in this case a low wall of fine-grain mahogany, and went straight to the witness box on Judge Sweeney's right. His testimony was brisk and surprisingly abbreviated. Although transcripts and tapes of his numerous interviews with Elizabeth were filed with the court as supporting documentation, what Updike wanted from the investigator was interpretation. The record would speak for itself, but the prosecutor wanted Gardner to put it into context.

When asked what first made him suspicious of Elizabeth, Gardner replied that it was the abrupt change in her statements about Margaret Louise. During the first interview Elizabeth was very defensive of her, but in a second interview eight days later she said that Margaret Louise may have committed the murders. Gardner said he asked her two years later, after she had returned from England under arrest, why she had given such conflicting statements about her friend.

"And what did she say?" Updike asked.

"She told me that she was just trying to save her skin."

Gardner also testified that he thought it was strange that Elizabeth made such implausible comments about Nancy Haysom's first husband and his alleged perversities and about how, when she knew investigators were looking for a motive, she sent them on a wild goose chase by claiming that her mother had a secret cache of money and that Annie Massie knew where it was. But what really made him and Investigator Reid suspicious, Gardner said, was the high mileage on the car they had rented to go to Washington.

Updike led Gardner through a quick overview of the case up until the time Elizabeth and Jens ran off to Europe. Then he called his second witness, Detective Constable Wright.

A lanky, bearded man with a receding hairline and a thick accent, Wright went into considerably more detail than Gardner had about the early days of the investigation of Jens and Elizabeth while they were being held for check fraud. Since Wright was the one who had laboriously plowed through the letters found in Jens's and Elizabeth's closet, Updike asked him to read many of the documents into the record. One of the most remarkable new facts that Wright contributed to the knowledge of Elizabeth's and Jens's saga was how close, how *really* close, the two had come to slipping away.

That April afternoon in 1986, when Elizabeth and Jens had been picked up for suspicion of fraud, they could have walked away free if only Jens had not agreed to let the detectives search their flat. If he had not consented, Wright said, he and Beever would never have known where they lived and they never would have found the incriminating letters and the journal, along with the bags of Marks & Spencer merchandise, the checkbooks, the bogus IDs, and the travel documents showing their true identities.

Updike's third and final witness in the first phase of the hearing was Detective Constable Beever. When he took the stand, his strong voice rang melodiously throughout the courtroom, his Upcountry accent a marked departure from Elizabeth's rounded tones.

In a crisp, professional manner Beever picked up the tale at the point where Updike and Gardner arrived in London and Jens and Elizabeth were remanded to the Richmond jail for a long weekend. Since it was Beever that Elizabeth chose to confess to, Updike asked him to go sentence by sentence through the June 8–9 statements. It was a long process and ate up the rest of the afternoon.

THE NEXT MORNING, TUESDAY, BEFORE A FULLER COURTROOM, GARDNER was recalled by Updike so he could go through, in detail, the long statement Elizabeth made to him on the night she returned from England. Updike wanted to know if Gardner had asked Elizabeth the question he had not yet found a satisfactory answer to: Why her parents were dead?

Yes, he had asked her that, Gardner said. "Okay," Updike prompted, could you read your question and her response?"

Gardner read:

Question: Okay, let's go back to the original question, and I think that was why your parents are dead. Was the main motive for their murders the fact that you and Jens were so much in love and that they were bitterly opposed to any future that you and Jens may share together?

Response: Yes. And I also—also looking at my brothers' situations, although they were cut away from the fold, my family living far away, their daily lives were still manipulated and interfered with by my parents and I wanted them to, I suppose, really to leave me alone.

When it came time to cross-examine, Davis hammered away at Gardner, trying to show that Elizabeth's statements to him were merely attempts by her to protect herself from Jens. Did she not often tell him, Davis asked the investigator, that she was under pressure from Jens, that she was afraid of him, and that she had lied repeatedly to protect him? She had, Gardner agreed. Rifling through a copy of Gardner's May 14 interview with Elizabeth, Davis found a comment from Elizabeth indicating her reaction to Jens's post-arrest letters. She had told Gardner that she felt she was betraying Jens by telling the truth, but she was not prepared to go on lying any longer—her list of betrayals had gotten too long.

When Gardner finished, Davis quickly pointed out that Elizabeth had voluntarily proffered Jens's letters. He wanted to make sure Judge Sweeney understood that she was trying to cooperate.

Having made his point, Davis pulled a sheet out of the stack. It was, he said, a letter Jens had written Elizabeth on November 11, 1986, before she had told him she was going against his wishes by deciding not to fight extradition. "Jens said," Davis began, reading slowly, " 'I really don't think you have anything to worry about, especially since you're not even guilty.' " He paused and looked at Gardner for confirmation.

"That's true," Gardner said. "That's correct."

"And as you understand it, that's an accurate excerpt from his letter to her of November 11, 1986?"

"Yes, sir."

Davis also asked Gardner to confirm that Elizabeth admitted to him in an unrecorded interview that she had been lying about being with Jens when he bought a butterfly knife on the morning of the day her parents were killed.

She had, Gardner admitted.

"Was she physically shaking when she was talking to you about Jens Soering?" Davis asked, anxious to demonstrate that Elizabeth was deathly afraid of her former lover. "Was she trembling?"

Gardner nodded. "She was nervous, yes, sir."

"Trembling?" Davis pressed. He wanted *that* specific admission in the record.

"Yes, sir," Gardner agreed.

Both the prosecution's presentation and the defense's cross-examination were accomplished quickly, much more speedily than they would have been in a trial, but at the same time in more detail than at a normal guilty plea proceeding. Usually in a case involving a guilty plea, Updike presented only enough evidence to substantiate the charges, like the player in a hand of draw poker who is asked to show his openers. But this time Updike went beyond what was simply necessary. For one thing, he wanted to establish a good base for questions when he got to cross-examine Elizabeth. For another, he was building a file for the eventual trial of Jens. It took him a day and a half to make his points. When he finished, it was the defense's turn.

But Elizabeth's lawyers, not surprisingly, asked for additional time to prepare their case. Judge Sweeney agreed because he also wanted time for a probation officer to put together a presentence report. He gave Davis and Jones seven weeks, until the first week of October.

As soon as Jones and Davis left the courtroom, they flew into a new frenzy of fact-finding, which would include still more caffeine-boosted sessions with Elizabeth and a trip to England.

Not everyone went away as gratified as Jones and Davis. A number of observers felt cheated when the proceeding was interrupted. They had heard dramatic evidence from investigators Gardner, Beever, and Wright, and they had sat spellbound as the officers took them through the process they followed in uncovering Elizabeth's participation in the murders of her parents. But the public's appetite was only whetted, not satisfied. They had not heard from Elizabeth herself. She had sat meek and silent during the hearing, sandwiched between her two protectors, Jones and Davis, like a rare flower pressed between two panes of glass. And from an observer's point of view her response to the state's presentation had been disappointing. Only rarely did she show any emotion, no matter how damaging the testimony

seemed. Although her reputation for theatrics was firmly established, thus far she had chosen not to demonstrate her profi-
ciency. Even Updike was puzzled by her docility. From what he
knew of her and from what he imagined her to be—at that point
he and Elizabeth had not exchanged a single word—he expected
a more vibrant, more aggressive woman. But from what he had
seen, her submissiveness was total. He didn't trust his own reactions; he knew in his gut that there was more to her than she had
let show.

43

On Tuesday, October 6, the State of Virginia's case against Elizabeth Haysom for the murder of her parents moved into its last phase. Thirty months and four days after Nancy's and Derek's bodies had been found, 16 months and a week after she had been arrested in a London suburb, Elizabeth was nearing the end of her adventure. She was almost, but not quite, there. Before she could take the stand to testify in her own defense, she had to wait her turn in the queue.

The first witness that bright, early fall morning was Ricky Gardner, summoned yet again by prosecutor Jim Updike. Suspecting that something was coming, Updike was anxious to get one particular issue clearly on the record, the issue of the butterfly knife: who bought it and when, or, actually, *if* such a knife was involved in the Haysom murder case at all.

Butterfly knives, sometimes called *balisongs,* are illegal in many states. They are fearsome devices built on the same principle as a switchblade, such that the blade can be instantly accessible. Unlike a switchblade, which contains a spring to flip the blade into an "open" position, a butterfly knife relies totally on wrist action. The blade in a butterfly knife is encased in a handle that is split horizontally and is hinged at one end. With a flick of the wrist, one half of the handle flips open, exposing the blade. The two halves of the handle then fold together to form a solid grip.

It is not a weapon for amateurs; it takes practice to manipulate a butterfly knife.

At Updike's prompting, Gardner said he had no inkling that a butterfly knife may have been used to kill Derek and Nancy until Elizabeth had brought it up. Indeed, a murder weapon was never found. Elizabeth said that she and Jens had gone together on March 30, 1985, to buy such a weapon from a martial arts store in Maryland. She told investigators that Jens had the knife with him when he left her to drive to Boonsboro, thereby implying that it could very well have been the murder weapon. She added that Jens had never told her exactly what weapon he had used to kill her parents. However, she obliged detectives by drawing a picture of the knife that Jens had allegedly selected and she had paid for.

Under cross-examination from Drew Davis, Gardner admitted that Elizabeth told him later in an off-the-record interview that she had fabricated the entire story about the butterfly knife.

Interviews with Jens could shed no light on the subject, Gardner agreed, because he consistently refused to talk to investigators about a knife, claiming an admission that he had a weapon of any kind when he went to Loose Chippings would indicate premeditation to murder.

After Gardner's third and final appearance on the stand it was the defense's turn. Before getting to Elizabeth, however, Jones and Davis called a string of minor witnesses to testify about the bright sides of Elizabeth's character or to support issues she would later testify to herself.

First up was Cheetah Haysom, Derek's niece and Elizabeth's first cousin. An attractive woman with short blonde hair and outsize earrings, she explained in rounded Oxbridgian tones almost as fine as Elizabeth's that she did not know Elizabeth well until her family spent some time with Derek, Nancy, and Elizabeth when Elizabeth was about eighteen. But after being around her for a while, Haysom said she was "very impressed" with her. Elizabeth, she said, was a "remarkably responsible and well-behaved teenager."

Davis, eager to establish Elizabeth's character as a devoted daughter, asked Cheetah Haysom about the relationship between Elizabeth and her mother.

"She appeared to be a very dutiful and respectful daughter," Cheetah Haysom said. "She responded very well to her mother."

Elizabeth sat expressionless at Jones' elbow, staring placidly at her cousin.

WITH A CHANGE IN WITNESSES, THERE WAS ALSO A CHANGE IN ATTORNEYS. Jones, his blond hair dipping over his forehead, rose slowly to his feet and called the second witness, Elizabeth Watson, a woman with a deeply lined face and striking silver-blue hair. Sitting uncomfortably in the witness chair, nervously twirling her strand of pearls, she told about attending a dinner party with Elizabeth and her parents.

"Elizabeth was telling me about when she was in school that a Middle Eastern sheik had offered her father a number of camels for her hand and her father corroborated it. And I said, 'Elizabeth, how old were you?' And she told me. I don't remember exactly the age, but she was very young."

She and Elizabeth got to be friends, she said, and they were close enough that Elizabeth later felt comfortable enough to write her asking for advice in her romance.

"She was a student at the University of Virginia and she wrote to me that she had met a man she wanted to spend the rest of her life with, but that her relationship with him was destructive to her relationship with her parents and vice versa. That bothered her very much, and she asked my advice because something had to be done about it. So I wrote her a letter to the effect that as we're growing we differ with our parents but in the end we would find what they wanted for us was the best that they knew."

IN CROSS-EXAMINATION UPDIKE ASKED HER IF SHE WAS AWARE OF Elizabeth's acting abilities.

"She is a very talented young lady," she replied. "She's very versatile."

"Also," Updike asked, "aren't there occasions when you have had to doubt the veracity of what she tells you?"

"I think there certainly were," Watson agreed, "but I attribute that to drugs."

"You attribute that to drugs," Updike repeated, sounding almost sad.

"Yes," she said, "but I don't think today you need to be concerned about her veracity."

THE DRUGS ISSUE WAS EXPLAINED IN MORE DETAIL BY THE NEXT WITNESS, a former neighbor and friend of the Haysoms named Jeff Taylor. A large, heavy-set man with a round face and a dark beard, Taylor testified that three months earlier he had received a letter from Elizabeth, who was then in the Bedford County Jail waiting to appear in court on the murder charges. At Jones' urging, Taylor read from the letter, which eerily resembled, in style and tone, some of Nancy's correspondence with Colonel Herrington:

> For a long time I had a serious drug problem. Even after I was arrested in April of '86, I was still using. In fact my habit grew with easy availability of drugs and alcohol in the English prison system. It took me eight months to finally realize that I indeed had a problem . . . so I became a member of Narcotics Anonymous and have been clean since January 2nd, 1987, seven months. That was or is something to be proud of and grateful for. It was not easy but my goodness, it has been better.

Thanks to the guidance offered through that program and others, she continued, she was looking at life differently. Writing in July, she said she was anticipating the August court hearing because it would allow her to "truly be able to close" an era of her life that began when she first was sent away to boarding school and thus began a spiral that resulted in the deaths of her parents. It would give her the opportunity, she wrote, to "build a real and positive and active future without anger and bitterness, fear and resentment." She never would be able to outlive the guilt and shame she felt, she said, but she had learned to lead a construc-tive, as opposed to destructive, life. "As we say in NA," she wrote, "I am not responsible for my disease, but I am responsible for my recovery."

Taylor was making a good impression, Jones thought. He was a believable witness, and he was giving testimony that was good for his client. Jones had only one more question for him: "Based on your personal contact with her, do you feel the thoughts she expressed in this letter were sincere?" Jones asked.

"Yes," Taylor responded. He thought she was very sincere.

Elizabeth's alleged drug problem was further elucidated by Johnny Horton, the defense's next witness. A small, thin, balding man with a dark mustache, Horton explained in sometimes hard-to-understand regional British argot that he was an ex–mental patient and a recovering drug addict and alcoholic who had been arrested more than a dozen times for armed robbery, robbery, and drug violations and, once, for attempted murder. Then, he said, he broke his addiction, got a regular job and became a counseler helping others break away from substance abuse. He was, he said, a cofounder in Britain of the program known as Narcotics Anon-ymous.

An NA member in Holloway Prison put Horton in touch with Elizabeth and he began visiting her and counseling her. "What impressed me about Elizabeth," he said, "was that she was trying. I saw that she was very mature and very honest, and I trusted where she was coming from." All told, he said, he had met with her about thirty times.

"Did you and I talk about Elizabeth conning you and every-body else?" asked Davis, who had alternated with Jones.

"Yes," Horton replied.

"And what did you tell me about that?"

"What did I tell you? Well, I'm not now, but I used to be a con man. That means I could manipulate and lie. And I can tell if somebody else is doing the same, and I believe what Elizabeth has said to me was real and she was honest."

Under cross-examination, Updike pointed out that Elizabeth did not try to contact NA until soon after she had been ordered extradited to the United States.

"Yeah," Horton agreed, "we have to make that contact sometimes."

"That's true," said Updike. "And you said that you were a con man. She, of course, was locked up there for being a con, wasn't she? Defrauding, bouncing checks, flim-flam, that kind of thing?"

"I'm sorry, sir," said Horton, "but I don't judge other people."

"I'm not asking you to. I'm asking what your English judicial system did. They found her guilty of that, didn't they?"

"Yes," Horton mumbled.

"And they incarcerated her as a result of that?"

"Yes."

"So she's something of a con herself, isn't she? I mean, you have been asked your expert opinion as a former con man."

"Exactly. And what I see is that we all make mistakes."

"Yes, that's true. Sometimes people die as a result of those mistakes, too, don't they?"

Horton nodded.

On re-direct, Davis pointed out that Elizabeth pleaded guilty to the fraud charges in Britain and was not found guilty in a trial. "Is that your understanding?" he asked Horton.

"Yes," he replied.

The defense's fifth witness was a preppy twenty-three-year-old former fellow student named Christopher Keland who later shared a house with Jens and Elizabeth before they ran away to Europe.

Elizabeth was "an extremely neat lady," Keland said in a resonant radio-announcer's voice.

Asked if he had ever met Derek and Nancy, Keland said that he had, in the winter of 1985, when they had come to Charlottesville to help Elizabeth find an apartment. They had spoken to his mother, who had several units for rent.

"Would you please tell us what you observed of that encounter," asked Jones, "particularly how Elizabeth seemed to relate to her parents."

"It was very interesting," said Keland, "because she did what a lot of college students would do when their parents are around, which is act a lot more like your parents. She seemed perfectly happy to be with them, but they are people who really did just drip with charm. When you walked into a room with them, you kind of straightened up your backbone and decided to all of a sudden to be very witty and very clever and very charming. I think Elizabeth had the same natural reaction. She acted a great deal like her mother and father."

"Did you detect any animosity between them?"

"No, certainly no animosity," Keland said.

Two or three months before the murders, Keland added, he was chatting with Elizabeth and the subject of parents came up. He asked her how she was getting along with hers. "And she said, 'Well, a year ago or two years ago I really didn't like them that much, but I'm really starting to like them, and we're really starting to get along.' "

As far as drug use went, Keland said that Jens did not use them and neither did Elizabeth when she was going out with him.

"How about on other occasions?" Jones asked.

"Previous to that I think she undoubtedly used drugs, but nothing particularly serious. There were other people in the dorms who would have done a lot more drugs than she would."

During the period he and a girl shared a house with Elizabeth and Jens, Keland said, he noticed that Jens was unable to control his temper. "He threw temper tantrums, but they never became violent."

Jones asked for an example.

"Well," Keland said, "it was just if a piece of machinery wasn't working properly. If the toilet plugged up or something wasn't working in the kitchen, he would just lose his temper over that. He just really got extremely upset for no reason."

From when he got to know them, Jones asked, which seemed to be the dominant personality?

"I do not believe that there was a dominant personality in that relationship," Keland said. "They worked very well together as a team, and they both had very clear goals in life. They worked very carefully together to achieve those goals. I didn't see one domineering the other, either in personal moments or in what they wanted to do with their lives. I'd say they were very much equal partners in the relationship."

THE LAST DEFENSE WITNESS BEFORE ELIZABETH TOOK THE STAND WAS HER half-brother Veryan, who was Derek's first child by his first marriage. Of all the siblings he probably had the least chance to know Elizabeth because he was twelve when his father and Nancy were married and sixteen when Elizabeth was born.

A criminal defense lawyer in Mahone Bay, Nova Scotia, Veryan Haysom said he had read news reports about Elizabeth's reaction to the murders and was worried about her possible lack of remorse. Nevertheless, he said, he was encouraged when she decided not to fight extradition and when she pleaded guilty to the murder charges.

"Would it be," asked Jones, "that you're saying that her actions are speaking louder to you than the words?"

"Well, we haven't exchanged that many words, really," Veryan Haysom said, "but I took as very positive signs the ways she has dealt with admitting her guilt."

Jones drew an objection from Updike when he asked Veryan Haysom what he thought Elizabeth's sentence should be.

Judge Sweeney said he agreed with Updike in general. "I think by and large that's my job." However, he told Jones he thought it would be appropriate for Veryan Haysom to give his general feelings on the subject.

Inching his chair closer to the microphone, Veryan Haysom shot a glance at his half-sister, who sat emotionless, staring straight ahead. "I accept," he said, implying he had given the matter some thought, "that one day she will be back in society, and I just question what it will be that returns to society. Whether there is a person there who is capable of rehabilitation. It would be my real desire to see that happen. I don't want to see her languishing in jail for a period of time. That does nobody any good. I just worry that simply forgetting about her and putting her in prison is not going to serve her or anybody's long-term interest."

When Updike rose to cross-examine, the matter of her punishment was the least of his concerns. The prosecutor was far more interested in talking to Elizabeth's half-brother about the allegations Elizabeth had made to investigators concerning her sexual relationship with her mother and about the news stories concerning those allegations.

"To your knowledge and understanding, are those allegations true?" he asked.

"They are unfounded in anything within my experience," he replied firmly, "and within anything within my knowledge of my family."

44

FOR HER PREMIERE APPEARANCE, ELIZABETH PICKED FROM A HANDFUL OF dresses brought to her by loyal friends a beige dress with long sleeves and a shawl collar, not unlike a monk's robe. Her hair was combed straight back. It hung loose over her shoulders and behind her ears, exposing small pearl earrings. Her heavy brows cut straight across her forehead, giving her eyes a more sunken look. She wore no makeup, so her childhood scars on chin and cheek stood out prominently against her pale skin. In a soft voice, at Jones' gentle prodding, she went through her life, beginning with her birth in Rhodesia, now called Zimbabwe.

As she went along, she gained confidence. Her voice got stronger, and she swallowed less frequently, bit her lip less often, and stopped fingering her left hand. Her tone was different from the one she had taken with investigators. In the courtroom she was more submissive, more cooperative, more anxious to please. Her story changed, too, in sometimes small, sometimes radical, but always significant ways, both in content and in manner. This was her first time to tell her tale under oath, and from now on it would be impossible for her to change it yet again. The questions put to her and the way she answered them more strongly implied her innocence. If she could, she was going to dump everything on Jens.

Her deviations from what she had said to investigators earlier began with her explanation of the statements she made in her diary-like letter to Jens written during the Christmas holiday period in 1984 and a separate letter written to him from Colorado several weeks later. In her testimony she painted herself as an unwitting instigator of murder. She had been ingenuous in her letters, she said. She had been dealing with subjects metaphorically, but Jens was taking her literally. Even when she had written that she and Jens could either wait until they graduated and leave her parents behind or "get rid of them soon," she had not intended for Jens to take her literally. "What I was saying," Elizabeth explained, "is that we can either wait until we graduate and leave them behind or we can leave them behind now."

She looked at Jones, waiting for direction. His job was that of a guide, someone to help her navigate through the labyrinth of words that she had spoken and written and lead her down the path that would show her to her best advantage. What did she mean, he wanted to know, by her written reference to practicing voodoo on her parents?

Elizabeth was eager to answer that. As she had told Gardner in one of the interrogating sessions, and as she now wanted to tell the world, she had merely been taking a dig at Jens, who had a lot of crazy ideas anyway, half-baked theories about pop-psychology and psychological warfare. "I used to ridicule him about it, mock him about it," she said as easily as she would have confessed to teasing him about his hair style. "I'm mocking him and his theories on these things rather than referring to my parents." Remembering to show the proper remorse, she added, "Although I should never have referred to my parents that way."

Jones nodded his approval. So far so good. His next question went a little deeper. When she was writing those letters, he wanted to know, had she ever considered the actual death of her parents?

"No," Elizabeth said emphatically.

"Was it ever in your mind?"

"No." It was Jens, she added, who had misconstrued what *she* was saying.

"Now before you left on Christmas break, had you had any conversations with Jens about your parents and your feelings in that regard?" Jones asked her.

"I had general conversations with him about my parents,"

Elizabeth admitted. "He would discuss his parents at great length, and at some point I sat down with him and said to him we all have problems." Looking slightly embarrassed, she added lamely, "I did voice some resentments and anger."

"Why?" Jones wanted to know. "Did you anticipate problems?"

Elizabeth looked slightly shocked by the suggestion. "Well," she replied, "I said that we all had problems at home and expressed some of the problems that I had."

Jones wanted a more comprehensive answer. What did she mean? he asked encouragingly.

She thought for a moment. "They didn't like any of the young men I saw." As an example she told how she had invited a male classmate to their home in Boonsboro one weekend so her parents could meet him. "My mother was very charming to him," she said, "but she didn't like him because he was Jewish."

JONES LEFT THE ISSUE OF THE LETTERS ALONE TEMPORARILY WHILE HE pursued what he insinuated was Jens's growing emotional dependence on Elizabeth, which colored his attitudes toward both her and her parents. To make his point, he brought up a comment she had made in a note dated January 6, 1985, in which she suggested that the two might be friends rather than lovers.

Jens had reacted strongly to that, Elizabeth said, telling her he wanted to be overwhelmed by her love. It was clear to her in retrospect that Jens "needed" her more than he "loved" her. "He wanted to be loved beyond reason. And at that particular time, when I wrote that letter, I was suggesting that I didn't love him beyond reason."

However, as time went on, the relationship became closer. "I still tried to escape from him from time to time. I still tried to acquire space, and there were arguments with my roommate about it. But we did become increasingly obsessed with one another."

ELIZABETH DELIGHTED IN GIVING EXAMPLES, IN UNDERLINING HER POINT with an anecdote. To show how unreasonable Jens had become in his attachment to her, she told about how she was studying in her room one day when Jens unexpectedly charged through the door. Without preamble, he screamed, "I could blow their bloody heads off!"

"What prompted that outburst?" Jones asked.

"I'm not sure," Elizabeth replied, suggesting it may have been because her parents had ordered her to go on a skiing trip to Colorado with her half-brother Howard after she had promised Jens she would stay at the university during the spring break and work with him on a class project. That may have been the trigger, she said. But Jens was so unpredictable that it may have been something else entirely. "I don't really know what it was. I was in my room. I was reading. He walked in. He said it, and it was definitely apparent that he was serious. He was angry, and he meant what he was saying."

Jens hung around another half hour after that, she said, and she calmed him down. But the tantrum bothered her. Later, she wished she had suggested to him that he get some counseling. Perhaps she should have gone to the police, she said, or at least to her parents. For some reason, she and Jens were not on the same mental wavelength. "It has become more and more apparent to me as I have gone over Jens's correspondence that he was not thinking the same way I was thinking. I was indulging in some grotesque, childish fantasies. I was feeling hate and resentment and frustration," she said in majestic understatement, "but I wasn't thinking about murder. And it seems that he was."

IN HER OWN NAIVETÉ, SHE SAID, SHE MAY HAVE MADE JENS'S PROBLEMS worse. One example of that was a long letter she wrote to him from Colorado while she was on the very ski trip he had been against. In the letter, she said, she let her imagination run wild while describing to Jens a whole series of circumstances that were totally untrue.

In the letter she told Jens that she would inherit a considerable amount of money from her parents, but only if she did exactly as they wanted. Jens had been pressuring her to go to Europe with him during the summer vacation, but she warned that her parents would never approve. If she went, she would risk losing her inheritance. So she passed the decision to him, appealing to his desire for financial security. "If you want to be rich we can't go to Europe," she had written to him. From the witness stand she confessed that the letter was a complete fabrication, an attempt by her to convince Jens to leave the university and run away with her.

"Was there any intent in your writing of that letter to encourage him to murder your parents?" Jones queried.

Elizabeth did not hesitate. "No," she said, "not at all."

Jones took his time in his questioning, leading Elizabeth down one trail and then another. On one trip he led her to the weekend of her father's birthday, the weekend before Derek and Nancy were murdered. Jones was interested in trying to prove that the weekend had been a glorious one for Elizabeth—that it went so swimmingly that the last thing in her mind was getting rid of her parents.

"It was a really wonderful weekend," she said. "I managed to sit down and talk with my parents. We discussed many issues which needed to be discussed. And there were some problems in the nature of the discussions, but we had progress. It was a lot of progress between myself and my father about the future."

They agreed, she added, that they would allow her to move out of the dormitory and into an apartment. Her father also promised to open a bank account for her and discontinue his practice of simply giving her an allowance. Best of all, she said, they talked about how she was going to spend her summer. She was either going to work with an organization called the Goethe Institute, so she could really learn German, or she was going to work for the United Nations in Vienna.

As soon as she got back to the university, she ran to tell Jens the good news. "I was jubilant. I was overjoyed. And I steamed up to the dorm, and I said, 'It's fantastic. It's everything that I have been working for. Everything that we've talked about is going to happen.'"

Jens, however, was less than enthusiastic. He felt threatened, she said, about her moving into an apartment without him. "He was very angry," she said. "He felt that I was letting him down, abandoning him in some way."

SATISFIED THAT HE HAD BUILT A FOUNDATION DEMONSTRATING HIS CLIENT'S good intentions while simultaneously illustrating Jens's instability, Jones progressed to the weekend of the murders and Jens's and Elizabeth's decision to go to Washington, D.C.

Originally, Elizabeth said with minimal guidance from Jones, she planned to stay in Charlottesville that weekend because she had to sign a lease on her new apartment. When the signing got postponed, Jens suggested they go to Washington. Jens, she said, was deeply troubled by his impotence, and he felt he might be able to overcome it if they could get away by themselves for a few days. Since they had virtually no privacy at the university, it might help their relationship to check into a motel far away from the pressures of the university.

She readily agreed, she admitted, not only because she wanted to help Jens but because she was running low on money and she wanted to sell some of her jewelry to help get her through until the next allowance check arrived from her father. She could get a much better price for the pieces in Washington than she could in Charlottesville, she added.

When she said this, Updike's draw dropped. Never in all her statements to investigators had she ever mentioned anything about selling her jewelry.

Almost on impulse, she said, she and Jens took off for Washington that Friday afternoon, March 29.

Never mind what she had told investigators about how she and Jens had planned the trip in advance, Updike thought. Never mind about how she had said the whole purpose of the trip was to create an alibi. He clenched his jaw. He knew what was coming next: She was going to deny everything she had said about how she and Jens had gone to buy a knife to use on her parents.

He was right.

On Saturday morning, Elizabeth testified, she made the rounds of capitol pawn stores. When she was through, she had several hundred dollars in her purse. Overjoyed, she invited Jens to lunch to celebrate her largesse and split the money with him since they divided everything half and half. Instead of being happy, however, he was angry, furious that her parents did not give her enough money to live on and that she was forced to sell her possessions to survive.

"He said my parents weren't providing me with sufficient funds, and they were supposed to be so incredibly wealthy, which was not true. He became very angry over that, and the conversation went into other resentments and angers about my relationship with my parents," she said.

You have to admire her, Updike thought, captivated by her tale. Her imagination is fantastic.

Jens was so angry, Elizabeth said, that he insisted on immediately driving to Boonsboro that afternoon to tell Nancy and Derek what he thought about their penny-pinching. At first she tried to talk him out of it because, first of all, her parents' money policies were none of his business. But worse than that, if he drove to Boonsboro, they would find out that she and Jens were spending the weekend together in Washington, and then they would be furious because they held her to very rigid moral standards. But the more she thought about it, the more she decided not to try to stop him. With him out of the way, she would be free to spend some of her new-found wealth on drugs. She would not be able to do that with Jens around because he disapproved intensely of her drug use.

"Once I thought about my drugs, I just became so self-centered, so selfish, so totally involved in my own desire to get my fix that I wanted to get him away from me so I could go and score. And so I didn't really care about the long term. I just wanted to get him out of the way."

Jens stewed about the situation for quite some time, she said. Then he got up from the table and headed toward the car, saying he was going to confront them. As he walked away he mumbled, "I could kill them."

Jones stopped her there. Didn't that ring some sort of alarm bell in her head? he asked. Didn't that make her worried?

Elizabeth shrugged. "At the time, I was so involved in my own selfish, tiny, stupid, irresponsible world of drugs and self-satisfaction, that I was just like, 'Yes, dear,' and went on with my business."

Before she continued with her story, Jones wanted to draw a moral from her experience. What did she think *now* of her actions *then?* he prompted.

She responded quickly. "Certainly in view of what happened and subsequent events, I felt I should have known, or I did know and didn't care, and that I could have done something to prevent it." When Jones nodded encouragement, she continued. "I feel that I should have done something, and because of my failure on so many occasions to do the right things, I'm indeed responsible for what happened."

He wanted her to keep going. "And is it your failure to do something at that time?" he asked. "Is that one of the reasons that you have entered the plea that you did?"

"That's part of it, yes, sir," she said. "And obviously I felt responsible because of the vehemence with which I wrote in my letters. It was irresponsible. They were unfair in what I said, the fact that I hated my parents—" She corrected herself. "Well, hated my mother so much at times. I feel responsible for that hate and for cluing Jens into it and then allowing him, in a sense, to have killed my parents."

Jones looked as though he wanted to cheer. Updike looked sick.

45

JONES WAS SATISFIED WITH THE WAY THINGS WERE MOVING, BUT THERE remained a number of issues to be cleared up before he turned Elizabeth over to Updike. For one thing, there was the very important point concerning Jens's and Elizabeth's alibi.

Elizabeth conveniently ignored everything she had told investigators previously about how she and Jens had planned the trip to Washington so they would not be suspects in the murders. The stories she had told police, she said when she took the stand, were what she and Jens had agreed to *after* the murders, not *before*.

When Jens came back to Washington and told her what he had done, her first reaction had been to try to protect him. So together they concocted a tale they would tell the police if they were ever asked. That had made her feel that she was demonstrating her love and loyalty to Jens. But now it was no longer necessary to take that position. To save herself, it was important that she renege on her earlier comments. If she continued to admit that she and Jens had planned the trip, she was placing herself in a position of responsibility equal to Jens's.

She did not retract everything. Some of what she had told police about what happened that weekend survived her trip to the witness box virtually intact. For the record, she repeated how Jens had picked her up on the street after the late-night movie, how he had been covered with blood, and how shocked she had been. It was essentially what she had told Gardner, Beever, and

Wright. Except for one important variation. What she had not told police, she said, was that when Jens picked her up, she had been so stoned that she could make little sense of the situation. She remembered thinking: "This is a bad trip. He's trying to freak me out." She was so high, she said, she couldn't understand what he was trying to say. At first, she thought he said he had killed a person. Then she thought he said he had killed a dog. Finally, it came through to her that he was saying he had killed her parents.

Her timing and sense of organization were impeccable. With her new story, Version 4 by conservative count, not only was she covering herself by, in effect appearing to lay all the blame on Jens while giving lip-service to her own responsibility, but she was further excusing her actions by saying she was under the influence of drugs. In essence, she was beating her breast and saying she was sorry out of one side of her mouth, while out of the other she was saying she had nothing to be sorry for because nothing was her fault anyway.

Then to her self-anointed attributes she added a highly developed propensity for self-preservation. After she had sobered up, Jones asked her, why had she not gone to the police?

"To be truthful," she said, "my first feelings were to save Jens, to save myself. I was stunned. The situation was so huge, so overwhelming, so definite, so final, so extraordinary. I mean, Jens is a wimp. You can't imagine him doing something like that."

The more time passed, she said, the stronger her desire became to protect Jens. But there was a flip side to that as well. By sheltering him, she increased her own dependency on him; she became an emotional cripple totally reliant on her lover. "It was pathetic, my need of this person, my total obsession and need for him," she said. "It was like a physical addiction; it overruled everything. It overruled all values, all concerns. I would have done anything for him, and I did do everything for him. I betrayed everything. I betrayed my family. I betrayed my friends. I betrayed my parents. And I sold my soul for him really because of this extraordinary need for him. And it sounds very peculiar, but after he killed my parents, I needed him more."

THINGS WERE GOING SMOOTHLY, JONES WAS CERTAIN, BUT HE WANTED TO help Elizabeth bury Jens a little deeper still. As undramatically as he could, he asked her if Jens's personality had changed after the murders.

As enthusiastically as she had gone into this subject with Gardner, Elizabeth leaped into it now. Yes, she said almost eagerly, he changed enormously. For one thing, he found his potency. For another, he became extremely domineering. Again, she used an anecdote to underline her point.

"There was a problem when my family came for the funeral," she said. "It was absolutely vital for me to spend time with my family, but Jens was very nervous and suspicious of me because I was spending time with them. He made verbal threats about different things that he would do if I didn't spend more time with him. He threatened to turn himself in and make sure that I went down with him. He threatened to kill himself and leave a message to convict me. He threatened leaving me, which was the terrible thing. He threatened lots of different things."

What made it especially difficult, she said, was that she was suffering alone. "In the public portrayal he was my loving boyfriend who was with me in my hour of need. But he didn't trust me out of his sight."

WHAT SHE HAD SAID UP TO THAT POINT WAS A PRACTICE SESSION, A warmup. With no more hesitation than a championship diver going off the high board, Elizabeth plunged into the very crucial issue of the knife.

The knife was important because it was the major indicator of her involvement. If she had, as she told investigators, gone shopping with Jens for the weapon, indeed had purchased it herself, then the rest of her courtroom story about how Jens had been acting on his own in murdering her parents would not stand. If she admitted that she bought the knife, she acknowledged her culpability. By doing that, she also would be adding to the evidence that she had talked Jens into the murders. And that was precisely what she wanted to deny.

In one respect Jens had been much more clever than she. Jens had refused from the first to discuss a knife at all, other than to say that Elizabeth bought one, because he correctly determined that if he told investigators he went to Loose Chippings with a weapon in his pocket, he would be demonstrating premeditation. Elizabeth, on the other hand, confessed to Beever and later to Gardner as well that she had bought the knife. That made her truly an accessory. Admittedly, she had pleaded guilty to that very charge, but if she hoped for leniency from Judge Sweeney, she had to minimize her responsibility. She had decided to do that by denying any involvement with a knife, and, by extension, denying any conscious attempt to manipulate Jens into committing the murders. The only reason she brought the subject of the knife up to begin with, she was saying, was because Jens made her.

Then she told a story she had never told before. When she and Jens first discussed the murder weapon, she said, Jens told her that that he had killed her parents with a steak knife. But they discussed the situation, and Jens felt she needed to be more a part of the crime of what had happened. So they devised the tale about how she should say that she had purchased a knife although she had not. Eventually, she said, it became a basic part of their narrative. But as far as the actual kind of knife it was, that wasn't decided until they had been on the run for several months. "It was in England," she said. "That was the first time he ever told me about a butterfly knife."

While they were in London, she said, Jens showed her an ad from *Soldier of Fortune* magazine. In the ad was a picture of a knife. "That's a butterfly knife," he told her. "If anyone ever asks, tell them that's the kind of knife you bought."

Later, when Beever asked her details about the type of weapon she thought was used in the murders, she drew for him, from memory, a picture of the butterfly knife she had seen in the magazine.

"Have you ever seen a butterfly knife?" Jones asked.

"Only a picture," she replied. "I've never seen a real one, no."

"Were you able to talk to Jens briefly after those statements in London were completed?"

"You mean on June 9?"

"Uh-huh."

"Yes, I was."

"And what was his concern at that time?"

"He asked me if I had told them about the knife."

JONES PERHAPS COULD BE LOOKED UPON AS A MASTER CHEF AS WELL AS A guide. He had to make sure just the right seasoning was added in the precise amount if he wanted his creation to be a success. At this stage he felt that it was time to throw in a dash of remorse, just to make sure Judge Sweeney had not missed Elizabeth's change of attitude once she had broken her bonds with Jens.

Now that she had time to reflect upon things, Jones wanted to know, how did she feel about her behavior through the whole unhappy episode?

Metaphorically, Elizabeth gave her chest a solid thump. "I was just disgusting," she said. "I not only lied to the police about what was going on when I had ample opportunity to do otherwise—I not only lied to them when I should have told them the truth, I betrayed my family." Thump. "It wasn't only just the betrayal, it was the whole acting out of this innocence." Thump. "I was betraying everything." Thump. "My behavior was completely unacceptable." Thump, thump.

JONES WAS PLEASED. THE DIRECT EXAMINATION WAS GOING LIKE CLOCK-work, but he sensed it was about time to give it up. If they had not made their points by now, they never would. But before surrendering his witness to the prosecutor, Jones wanted to make one more pass at Jens. Tell everyone again, he urged Elizabeth, about how Jens evolved overnight into a first-class bully.

Elizabeth seemed delighted to comply. "He made it very clear that there was no point in me thinking about trying to tell somebody about what had happened," she said, "although I have to admit that at that time I was not thinking about it. I loved him, I needed him, and I just wanted to blank out what he had done. But he was obsessed with the notion that I might speak to somebody. And he would say that if he went down, I would go with him."

At the same time, she said, he was insufferably proud of what he had done. "He thought he was some kind of hero." When he was in a mood like that, she added, he would brag about how he had done everything by himself: how he had plotted the murders; how he had carried them out; even how he had outwitted the police. "He thought he was incredibly smart for having outwitted Investigator Gardner."

As all investigators do, there were some things Gardner told his wife and there were some things he did not. One of the things he had not told her, at least not at first, was Elizabeth's assertion that Jens had planned to murder him. He had not wanted to tell his wife because he did not want to worry her. In any case, Jens was locked up now, and there was little chance he was going to get free anytime soon. But as the day for Elizabeth's testimony drew closer, Gardner began to wonder if he should not confide in his wife. He did not want her to hear it first from Elizabeth. The night before Elizabeth took the stand, after dinner, he had told her that she might hear something in the courtroom that could come as a surprise to her. Then he related to her what Elizabeth had told him. Afterwards, he was glad he had. Elizabeth, in her determination to hit Jens with whatever ammunition she had, brought it up.

"He felt threatened by Investigator Gardner," she said. "He felt he knew in some sort of way what he had done. So he plotted to kill him at his home, and I was to provide his alibi in Charlottesville."

Elizabeth could have stopped there, but she did not. She wanted not only to blacken Jens's name, but to put as much shine as she could on hers. So she made herself a quasiheroine in the situation.

"There wasn't any point in reasoning with Jens about killing people," she said. "No sense telling him it was bad, that you shouldn't kill people. He *had* killed people, and I wasn't in a position to moralize to him." So she interjected herself into the plot in the way in which she was most accomplished. She created a fictional situation. She told how she had invented a brain tumor and how that had distracted Jens so much that he forgot about Gardner. When she finished telling the anecdote, she looked very self-satisfied.

46

JONES WAS TRYING TO WIND UP. IT WAS LATE IN THE AFTERNOON AND Elizabeth had been on the stand for four hours. But before he quit, he wanted to make it clear who from his perspective had been manipulating whom in the Jens-Elizabeth relationship.

For Elizabeth's sake it would be helpful for Jones to help make Jens the villain. Proving this, however, required a great deal of skill. His client had backed herself into a corner by admitting numerous times that in the early days of their relationship she believed she had been manipulating Jens. Carrying this one step further, it was not difficult to infer that she had been manipulating him to murder her parents. But Jones wanted to go backwards and undo all the allusions to Elizabeth as the manipulator. He intended to try to persuade Judge Sweeney that even though Elizabeth thought she was manipulating Jens, he was actually manipulating *her*—that she was, in fact, the "manipulatee." It was a most Machiavellian point, and to present it convincingly, he would have to convince the judge, through Elizabeth, that Jens was a very clever fellow indeed. Furthermore, Jones would have to produce some physical evidence to substantiate the claim. Since letters were as common in this case as sunshine is in Arizona, it was not surprising that he picked a letter as his vehicle to try to underscore Elizabeth's naiveté.

Gingerly, he began laying the groundwork. Did she believe that Jens was acting as a result of her will? he asked Elizabeth.

"Very definitely," she said. "I felt that I was fully responsible for Jens's actions. For Jens's life. For what happened. For everything. I believed that I had manipulated him, that I had controlled him, that I had somehow made him do this."

Excellent, Jones thought. "But," he said, "based on what's happened since then, do you still believe it was your will?"

"No," Elizabeth said. Since then, she added, she had read letters and documents written by Jens that convinced her that she was the one being maneuvered. "Now I believe I didn't have any control over him whatsoever."

What really turned her around, she said, was a letter from Jens to a friend he had made in his first few days in prison, a youth named Neil Woodall. The letter was dated May 18–19, 1986, less than three weeks after they were arrested and some two weeks before Jens and Elizabeth were aware that Beever and Wright were beginning to put together the pieces connecting them to Derek's and Nancy's murders. The date it was written was significant because it showed how, even though they had been separated for only a short time, Jens already was trying to cut himself loose from her psychologically.

The rambling hand-written document was eleven pages long and dealt mainly with discussions Jens and Woodall had while they shared a cell for a few days. In it, Jens, who is prone to philosophize extensively in his writings in every case, closely examined his relationship with Elizabeth and delved into an issue he called "separateness," which was his euphemism for ego. The "self" was all important, he had written, and it was what he and Elizabeth had forgotten in their relationship.

When he and Elizabeth denied the "self" motive in their relationship they were fooling each other, denying their instincts in an attempt to get what they could from the other. At one point he wrote about the great joy he experienced in giving something to someone unconditionally. That, he felt, was fulfilling a perfect act of friendship. It was an example of a totally "selfless" act. At that phrase, in the margin of her copy of the letter, Elizabeth had scrawled that was precisely what Jens used to say about the murder of her parents—it was a completely "selfless" act.

Talking about the letter made Elizabeth angry, or at least it prompted her to feign anger successfully. She had first seen the letter only a few days before when she was sifting through the mound of documents collected for her to use in her defense, and she was still smarting from the shock. Up until then, she said, she believed she had been the manipulator and had assumed that role in talking to investigators. But once she read what her lover had written to Woodall, she realized she had been used. Once she read it, she said, she began putting together things Jens had told her and what he had said to others, including investigators. In retrospect, her first inkling of the true nature of their relationship should have been apparent to her almost a year previously, in November 1986, when she and Jens began to disagree on how to handle their defense. "Suddenly, he was no longer so subtle," she said.

But the real clincher was the Woodall letter. What it showed her, she said, was that Jens had been manipulating her all along. "He was using me. But it was more than that. He knew exactly, precisely what he was doing. It wasn't—it's not as if he even believes what he says to me. He states very plainly how to manipulate me. He knew what he was doing in his manipulations. It was deliberate." She sighed. "Now, on top of everything else I am a first-class idiot."

ALTHOUGH JENS'S LETTER TO WOODALL HAD BEEN A REVELATION, THE REAL turning point in her feelings for Jens had come the previous November, when she saw for the first time the photographs taken at Loose Chippings by investigators, the ones that showed in unrelenting detail how viciously her parents had been murdered. She was giving a deposition, she said, and the photographs were attached to another document she was shown at the same time. It was a profound shock.

"I lived with those photographs," she said bitterly. "They were in my cell. They were on my person. They were with me wherever I went, and they were in my mind's eye the whole time as well. As far as I was concerned, absolutely nothing, nothing, could justify what he had done, what I had done. Everything else just became irrelevant—the details of who did what to whom. He had butchered my parents. It was there, sitting in front of me. It wasn't just words, it was there. And I was in some way, shape, or form part of that. I was responsible for it."

Taking a breath, she continued. The really sad part, she said, was that up until then she had continued to be loyal to him. But after she saw the photographs, everything changed. "There was just no way, absolutely no way, no matter what I felt specifically for Jens, there was no way I could continue to have a relationship with him or to pander to his whims or needs. And if I felt lonely, too bad, because it was time to take a stand."

That, she said, was when she decided to plead guilty. Once she had made that decision, she also determined that she would try to see that Jens shouldered his share of the blame as well. That was why she emphasized premeditation in her interview with Gardner on May 8, why she had lied to the investigator. "I knew the line of Jens's defense. I wanted to make sure that was quite clear to Investigator Gardner because I want Jens to come back here and I want him to stand trial. I wanted to make sure that Jens was convicted."

Jones asked if she would be willing to cooperate with the prosecution in building a case against Jens.

"Absolutely," she said emphatically.

"If called upon by the prosecution to testify, would you do it?"

"Yes."

Jones and Elizabeth both looked exhausted. Almost simultaneously they glanced at Judge Sweeney.

"That's all the questions, Judge."

Sweeney leaned forward and warned the lawyers to make sure their witnesses who had not testified that day would be in court for the next day's session. Then he told everyone to go home and be back at 9:30 Wednesday morning.

He didn't have to be specific with the spectators. The next day would be what everyone had come to hear: Commonwealth Attorney Jim Updike's cross-examination of Elizabeth Haysom.

47

IN THE SPRING OF 1985 THERE HAD BEEN MUCH ANGER IN BEDFORD COUNTY about the murders. At the time it was almost universally felt that the electric chair was too good for whoever had carved up Derek and Nancy. But two and a half years down the road attitudes changed. When it turned out that the accused were the couple's daughter, a young woman who may have been subject to sexual abuse by her own mother, and the extraordinarily intelligent son of a German diplomat, the line softened. The fact that the daughter had pleaded guilty—had actually thrown herself upon the mercy of the court—helped. At the proceedings the previous August Elizabeth had indeed appeared contrite, a soft-spoken young woman who had admitted her role in the affair and was willing to accept the punishment. By now there was more than a little sympathy for her. No matter how tragic Nancy's and Derek's deaths had been, the feeling went, there was no way to bring them back to life. Perhaps, it was said, there *were* circumstances that made the murders understandable. Not justifiable, but understandable. Maybe it was time to temper justice with mercy.

Jim Updike did not feel that way.

ALL AFTERNOON MONDAY HE SAT IN DISGUST AS ELIZABETH CHANGED HER story still another time to serve her own purposes. Throughout the investigation he had watched in wonder as she molded her narrative to her own advantage, skillfully weaving truth and untruth into a credible whole. He marveled at how she could say one thing at one time and five days or five minutes later say something completely different. And in her tiny, shy-little-girl voice and an exotic accent make *both* versions sound completely believable.

At first Updike tried to put himself in Elizabeth's place, to understand why she was so unhappy with her parents. It was a position that was totally alien to him. His parents were working-class people who had to scrimp and save and make sacrifices. They had worked hard to make sure that he got an education, and he was grateful. He couldn't understand how someone who had all the privileges Elizabeth had enjoyed could appreciate them so little. Already disgusted by the viciousness of the crime, he was further repelled by her motive, or, as he saw it, her appalling lack of motive.

When the defense finally finished and turned Elizabeth over to him, Updike rose and stood quietly staring at her, sizing her up as though he were seeing her for the first time. His face was impassive, but his back was rigid, every muscle tense. He was wearing a light gray three-piece suit, a white button-down shirt, and a blue tie with small white figures. A gold watch chain stretched across his waist. He stared at Elizabeth, taking in her powder-blue short-sleeved dress with flap pockets on the chest that minimized her breasts. She was wearing the pearl earrings again, and around her neck was a pearl tear-drop pendant on a gold chain. She stared back, realizing her toughest ordeal was coming, that there would be no friendly, leading questions from this man. She clamped her mouth tightly closed, compressing her lips into a thin, pink, unlipsticked line. Her eyes were cold and wary. She seemed to age in a heartbeat, like the villainess in the horror movie who, having been kept youthful by a magic serum, is suddenly deprived of the potion. Before everyone's eyes Elizabeth's appearance changed from that of a demure fifteen-year-old to a hardened veteran of the streets who looked every day of forty.

Updike cleared his throat. Then he began, politely at first, in a friendly down-home drawl. "Ms. Haysom," he said, "the circumstances have been such that you and I haven't had the opportunity to talk before. It's not been appropriate before now. But in view of your lengthy testimony yesterday, as you can well imagine, I have a number of questions I would like to ask you." It was the fisherman's speech to the trout he was trying to catch. Soon enough, the dialogue would become heated; then Updike and Elizabeth Haysom would reveal their true personas. They were equally strong-willed people working to opposite ends: he to get her to incriminate herself, she to maintain her last-stated position as that of a naive young woman gulled by an evil killer. In a manner dictated by the surroundings the two began an absurdly polite, hushed-voice fight, a deceptively low-key battle that both knew was going to turn hostile.

Updike's drawl was exaggerated even for Virginia; his voice was quiet, but it dripped with sarcasm. Patiently, he repeated details from her personal history. Despite her advantages, Elizabeth viewed herself as underprivileged, a poor-little-rich-girl who had been given everything but in the end had nothing. In her testimony she tried to elicit sympathy for her plight.

Plight, indeed, thought Updike. A posh school in Switzerland. Even posher ones in England. Skiing vacations in Europe and the Rockies. Summers in Canada. Writing seminars in New England. Entrée into the best homes. Everyone should have it so terrible, he pointed out. In return what did she do? She lied, he said. She connived. She built up resentments and hatred for her parents who were trying to give her the best, certainly the best they could afford. She lied to her parents. She lied to her boyfriend. She lied to anyone and everyone, including investigators. She created her own world, which was based only in part on reality. She was living a play, but she called it life. In fact, one of her major interests was theater; one of her favorite pastimes was acting.

"While you were at Wycombe Abbey, you did quite a bit of acting, didn't you?" Updike asked.

Warily, she agreed that she had.

"A lot of Shakespeare, I see," he said, shuffling through his notes. *"Antony and Cleopatra* with you playing Cleopatra." But that was strange, he added, looking up. "I don't see *Macbeth* listed here." Why was that? he wanted to know, and he asked, "In one of your statements you referred to yourself as Lady Macbeth, didn't you?"

He was trying to get a rise out of her, trying to put her on the defensive, trying to get her angry enough to say something she perhaps would not say otherwise. "Did you see yourself as Lady Macbeth?" he pressed.

Elizabeth glared at him but kept her tone even, controlling her anger. "Yes, sir, I did," she said.

"Your Shakespeare is certainly much better than mine," said Updike, whose undergraduate degree was in English literature, "but it seems to me, if I recall, that Lady Macbeth encouraged old Macbeth to commit murder, didn't she?"

The replies came like gunshots.

"Yes, she did," agreed Elizabeth.

"Persuaded him—"

"Yes."

"Encouraged him—"

"Yes."

"And that's how you saw yourself," Updike said, making his point, "with reference to Jens Soering."

Elizabeth had to answer in the affirmative, otherwise she would contradict her own testimony. But she proved quicker on her feet than Updike expected. "I felt totally responsible for manipulating him at that time," she admitted, adding that she later came to realize she had misjudged her position and discovered that it was he who was manipulating her.

Updike nodded. Round one was a draw.

THE COMMONWEALTH ATTORNEY IS AN OLD-SCHOOL SOUTHERN gentleman, a man brought up in a culture that stresses politeness and respect. Especially respect. Even more especially, respect for one's parents. One of the most grievous sins a southerner can commit is parental slander. To Updike it was incomprehensible that Elizabeth could say such bad things about her mother and father, particularly her mother. Particularly if what she was saying was not true.

In addition to being a southern gentleman, Updike also was a prosecutor. He was not naive enough to believe that some parents were not cruel to their children—that some of them brought bad things upon themselves by the way they treated their offspring. Incest, he knew, could be a motive for murder. He did *not* know if that applied in this case. Elizabeth had made a lot of accusations against her parents, and she had been particularly critical of Nancy. Updike did not know if the things Elizabeth had said about her mother were true. But he desperately wanted to find out.

Riffling through his notes, he produced a thin sheaf of papers. He told Elizabeth the papers composed a presentence report that had been drawn up at Judge Sweeney's direction. It was based on statements Elizabeth had made to a probation officer, who then reported her remarks and made recommendations on what he thought her sentence should be. In some states presentence reports are part of the public record, available for perusal by anyone who takes the time to go to the clerk's office to look them up. In Virginia they are not; they are treated as confidential documents. Nevertheless, they can be used by prosecution and defense alike to make points during sentencing proceedings. Updike was anxious to go through the report on Elizabeth because it gave additional detail about the relationship between Elizabeth and her mother. That is, it gave detail from Elizabeth's point of view.

Nude pictures of Elizabeth had been found in her mother's bureau. Elizabeth had told Gardner that her mother often came into her bed naked and indulged in "some very affectionate" kissing and hugging. But Elizabeth had not told Gardner what she told the court officer who drew up the presentence report. Updike flipped through the document until he found what he was looking for. He read it to himself quickly one more time and then leaned forward, looking Elizabeth in the eye. "You stated to this man sitting here," he said, waving his right arm vaguely in the direction of where the probation officer was seated, "that from age eighteen to age nineteen you had a full-blown sexual relationship with your mother. Is that right?"

Elizabeth looked more angry than uncomfortable. "That isn't the way I put it," she said, explaining that she had gone into considerable detail with Ricky Gardner about the relationship.

Updike shook his head. That wasn't his question. He wasn't talking about Ricky Gardner, he said, but about the probation officer. "Did you make that statement to him?"

Elizabeth stood her ground, denying she ever called it a "full-blown sexual relationship." What she had told him, she said, was essentially what she had told Gardner—namely, that her mother had been "aggressively affectionate" and that she had craved attention.

Updike was getting angry. He wanted to put the issue to rest. He was offended by the way Elizabeth had been quick to blame her mother, and he wanted to determine for the record if there was a concrete basis for her statements. But he was having trouble doing that because Elizabeth was refusing to answer his questions in a straightforward manner. He put down the presentence report and shuffled among his papers until he came up with the transcript of Gardner's interrogation. " 'Question,' " he read, marking his place with his finger. " 'Was there some sexual activity there? Response: No, I don't think you'd call it sexual activity.' That's what you said to Investigator Gardner, wasn't it?"

"That's correct," Elizabeth said. "And it's true."

Then why, Updike asked, his voice rising, did you say something different to the probation officer? "After having made this statement that there was no sexual activity from your mother, what is this doing in this presentence report?"

Elizabeth looked down in her lap. She had said, she answered, only that she and her mother slept together.

Updike nodded. He could buy that. There were, he knew, times when Elizabeth came home from the university that there were no beds available and she and her mother would have to double up. But that was a long way from a full-blown sexual relationship. Updike wanted to show that Elizabeth had been lying to the probation officer, not so much to prove Elizabeth a liar—there were a lot of other ways to do that—but to protect the reputation of a woman who had been brutally murdered. A woman who was not there to defend herself. "It was perfectly innocent, wasn't it?" he asked, willing her to say yes.

Instead, she snapped at him. "That isn't an issue I want to bring up," she said curtly.

Updike looked surprised. "I don't want to bring it up either, ma'am."

"It's not something I want to discuss," Elizabeth said heatedly. "I don't think it's relevant. My mother isn't here—"

Updike had enough. "Exactly!" he yelled.

"And it's not something I want to discuss in public. This is a very private thing, and if the newspapers and people have wanted to interpret what I said about my mother in a sordid way, that is their filthy minds."

Updike wanted to let it drop, but he still did not have a direct answer. He had only one question for her, he said. Did Nancy sexually abuse her? "If she didn't," he implored, "for God's sake clear her name now."

Elizabeth paused, then answered in a soft but firm voice, pronouncing the words distinctly: "She . . . did . . . not . . . sexually . . . abuse . . . me."

Updike looked relieved. Grabbing for his notes, he was ready to move on to something else. But inadvertently he plunged right back into the swamp. He meant it as a footnote to the issue they had been discussing, but his question had a nuance he had not intended. "If there was any lesbian relationship, it was with Melinda Duncan in the summer of 1983, wasn't it?" he asked, meaning to clear Nancy's name. Instead, it set Elizabeth off.

"That's your terminology," she sniffed.

Updike was puzzled. He had not expected argument on that point. "Excuse me?" he said.

"That's your terminology," Elizabeth repeated angrily.

"Did you sleep with her?"

"Yes, like I slept with my mother."

To many, that brought the issue back to where it had begun: Was there a sexual relationship between Elizabeth and her mother? As was common with Elizabeth, what she said was frequently elliptical. It often had only a very tenuous connection with reality. Since no one doubted that the relationship between "Bunnie" and "Melie" had *not* been sexual, was this Elizabeth's way of admitting that her relationship with her mother also had been sexual?

Updike groped for a way out. He seemed to acknowledge to himself that the line he had been pursuing was reaping very few rewards. He had made an effort to get to the bottom of that conundrum but hadn't been successful, and he couldn't see wasting any more time on it. He dropped the incest issue and never brought it up again.

48

INSTEAD, UPDIKE HAMMERED AT HER CREDIBILITY. HE WAS TROUBLED BY her inconsistencies, he told her, particularly in the various ways in which she characterized her relations with her parents. In her first interviews with police, he pointed out, she said her parents were wonderful. Then, beginning with the admissions she and Jens made to detectives in London, they were terrible. And, in another reversal, on the stand a day earlier, they were back to being wonderful. She could not have it both ways, Updike said. Which was it going to be?

Updike lived, for all intents and purposes, in a black and white world. The law does not equivocate. There is right and wrong. Legal and illegal. Guilty and innocent. Elizabeth, on the other hand, lived in a world of gray, a dreamer's world. There was right (maybe) and wrong (maybe). Guilty (of some things) and innocent (of some things). Her parents may not have been cruel to her, she explained, but she *thought* they were, which was just as important. "A lot of my resentments were in my own head," she said. "My parents were wonderful, and they tried very hard. Sometimes my mother probably tried too hard. I believe one of her faults was that she loved me too much."

Elizabeth meant it as a throwaway line. Updike jumped on it. He shook his head and repeated in a sad voice: "Loved you too much."

Elizabeth, demonstrating how quick she could be on the uptake, saw where he was going and fell into step. "Yes," she said, determined to use it to make her own point. "And I think that possibly because she did love me too much, she did make me feel guilty because I had let them down so badly. They had such expectations of me, and I was so very imperfect and so very far from what they really wanted me to be that I felt guilty. So what I'm trying to say is that you're quite right. The problem was with me, not with my parents."

Updike saw an opening. "And despite all of these allegations that we've heard and talked about, especially concerning your mother, you say now that the main fault with your mother was she loved you too much?"

"I think that's very true, sir."

He delivered his punchline. "And she died because of it."

Elizabeth paused, then all but whispered: "Probably."

UPDIKE HAD LISTENED IN DISBELIEF THE PREVIOUS DAY AS ELIZABETH PLAYED her game about whether she had manipulated Jens or Jens had manipulated her. First it was the former and then it was the latter. He was not interested in her intellectual gymnastics. The way he saw it, Elizabeth had zeroed in on Jens, led him on with an amazing repertoire of lies and half-truths, and kept after him until she convinced him to kill her parents. Her explanation that Jens had simply misinterpreted her was about as credible to Updike as if she had said it had snowed in Bedford on July 4th. But there was a big difference between what he felt and what he could get her to admit.

He decided to begin at the beginning—to go back to the early days of their relationship and see if he could wring from her an admission that Jens had been totally under her spell.

Elizabeth saw him coming. When Updike asked if she had not talked to Jens about killing Derek and Nancy even before Christmas 1984, she firmly denied it. She told Jens only about her "frustrations," she claimed.

Updike thought he saw an opening, but she cut him off again. When he asked her to elaborate on what she called "frustrations," she found another opportunity to beat her breast. She thought the problem was her parents, Elizabeth said, but in reality the problem was her. "It was my attitude that was wrong," she said. Mea culpa.

The issue of whether Elizabeth manipulated Jens or Jens manipulated Elizabeth was temporarily lost while the prosecutor and the witness sparred over Derek's and Nancy's treatment of Elizabeth.

"It sounds like your mom and dad couldn't win," Updike said. "You didn't like it when they didn't give you attention, and you didn't like it when they did."

That was because they went from one extreme to another, Elizabeth explained. They were either sending her off somewhere or smothering her with affection.

How could she look at it that way? Updike asked. Her parents had given her every opportunity. Had sent her to the best schools. Had done everything they could to make her life full and rich. "What did they do that was so wrong?" he asked in exasperation.

Elizabeth switched tones, moving in a blink from argumentative to submissive. "Probably not very much, sir," she said.

Updike wanted to explore the field more thoroughly. He repeated his question. "Well, what did they do that in your estimation was so wrong?"

Elizabeth knew an opening when she saw one. The thing she really resented, she said, was they insisted on telling everyone that she was perfect and they made her feel guilty because she was not.

Updike took that to mean that they bragged about her accomplishments. If that was true, what was so wrong about it? Didn't parents have a right to brag about their children? Didn't they have a right to be proud of her?

"Yes, sir," Elizabeth answered meekly. "They certainly did. Except that they exaggerated my achievements, and I had to try and live up to those exaggerations. That," she said, "was difficult."

Cross-examining Elizabeth Haysom, Updike was learning, was a very frustrating experience. She was very adept at maneuvering, slipping away and not answering his questions. He had started out hoping to nail her on how she had controlled Jens, and he ended up letting her maneuver the dialogue and switch it to her advantage.

Let's get back to Jens, he said with a sigh. Let's talk about the things you wrote him during the Christmas vacation.

Despite his intentions he got no more than one or two questions in before she orchestrated a debate on whether her Christmas communication to Jens had been a "letter" or an entry for her journal. He had started out with the idea of making her defend her earlier statements that she had been writing only some random, personal thoughts about her relationship with her parents but that Jens had interpreted her remarks as expressing her desire to have them killed. Updike thought that theory was hogwash, and he wanted to demolish it. But he was having trouble getting started. Immediately, she challenged his presumption that she had planned to share those thoughts with Jens to begin with. She did not mean it to be a "letter," she claimed.

Updike could not believe this was happening. What did she mean it was not a letter? he asked. It was dated, was it not? It had a salutation that read, "My Dearest Jens." She had put it in an envelope, had she not? Jens's name and address were on the envelope. She had put a stamp on it. And she had dropped it in a post box. What did she mean it was not a letter?

Elizabeth was a shrewd witness. She knew when to take ground and when to give it. She had made her point, so she decided to give a little. But only a little. "I don't know when I began whether I intended to mail it to him," she said. "I did eventually send it to him, which I should never have done."

Updike rolled his eyes.

He tried again to pin her down. He used sarcasm. He used politeness. He used anger. He tried to be conciliatory. He ducked and dodged and poked and probed. But he hardly got anywhere at all.

Most of the time she answered evasively, trying to take his

questions off on tangents. When that failed, she reverted to breast-beating.

Why are you writing such nasty things about your parents to someone you had known only a short time? he wanted to know. What kind of letter is this to send? he demanded.

She retreated. "It's a disgusting, atrocious letter," she agreed.

Updike paused. How in hell was he supposed to respond to that? "Then we're in agreement," he said finally. "But why did you write it?"

She started to wander. He tried to pull her back. "I still don't understand *why*, Ms. Haysom," Updike said.

She repeated what she had told Hugh Jones during the direct examination. All of her references to voodoo and willing her parents to death were digs at Jens, nothing more.

Updike wanted her to confess that she was working on Jens, not tweaking his intellectual eccentricities. She would not go along. The fault was hers, she said, retreating without surrendering. "I was completely selfish and self-centered."

Updike sighed. He was going to give it one more try.

"ALL RIGHT, MA'AM," HE SAID PATIENTLY. "SO YOU'RE SAYING THAT THIS expression of concentration on their deaths, then, was mere fantasy of yours. Just yours?"

"Yes, sir."

"Why is it, then, that you communicated this fantasy to Mr. Soering? I mean, you can fantasize things—you can write them down and throw them away. You don't have to stick them in the mailbox. Why did you mail this fantasy to this young lover of yours?"

"We shared many things," she said, "and one of the things I think that was wrong about our relationship was that perhaps I shared too much with him. I indulged my resentments, my self-pity, my frustrations with him. I exaggerated them. I let them run away with themselves."

"Did he know these were merely fantasies?"

"Well, this is one of the problems that we obviously had. He would discuss with me his fantasies as he describes them in his letters, some of his bizarre sexual fantasies, and I told him my fantasies."

So far so good, Updike told himself.

One of *her* bizarre fantasies, Elizabeth explained, was of a life without her parents. The problem was, Jens had taken her seriously. He had not known she was fantasizing. When she had said "life without her parents," he had understood her to mean life with her parents dead. He had "misinterpreted."

"That's right much of an understatement," Updike commented laconically. "Wouldn't you say?"

"Yes," she agreed.

BUT THAT DID NOT EXPLAIN JENS'S REACTION, UPDIKE POINTED OUT. IN HIS letter to her on the same date, he was expressing similar thoughts. While she was writing about voodoo and life without her parents, Jens, who was several hundred miles away at his parents' home in suburban Detroit, was writing to her using phrases like "that instrument for a certain operation on somebody's relatives." Updike wanted to get her to admit that they were plotting—that they had, jointly, begun thinking about murdering Nancy and Derek. "So about the same time you're fantasizing about their deaths, he's talking about using an instrument on somebody's relatives, isn't he?"

Elizabeth tried to slip away, seeking refuge in Jens's intellectualism. "I believe he discusses this weapon, or instrument, and it is, what does he call it? Neurolinguistic programming. Psychology. Hypnosis. All his pseudo popularized psychology."

Updike was not going to let her get away that easily. He pointed out that Jens had further discussed what he called "the ultimate weapon." At one point he had written that Elizabeth's father could "could quite well die from a confrontation." At another, he had commented that he "had the dinner scene planned out." Hanging in the courtroom air was the knowledge that Derek and Nancy were murdered at dinner. "Was it just coincidence that he is fantasizing about their deaths while you are also fantasizing about their deaths?" he asked.

Elizabeth hedged. "I believe you'll find he also fantasized about his own parents' death as well in that letter."

She's wiggling away again, Updike realized. He tried to get her back. "I'm not concerned with that here today, Ms. Haysom. I'm concerned with why your mom and dad got butchered like they did and why y'all were writing these things at the same time. His diary is full of references to weapons against your parents, isn't it?"

Elizabeth refused to concede. "If you examine what he describes as the weapons," she said, "they are things like emotional blackmail."

Updike was frustrated with the bantering. There were other avenues he wanted to explore. Elizabeth, however, had another idea. She decided to use Jens's words to prove the opposite of what Updike was saying. The prosecutor was anxious to demonstrate that a conspiracy existed between Jens and Elizabeth to murder Derek and Nancy. Elizabeth wanted to demonstrate that all she had been doing was exercising her right to complain to her boyfriend about her relationship with her parents and that Jens had taken it from there. He read something into her words she did not mean and used that to begin manipulating her.

"Jens Soering manipulated my resentment and my frustration," Elizabeth began. "He began talking about a dinner scene three or four months before it happened."

Updike nodded.

"So I don't see how I could have manipulated him to plan those sorts of things when he already had it planned," she said, willing to drift wherever her thoughts carried her. "We had been discussing these things, my hatred and my resentments, and he takes it one step further," she added, building steam. "I told you, I admit fully that I had macabre and dreadful fantasies for many years about . . ."

Updike cut her off. This was getting nowhere, he perceived, and he had his own agenda. "If we could move on, please," he said impatiently. "We've covered those letters then." It had been a disconcerting hour.

49

JIM UPDIKE'S MISSION WAS TO EXPOSE ELIZABETH HAYSOM. HER PARENTS, he was convinced, were dead because of her. She may not have killed them. In fact he had already conceded that she was not even present when they were murdered. But that did not diminish her responsibility, legal or moral. They were dead because of what she was. And she was a liar, a manipulator, a conniver, a seductress, and a self-centered, ungrateful daughter, not to mention a confessed accessory to murder. She also was proving to be a very articulate and astute witness. While Beever had noted that Jens had a way of answering a question with a question, Elizabeth's technique was different. She *appeared* to be answering a question, but when she had finished, it was apparent that she had not answered it at all. She was a world-class evasionist.

Part of Updike's plan to expose her consisted of demonstrating how virtually nothing she said could be believed. Not even the little things, the irrelevant things. Things like whose idea it had been for her to go skiing in Yugoslavia during the Christmas vacation in 1984. If Updike could show that she lied about things like that, he could prove that she was capable of lying about almost anything concerning her parents' deaths.

Elizabeth claimed that she hadn't wanted to make the trip, but that her mother had made her. Updike wanted to show that she was lying. Annie Massie had told investigators that Nancy had told her that it was Elizabeth who had begged for the vacation. Updike wanted to get to the heart of this issue.

"If one of your mother's friends, Mrs. Massie for instance, testified that your mother was concerned about you going to Yugoslavia, but that it was your idea to go anyway, and she consented to your wishes—"

"I'm sure my mother said that."

"But you still maintain it was her idea, not yours?"

"Absolutely."

"And then if your mother said that to Mrs. Massie, your mother was not telling the truth. She lied in other words?"

"Yes," Elizabeth said.

Updike bored in. "Would you agree that you're calling her a liar?"

"I would say she wasn't so much of a liar as somebody who—"

"Didn't tell the truth."

"Had fantasies."

Updike pointed out that Elizabeth had written to her rescuer from Berlin, Colonel Herrington, about the Yugoslavia trip and that in the letter she had told him that it was her decision, not her mother's.

Elizabeth responded that she was obliged to say that because her mother read all her letters.

Updike looked steadily at her. He felt he had made his point. "Ms. Haysom," he said solemnly, "it seems that you pass responsibility for everything to somebody else, don't you?"

Elizabeth wanted the last word. "I have done that," she confessed.

UPDIKE WAS CURIOUS ABOUT AN INCIDENT SHE HAD DETAILED DURING HER direct examination: the time Jens allegedly walked into her dormitory room and said, apparently without provocation, that he would like to confront her parents because he "could blow their bloody heads off." Elizabeth had not mentioned that in any of her interrogations. Was it another of her fantasies? If it had occurred as she described, he asked her, what had she tried to do to stop him?

"Absolutely nothing, sir, and that's why I'm guilty."

Her response surprised him, but Updike was not interested in more of her self-flagellation. He wanted to know if such an incident had actually occurred and what her response had been.

It would seem to him, he said, that unless someone actually wanted his or her parents dead, that person would react very strongly to a comment such as that.

Elizabeth repeated what she had said before. Several times. "I did not want my parents murdered," she insisted. "But there was a large part of me which did want my parents out of my life."

Updike considered that another nonanswer. He wanted her to be more specific. "Couldn't you very well have said to Jens Soering, 'Look, Jens, I don't want them dead. I would like them out of my life, but I don't want them dead. I love you, but don't you ever say anything of that nature against my mother and father again.' "

Elizabeth conceded that the statement had made her angry and that she had told Jens it was a "disgusting" thing to say. Then she added: "But he obviously knew from my letters that I didn't want them in my life."

That was what Updike was driving at. She had already primed him with her letters about wishing them dead, and therefore he had been ready to act on her wishes. "So you admit that you placed the idea of your parents' deaths in the mind of Jens Soering?" he asked, thinking he had boxed her in.

But she jumped away. "No, sir," she said.

He exhaled. "You did absolutely nothing. You said absolutely nothing. And you say that you did not want them dead. So you just ignored that statement, is that correct?"

"To a certain extent."

"To a certain extent!"

"What is your question then, sir?" she asked indignantly. "Excuse me, maybe I misunderstood."

"Let's just move on, Ms. Haysom," Updike mumbled in frustration. "I think I've plowed that ground, and I'm not getting anything but rocks."

He hoped to find more tillable soil in Colorado. Digging in his documents, he produced a copy of the letter Elizabeth had written Jens during the spring break in 1985, shortly before Derek and

Nancy had been murdered. On stationery from the Ramada Inn in Denver, Elizabeth had composed a fictional tale about how she had inherited valuable property in London from her cousin, Lady Astor, and about how her parents were wealthy but miserly and she would never get any of their money until they were dead. She wrote this, Updike emphasized, knowing that Jens was obsessed with financial security.

She nodded. "I tried to manipulate him in that letter," she acknowledged.

"Ah," said Updike, brightening. "You said that: 'Tried to manipulate.' "

"Unsuccessfully, too," she added hastily.

"At any rate, you are giving him an ultimatum here, aren't you? That the only resolution to the dilemma, the only one, the only way you could have everything, is to kill your parents. Isn't that what you were saying?"

"No, sir," she said, refusing to give ground. "What I'm trying to do in this letter is I'm trying to manipulate him."

"To do what?"

"To leave the university with me. That is why I go into this incredibly flamboyant and nonsensical description of how it's okay to leave, that everything's going to work out, that you can find money, do whatever is necessary."

Updike paced. He had to find a way to break through her resolve, a way around her evasions. "What you were doing was you were emphasizing your background, your heritage, your potential wealth to this young man who was concerned about financial security, weren't you?"

"No, sir," she began, then paused. She made a slight concession. "Well, yes, you're correct in a way," she told Updike, who welcomed the small victory. "I was emphasizing the fact that there was lots of money there. But I was emphasizing to him that that money would never be available to me."

"Unless your parents died?" he pressed.

She had given enough. She wasn't going to bow too much. "No," she said flatly.

Updike backed away slightly, preparing for another rush at the fortress wall. What she was doing, he suggested, was manipulating Jens.

She admitted that she was, and Updike considered that a major step forward. Encouraged, he pushed harder. "Your purpose, in this reference to the young man who's talked about blowing their brains out, is to encourage him to free you so the two of you will have the freedom and the wealth to do whatever you want."

She repelled the charge, denying that was her intent.

Well, why did she write that letter then? Updike all but screamed in frustration.

"I wrote it to manipulate him to leave the university with me," she said, happy with herself.

Updike silently cursed to himself. Trying to pin Elizabeth down was like trying to grab a handful of smoke.

"Two weeks later, Ms. Haysom, you were in the Washington Marriott, and Jens Soering was on his way to Loose Chippings." On his way to murder her parents, he added. "And now you are saying that this letter and the statements he made in February and the letters you wrote in December had nothing to do with it?"

Elizabeth refused to be cornered. Her strategy was first to evade, but when that was no longer viable, to deny. This time she denied. "No, I'm not saying that, sir."

What was she saying? Updike asked. She had already said she wanted her parents dead.

"I did not want them murdered," she repeated, insisting there was a difference between them being dead and them being killed. "I know to you who obviously are very logical and very clear-headed that doesn't make any sense," she said carefully. "I wanted my parents out of my life. I had this immature, ridiculous fantasy of them being dead. Not murdered. Not in actuality. Not in reality. My letters, my writings, they all have a very surreal and fantastic nature. It was in my head, and Jens made it reality. But it wasn't reality that I wanted."

"You wanted them *dead,*" Updike persisted.

"I wanted them dead *to me,*" she said. "I wanted them disconnected from me. I wanted them to be out of my life."

Updike was exasperated. "So this is just, oh, a lack of communication between you and Jens Soering, is that right?" he asked sarcastically.

Elizabeth was affronted. "I think that's a very gross understatement."

Updike shrugged. One more time, he told himself.

HE APPEALED TO HER SENSE OF LOGIC. THE STORY SHE WANTED HIM AND everyone else to believe, he pointed out, simply was not logical. Would she at least agree with that?

Yes, she conceded. Then she retreated into humility again. "You've said several times that I'm awfully bright. Perhaps that's an overestimation of my abilities."

Updike ignored that. Laboriously picking apart her latest version of what had happened in Washington, he pulled out several things that he could attack, statements he could point to and make her admit that she had lied to investigators.

"I know, sir," she admitted. "I lied."

That was a step in the right direction, he thought. "You're capable of lying and deceiving, should doing so meet your needs then?"

"I have lied, and I have deceived," she admitted.

"To suit your own purposes at the time?"

"Yes, sir."

But basically he was unable to shake her. She was especially stubborn about insisting on the different nuances between her wanting her parents dead but not wanting them murdered. "I'm sure you can tell from my letters that I lived in a world of fantasy to a large extent," she said. "I deceived people. I lied to them. I exaggerated things. I played roles. But I had never known anybody who was particularly violent or criminal. To kill somebody—it's so very definite and so very real. I just never imagined somebody could do that. That somebody *would* do that. It's just not something that people do. They don't go around killing other people even if they have talked about it, have written about it."

Updike was convinced she was evading again, that she knew exactly what Jens had had in mind when he had left her in

Washington and driven to Boonsboro. *"You* knew what he was going to do, didn't you?"

Elizabeth leaned forward, looking very intent. "What I want you to understand," she began in a school teacher-ish tone, "and I don't mean to minimize my guilt, is that what I did, what I said, what I failed to do—my irresponsibility, my manipulation of Jens—yes, in that I'm totally guilty. I'm totally responsible for my parents' deaths. I accept that. But what I want you to realize is that Jens acted of his own free will. He had a choice. He had a four-hour drive. No matter what I said to him before that, no matter what I had written to him in the months before that, he had a choice whether he killed my parents or not. He sat and talked with them. He had some kind of meal with them or something. He didn't *have* to do anything. Nobody forced him to do anything. And I never once believed that somebody like Jens could do something like that."

It was Updike's turn to clarify his position.

"Please don't misunderstand me," he said. "I'm not trying to minimize Jens Soering's guilt. And if I live long enough, the time's going to come when he's going to be here. His day will come, so I'm not trying to minimize his involvement. I'm trying to lay a foundation for the court to determine *your* involvement. That's why we're here."

Elizabeth nodded. "I understand that, sir."

50

UPDIKE CONTEMPLATED THE SITUATION, STARING AT THE WALL OVER JUDGE Sweeney's shoulder while he gathered his thoughts. This was his first and last chance to question Elizabeth. The law allowed considerable latitude when determining mitigation, so his inquiries could be broad and far-reaching. But just how broad, how far reaching, did he want to make his inquiries? His goal was to prove that Elizabeth was deeply involved in the murder of her parents. Even though she had pleaded guilty, her testimony was designed to absolve her of culpability. Updike's aim was to prove that that was not true—that there was no reason for Judge Sweeney to show leniency. The only mitigating factor that had not yet been discussed was her mental condition, but Updike did not see any problems from his end on that score. Still to come was testimony from a psychiatrist who had examined her, but Updike expected that to be simply another mitigation claim. She was not going to assert that she was legally insane even though her psychiatrist undoubtedly would say that she suffered from a certain amount of instability, enough anyway to reduce her accountability. What Updike needed to do before he let her off the stand for good was to hammer some more at her, see if he could rattle her enough to make her change her story yet again. He needed to get her to admit all the opportunities she had to influence Jens, to confess that there was a dialogue between them that centered on murdering her parents. So far he had not done that. He was not surprised at her reluctance to admit her involvement, but he was frustrated by her shrewdness, her ability to work her way out of a trap no matter how skillfully he thought he had sprung it. He took a deep breath. Time to get on with it, he told himself.

He decided to begin with the knife and her ever-changing tale about the possible murder weapon. Undeniably, Derek and Nancy had been killed with a knife. But since the weapon had not been found, investigators could only guess about it. They thought they had a good lead when Elizabeth volunteered that she had bought a martial arts–style knife for Jens on the morning of the murder. Then, inexplicably, she flip-flopped. On the stand, she testified that her original story had been a lie, a tale she and Jens had concocted as a loyalty test between themselves. Updike was still puzzled by this. How was he, or anyone, to know what was true? he asked her. Did she initially conceive of the story as part of her alibi? he asked.

Elizabeth pondered the question for several seconds. No, she said finally, the story about the knife had nothing to do with the alibi. "It was an admission of guilt," she said, explaining that Jens, when he feared he was going to be arrested, asked her to share the burden of the crime. The best way he could think of doing that was to have her become a part of the events that transpired. "I was supposed to say that I had bought the knife and that I had bought a can of mace and that I had given them to him and that I had made him go down there and do it."

She paused and looked at Updike, who was standing almost within arm's reach, waiting expectantly for her to continue. "That's what I was *supposed* to say," she added. "But when I actually came to saying it, I talked nonsense about his little brother's birthday and ended up saying that we both purchased it. However, I did say that I paid for it."

Updike shook his head. "Help me understand," he pleaded. To him, it made no sense because her alleged involvement did nothing to reduce Jens's responsibility. Even if she *had* bought it, he still was the one who used it. How did her story help him?

Elizabeth tried again to explain Jens's convoluted reasoning.

Her desire to make herself clear on this point was evident. She displayed more patience now than she had so far with any of the prosecutor's questions. Jens took the position, she said, that she had forced him to commit the murders. "He believes—as he has portrayed very convincingly—that he's an innocent young lad who was led astray by an older, more experienced woman." This had to be kept in mind, she said as she continued her explanation that he developed the idea that she should acknowledge her culpability in some fashion. "His point was that I was to shoulder the responsibility for what he had done, that I was in control of his actions." The best idea he could come up with for demonstrating this was her saying she was involved directly in the murders through the purchase of the knife.

Updike nodded. He understood what she was saying, he told her, but that story fell apart when she changed the other part of her story too. Her "knife" story worked only as long as she agreed that she had been manipulating Jens. If Jens had actually been manipulating her, as she said she later came to believe, why had he insisted on the knife story?

Elizabeth shook her head. That was the irony of it, she said. When she and Jens later underwent a role reversal, and he became the dominant party, it was he who began to manipulate her. It was then that he developed the belief that it helped him to have her admit to buying the knife. But he told her it was because she had manipulated him. "I believed very firmly that I had been the manipulator," she said. "I believed what Jens said, that I had made him do it. I believed that I was the cause of his actions." But then, she added, she realized that was not true. Her attempt to make him leave the university had not been successful, so she realized her influence had been minimal. "Since then," she said, "I have seen correspondence of his where he discusses deliberately manipulating me to believe those things."

Holy moly, Updike thought. Talk about intricate plots— wheels within wheels within wheels. Still, he remained unconvinced. But no matter whether he believed her or not, he could see no advantage in pursuing this issue further. "I see," he told her, jumping to a subject that had worried him from the first: motive.

IF JENS HAD INDEED BEEN MANIPULATING HER, HE HAD TO HAVE HAD A reason for what he did. What did *she* think that reason was?

Elizabeth was not as eager to answer that as she had been to respond to his queries about the knife. First, she said it was her belief that sooner or later Jens would have murdered someone. It had been bad luck that their paths had crossed and that she had unburdened herself to him about her frustrations with her parents. This had given him a target and an excuse.

Updike shook his head. Her story did not sound right to him. He invited her to try again.

And again she evaded him. "I've asked him that many times," she said, as if that were explanation enough.

Updike's patience was giving out. He gave her a withering look. Come on, he told her, she could do better than that. They were lovers, he pointed out. They traveled all over Europe and parts of Asia together. They shared a bed and all their secrets. Certainly, in all that time, the two of them talked about what had happened. "Did it ever occur to you," he asked sarcastically, "to say to Jens Soering, 'Why did you do it?' "

Yes, she said grudgingly, she had asked him that. The first time had been when they were in Lynchburg soon after the murders.

And what did he say? Updike asked impatiently. What was his answer?

He didn't say anything, she said. He just reached into his knapsack and pulled out a stack of papers. They were the letters she had written him.

Updike smiled inwardly. "Your letters did it then?" he said, struggling to contain his elation. "Okay, I won't argue with you there."

DURING HIS OPENING STATEMENT UPDIKE HAD SAID THERE WAS A WITNESS who claimed to have heard Elizabeth make a grotesque comment about her father's brains being splattered on the fireplace that she was cleaning. If he could get her to admit that she had been so unfeeling, the admission would show how little remorse she actually had about her parents' murders; it would give the lie to the story she told in court about how disturbed she had been about Derek's and Nancy's deaths. Was the witness right? Had she made such a statement?

Not exactly, Elizabeth said guardedly. She tried to evade an answer by claiming that she had been standing by the door, not the fireplace. When Updike contended it was why she had said it that was important, not where she was when she said it, she challenged his respect for the facts. "We're supposed to be dealing here with accuracy of what happened and what did not happen," she lectured.

Updike could not believe her arrogance. "Thank you, ma'am," he said, bowing slightly. "But you did make the statement nevertheless, didn't you?"

"No," she said coolly. "I did not make that particular statement."

Here we go again, Updike thought. Placing his hands on the witness box rail, he stared at her. "If you did not make it," he said just as coolly, "how do you know where it occurred?"

Elizabeth appeared not at all flustered. She said that her brother Howard had asked her to come to Loose Chippings to help clean up the bloodstains. She was working on the door when she saw several of her father's hairs glued to the surface with dried blood. When she saw that, she said, she gulped and announced that she thought she was going to be sick.

Updike looked at her closely. "How in the world did that get confused?" he asked. "How did it come out, 'Well, I'm just cleaning up Pop's brains'?"

"I did make some comment about these are the hairs of my father's head," she said. "Then I went to the bathroom, and I was sick."

Regardless of the exact words of the statement, Updike said, he was curious as to why she was there to begin with. When Updike had interviewed Howard Haysom, Howard had told him that going to clean up the house had been Elizabeth's idea, not his. Even though Howard was a surgeon and saw blood all the time, cleaning up the blood of his mother and stepfather was something else. He had suggested they hire a professional cleaning crew, but Elizabeth had insisted that they do it themselves.

"I want to make sure of this," he said. "You're saying that Howard Haysom, your brother, asked you to go there?"

"Yes," she said emphatically.

Updike made a mental note to be sure to ask Howard about that when he took the stand.

UPDIKE WAS FASCINATED BY ELIZABETH'S STATEMENTS CONCERNING JENS'S metamorphosis. He simply did not believe that a person could change so quickly, that one could go literally overnight from a submissive person to a domineering one, that after months of sexual inadequacy Jens could suddenly develop potency. He wanted Elizabeth to run through that one more time. Was it true, he asked her, that it was only on the night of the memorial service for her parents that she and Jens made love for the first time?

It was true, Elizabeth acknowledged, only if you could call what they did making love. After the memorial service they went to a friend's house to spend the night because they could not go back to Loose Chippings. She had been sleeping in a separate room with her college roommate when Jens awakened her and asked her to return with him to his bed. He said he was lonely and frightened. Thinking nothing of it, she said, she went with him since up to then he had been impotent. Because she was so upset by events, she had been taking sedatives, and when she got into Jens's bed, she fell asleep again immediately. Sometime later, she said, she awoke and Jens was making love to her.

"Making love to you?" Updike repeated.

"Well," she replied, "for want of a better term you could say *making love.*"

"Are you saying he raped you?" Updike asked, intrigued by her response.

"No," she said, she would not call it *rape* because she had not put up a struggle.

Updike shook his head sadly. "This is the man known to you as the murderer of your parents," he said. "The funeral service, the remorse that we have heard about, the attendance at the service for your slain parents must have had no effect on you, did it?"

To the contrary, Elizabeth answered heatedly, it had a very profound effect on her.

"Then how in the world could you lie in the same bed with the man who had killed them and make love to the man?"

She mea culpa-ed. "I don't know, sir. I'll never forgive myself, and I don't expect anyone else to either."

Updike thought he knew why. "The only logical explanation is that this lover had done as you requested," he said. "Isn't that it?"

She was not to be trapped. "No, sir," she said, glaring at him.

IT WAS ALMOST TWO O'CLOCK AND THEY HAD NOT YET TAKEN A BREAK FOR lunch. Elizabeth had been on the stand for nearly four hours. Updike was sure he was not going to get any more direct answers out of her than he had already, but there was still one question he wanted to ask, one issue that was haunting him. He wanted to know why *she* thought Derek and Nancy had been murdered. "Why did your parents die?" he asked.

She did not hesitate. "My parents died because Jens and I were obsessed with each other and he was jealous of anything else in my life."

Was that why he killed them? Updike asked. Out of jealousy?

Yes, she said. He killed them because he knew how important they were to her and because she had told him that she was reconciling with them. He feared that he was going to lose her.

Updike flipped through a copy of her May 8 session with Ricky Gardner. What she had just said was interesting, he said, but it was not what she had told Gardner when he asked her the same question. She had told the investigator that she believed Jens had killed them because he believed that Derek and Nancy were determined to break them up.

That was true, too, Elizabeth answered quickly. "They were making arrangements for all of us to leave Virginia and Jens did not like it."

Updike flipped through his papers some more. At another time, he said, she had claimed that her parents were murdered because *she* wanted her freedom. She asserted that her parents had controlled her siblings' lives and now they were trying to control hers as well. But she wanted them to leave her alone.

That was true as well, Elizabeth agreed. In fact she had said that earlier in the day.

"You felt that they were interfering with your life and you felt the only resolution was for them to be murdered?" Updike asked, anxious to clarify the issue for the record.

"No," Elizabeth shot back. "I didn't mention anything about murder. I said I wanted them to leave me alone." That may have been Jens's motive, she added, or at least one of them. But it was not hers. She steadfastly maintained that she had never wanted them killed.

Updike swallowed hard. He knew she was not going to give him an honest answer. "You're just trying to minimize your involvement," he said angrily. "Isn't that what you're trying to do?"

"No," she snapped, "that is *not* what I am trying to do."

All day Updike had been trying to provoke her into making an uncontrolled response. Now, just as he was about ready to give up, he had succeeded. She poured out a torrent of words about how badly she wanted Jens to be convicted of the deaths of her parents and how she had lied, particularly about the knife.

Updike's eyes widened in surprise. Before he could interrupt to ask about the knife, she told him.

She had told Gardner about the butterfly knife, she said, because Jens had told her he had used a steak knife to kill her parents. She was worried that if Jens came to trial and he had told her the truth about using a steak knife, his lawyers could argue that he had not been involved because the wounds on her parents' bodies could not have been made by the knife *she* described; therefore Jens would be liable to get off on a technicality.

Updike's head was spinning. Elizabeth Haysom was totally unpredictable, he told himself yet again. She could change her stories quicker than a camera flash. How could anyone tell when she was speaking the truth? He turned his attention back to her. She was still explaining her latest tale about the knife.

No matter what the murder weapon had been, Elizabeth said, she was convinced that Jens had planned to kill them. "When I came over here, I believed that if I was convicted of premeditating this murder with him, that he also would have to be convicted of premeditated murder and that he would not be able to give an insanity plea or to give a self-defense plea or to get a second degree murder conviction. I was trying to help you," she told Updike angrily.

That is not true, Updike thought. She is not trying to help me. She is trying to help make sure that Jens is convicted. And that she gets off as lightly as possible.

"I'm sorry if it appears I'm trying to minimize my guilt," she said. "I believe that I am thoroughly guilty, thoroughly responsible for what happened. I agree that I have betrayed, lied, and deceived, and I wouldn't be in this position if I had not done those things."

UPDIKE KNEW WHEN TO QUIT. HE COULD ASK HER QUESTIONS INTO NEXT week, and they would never get any closer to the truth than they had already. He felt he had made some points, not nearly as many as he had wanted to, but he was not going to get any further. I have to look at the proceedings objectively, he told himself. The only opinion in the courtroom that matters is Judge Sweeney's. I just hope he has not been fooled.

She could go, he said. He had no more questions. He slumped into his chair. He needed a breather. Elizabeth's psychiatrist was still to come, and he wanted to be as fresh as possible for him. He knew that was going to be another fight.

51

AT MIDAFTERNOON, JUST WHEN THE AFTER-LUNCH BLAHS WERE STARTING to settle in, Drew Davis decided to enliven the proceedings. He called the psychiatrist, C. Robert Showalter.

In answer to Davis's summons, the author of a lengthy psychiatric evaluation of Elizabeth strode briskly to the stand, jutting his chin and swinging his arms like a soldier on parade. A compact man with startlingly white hair covering the tops of his ears, Showalter had a florid, outdoorsy look that contrasted markedly with his expensive dark suit. His voice was pleasant and well-modulated, but when he opened his mouth, his speech was as distinctive as Elizabeth's, although in a different way. Elizabeth spoke pure English; Showalter's language was psychiatric jargon, liberally peppered with phrases such as *impetus stimulus* and *threshold criteria*.

In the beginning, though, he was understandable enough, explaining that he had been a practicing psychiatrist for twenty-four years, had testified in hundreds of court cases, and currently was associate medical director of the Institute of Law, Psychiatry, and Public Policy at the University of Virginia.

As far as Jones and Davis were concerned, Showalter was a star. He could be invaluable to their case if he could convince Judge Sweeney, as they hoped he would do, that Elizabeth had not been totally to blame for her actions because of a long-standing psychiatric condition. Next to Elizabeth herself, he was the defense's most important witness.

However, he did not rank as high in Updike's book. As the psychiatrist listed his credentials for the record in his resonant voice, Updike sat a few feet away with a deep frown on his forehead, angrily flipping through Showalter's thirty-nine page report. The defense had waited until the psychiatrist was seating himself in the witness box before giving the prosecutor a copy. The stratagem did not put Updike in the best of moods.

Just as Jones had done with Elizabeth, Davis treated Showalter gently and only occasionally gave him a verbal nudge or politely interrupted to get him back on track.

The first thing he wanted to make clear, Showalter said, was that Elizabeth's psyche was not so out of balance that she was not competent to stand trial. Nor had he found any indication, he added, that she had been sufficiently disturbed at the time the crimes were committed to meet the legal definition of insanity. He and the other scientists at the institute who examined Elizabeth or interviewed her friends and family members came away feeling that she was a very bright, articulate young woman. Not that she didn't have problems. Serious problems. She did, in fact, show symptoms of a serious psychiatric "dysfunction" known as a *borderline personality disorder.*

In layman's language, *borderline* means neither here nor there. Someone on the borderline is in the middle. In psychiatric terms, however, there is nothing in the middle about a borderline personality disorder. In mental health jargon, *borderline* has a much more rigid meaning. A borderline personality disorder, the psychiatrist explained, is a condition that develops early in life but commonly does not become apparent until the person reaches puberty or later. A person suffering from a borderline personality disorder commonly has trouble maintaining personal or social relationships. Generally, he or she does not function very well in day-to-day life. He or she has a lot of hang-ups.

Personality disorders, he said, differ from each other in the symptoms displayed by the sufferer. All the symptoms of all the disorders are enumerated in a huge tome called the *DSM III,* the third edition of the *Diagnostic and Statistical Manual.* It is the mental health worker's Bible. Symptoms of a person suspected of suffering from a personality disorder are listed by a diagnostician, then the listed symptoms are compared with the ones inventoried by the *DSM III.* The book catalogs eight clearly identifiable criteria for a borderline personality disorder. Mental health workers agree that anyone exhibiting five of those eight criteria can be judged as suffering from the disorder. Elizabeth, Showalter said, exhibited seven of them.

She tended, for example, to judge others in the extreme. Either the person could do no right or the person could do no wrong. "Her mother was seen as seductively attentive yet critically rejecting," Showalter said. "Melinda was an understanding albeit possessive friend with whom Elizabeth lived and traveled, and then from whom she abruptly separated. Jens was her passionate paramour with whom she played out highly charged physical and emotional scenes." In each of the relationships Elizabeth found herself bouncing between submissive and dependent or resentful and manipulative.

She was also impulsive to the extreme; she was frequently depressed; she mutilated her own body—once, at age eleven by trying to cut away a mole on her chest, and at other times by slicing her wrists or sticking pins in her feet. She suffered from a poor self-image and a confused sexual orientation; she often felt lonely or bored; and she felt incapable of standing up to her mother. This last compulsion was particularly strong for Elizabeth, Showalter said. Instead of rebelling against Nancy, Elizabeth "felt compelled to placate and appease her, agreeing even at one point to pose nude for her upon request." The same compulsion, he added, made her accept "physical beatings" from Jens and "participate in his bizarre sexual interests."

The only criterion of the borderline personality disorder that she failed to exhibit, Showalter said, was an inability to control her anger. With prompting from Drew Davis, Showalter agreed that this probably indicated that Elizabeth was basically a nonviolent person.

Despite such a plethora of psychiatric problems, Elizabeth's real troubles did not begin until she met Jens Soering.

JENS AND ELIZABETH FIT TOGETHER WELL INTELLECTUALLY, SHOWALTER said. Indeed, they fit together too well for their own good. One of their favorite activities was playing "head games" in which they would try to work out extremely difficult, perhaps unsolvable problems. One of those head games included plotting several murders, such as those of her parents and Jens's parents. Talking about these things helped relieve "tension" for Elizabeth, Showalter said. It helped to bring her "a little closer to a reasonable level of psychological functioning."

Despite their discussions, Showalter said, in his opinion Elizabeth never felt that Jens would actually kill her parents. Murder was not reality to her—murder was "something that happened in a metaphorical, fanciful mental life."

Davis asked Showalter why he thought Elizabeth was so loyal to Jens after the murders, why she stood by him and made alibies for him.

The psychiatrist replied that her doing so proved a basic tenet of the mental health fields—namely, that to some people negative attention was better than no attention at all. "She so craved and was so starved for some type of relationship that the negative aspects of the relationship were somehow denied or attenuated to a level where they could be tolerated," he said. "Her fear of being alone, her fear of being unloved, was so intense that she paid virtually any price to have a friend."

During Elizabeth's testimony there was a lot of discussion about Jens manipulating Elizabeth and Elizabeth manipulating Jens. Who, Davis asked, did Showalter think was the dominant party in the relationship?

Showalter showed no hesitation at all. "There is no question in my mind," he said, "that throughout this relationship Mr. Soering was the dominant, the stronger of the two personalities." This, he said, was made abundantly clear by the Neil Woodall letter. In it, he said, Jens clearly outlined his philosophy on a number of things, especially on his relationship with Elizabeth. "I think that this letter should very clearly establish the fact that Mr. Soering saw himself as the sort of prime mover and certainly as a self-contained young man fully capable of carrying out whatever deeds or acts he wanted to do," he said.

Showalter also had an opinion on Jens's motive in killing Derek and Nancy. "I think after extensive research and study, it's my impression that Mr. Soering carried out the murders largely motivated by his fear that he was losing Elizabeth."

Jim Updike was fidgeting in his chair. Having finished skimming Showalter's report, he listened skeptically as the psychiatrist made every explanation he could for Elizabeth. What really struck the prosecutor, Updike said in the courtroom, was the similarity between the points Showalter made in his presentation and the points Elizabeth had made in her testimony. Already frustrated by Elizabeth's dogged evasiveness, irritated by the defense ploy not to give him a copy of Showalter's report until the psychiatrist was literally on the stand, and bothered by the similarities in the testimony, Updike could hardly wait to get his shot at Showalter. He did not have to wait long.

52

FOR WHAT SEEMED LIKE A LONG TIME, UPDIKE AND SHOWALTER SIMPLY stared at each other. It was not love at first sight. As a veteran expert witness, Showalter had seen his share of highly aggressive prosecutors. He was not intimidated by Jim Updike. For his part, Updike was unconvinced by Showalter's explanations of Elizabeth's psychiatric condition. The psychiatrist was too glib to suit Updike, his judgments too unpersuasive. Showalter was not the first psychiatrist Updike had cross-examined, and he was not going to be cowed by what he considered to be Showalter's elusiveness.

Updike was entitled to throw the first blow. Slowly he walked around the table and stood close to the psychiatrist, who glared up at him. "You've made some rather broad statements here today, haven't you?" Updike drawled. "I mean, you've not only offered a psychological analysis of the defendant, but you've offered an analysis of the facts of our case as well, haven't you?"

Showalter was tense but unperturbed. "No," he said, locking eyes with Updike. "By no means."

It promised to be a bloody fight.

THERE WAS NOT MUCH OF SHOWALTER'S TESTIMONY THAT UPDIKE DID NOT attack, from the way the report was compiled to the conclusions it drew. Updike was particularly critical of the way the psychiatrist had described Elizabeth's position in what Updike felt were simplistic terms. Showalter had been too eager, Updike said, to conclude that the entire plot to kill Derek and Nancy had been conceived and carried out by Jens. "It seems to me what you're saying is that Ms. Haysom had nothing to do with this really, other than through some mere fantasies," Updike said. It also seemed to him, he continued, that Showalter felt that Elizabeth had not participated in the attempt to create an alibi. If Showalter were successful in advancing that opinion, Updike believed, he could destroy the prosecution's case against Elizabeth as an accessory before the fact. He leaned close to Showalter. "Do you feel she had *any* participation in advance of the murders?" he asked belligerently.

The psychiatrist was not flustered. In his opinion, he said, Elizabeth's participation occurred primarily at the "head game" level, but even that left her with a huge load of guilt. "She feels intensely guilty," he added.

Updike paced. Turning on his heel, he fired another question. "What you're saying is that she played some mind games and that those were misconstrued by Mr. Soering. Is that it?"

Showalter, who had been intently following Updike's progress around the room, agreed with the prosecutor's assessment. Either that, he said, or he had acted upon their joint fantasies when Elizabeth had not expected him to.

"So you don't think she encouraged him at all?" Updike asked.

"Well," Showalter allowed, "that depends on how you define encourage."

UPDIKE WAS BOILING. HE COULD NOT UNDERSTAND HOW SHOWALTER could have examined any substantial amount of documentation in the case, interviewed the people involved, particularly Elizabeth, and come away with such conclusions. It was obviously crucial to his case that he discredit Showalter's findings. He was going to do this, apparently, by showing first of all that the material in the doctor's report was incomplete.

In long strides he made his way to the prosecution table and picked up his copy of the psychiatrist's report. Thumbing through it, he called out the names of people interviewed in connection with the study. When he reached the end, he looked up at Showalter and asked if he personally had talked to them. Showalter said he had not, that they had been interviewed by members of the institute's staff. Updike nodded. Turning back to the report, he read the list of documents, noting that the report enumerated thirty-five. He asked Showalter if he knew what any of them said, citing particularly a document identified as an affidavit from him. Showalter said he did not remember.

"Was it my grocery list?" he barked at Showalter, "Or did it have some pertinence to this case?"

Everything listed had some pertinence to the case, Showalter responded. "That's why it's there."

That was what Updike was hoping he would say. "No, sir," he fired back. "That's not why it's there. That affidavit was required by the State Department to state the law of this Commonwealth for purposes of extradition. It had nothing at all to do with this woman's psychological status at any time in her life. Yet it's listed here, and it doesn't even seem that you know what's in it."

Updike looked at the list again. What about Ricky Gardner? he asked. The report listed an affidavit from the investigator as being among the documents. Did Showalter know what it said?

Showalter admitted he did not. "I'm not going to play that game," he told Updike angrily.

Updike pounced. "I'm not asking you to play a game," he said. "I just want to know the essence for these wide, far-reaching opinions that you've stated."

His opinions, Showalter responded, dealt only with Elizabeth's psychiatric condition.

HAVING MADE HIS POINT ABOUT THE DOCUMENTS, UPDIKE MOVED ON TO what he considered the most vital issue: that Showalter had based his opinion on Elizabeth's mental state almost exclusively on what Elizabeth herself had told him. If he could get Showalter to admit that, he felt, he would be able to demolish the report because everyone in the courtroom had seen what a changeable, unreliable witness Elizabeth was. But Showalter himself was a savvy witness and would not be easily trapped. Updike was going to have to hammer away at the report item by item and hope when he finished that Judge Sweeney would agree with his assessment of its unreliability.

Turning to Showalter, Updike abruptly asked the psychiatrist why he had assumed that Nancy had *forced* Elizabeth to pose for the nude photographs later found in Nancy's bureau.

Elizabeth told him that, he said.

That's what he meant, Updike shouted. *"Elizabeth told you.* And based upon that you assumed that she was telling the truth and you used that in formulating your opinion, didn't you?"

Showalter was not to be that easily cornered. That was only one tiny bit of information that went into the report, he said. There were many other pieces as well.

FOR THE BETTER PART OF AN HOUR, UPDIKE AND SHOWALTER BATTLED. Often, the conflict went beyond the give-and-take expected when a prosecutor is cross-examining an unfriendly witness; it was obvious that Updike and Showalter did not like each other. The animosity was evident.

At one point Updike questioned Showalter about his frequent use of the word *metaphorical* to describe Elizabeth's actions. She metaphorically plotted their murders. She metaphorically hated her father. She metaphorically encouraged Jens. "What is it, Dr. Showalter," Updike asked sarcastically, "that indicates all this was metaphorical? Mr. and Mrs. Haysom are not metaphorically dead."

Showalter conceded his point.

AT ANOTHER TIME, UPDIKE HAMMERED AT SHOWALTER ABOUT THE BASIS for determining when Elizabeth was telling the truth. How could he tell? the prosecutor asked.

Showalter said he made his judgment after hours of interviewing and of assessing and evaluating her responses.

Updike reminded Showalter that he had interviewed her for

hours on the witness stand and all he got was a number of different answers. "It comes across to me," Updike said, "that the truth is the same every time you tell it, and when she's telling things different ways each time, she's lying." Thinking to zing the psychiatrist, Updike added, "And she is capable of lying, isn't she?"

A grin flickered across Showalter's lips. "Anyone is capable of lying, Mr. Updike."

THEY HAD BEEN GOING AT IT FOR ABOUT THIRTY MINUTES WHEN Showalter agreed for at least the second time that much of the information on which he based his conclusion had come from Elizabeth. When he said that, Updike appeared to be relieved. His tone softened slightly. At least it was less combative. "You've got this extremely bright young woman," he said almost conspiratorially, "who knows what she's charged with, knows she's pleaded guilty, and knows that you're going to be down here one day testifying in her defense. And she has this very good capability of deception as you've already admitted. Talking to her for a few hours, it's right hard to tell whether she's deceiving you or not, isn't it?"

"It can be difficult," Showalter agreed. Then he qualified his statement. "But it's less difficult for a clinician, I think, than for someone else."

That set Updike off again. "What is it about being a clinician," he said aggressively, "that tells you whether she is lying?"

"A clinician has a special ability to listen to a case history, to listen to the facts, to knit it together, and make it mean something," Showalter said.

"I got the idea," Updike said drily, "that's what the judge was for."

ONE OF THE THINGS THAT WAS REALLY EATING AT UPDIKE ABOUT SHOWALTER'S testimony was how closely his opinion of events paralleled Elizabeth's. Updike explained to Showalter, who had not been allowed in the courtroom while Elizabeth was testifying, that when Elizabeth got on the stand, she changed her story from what she had told investigators. Rather than admitting her involvement in manipulating Jens, in formulating an alibi, and in buying the knife, as she had to Beever, Gardner, and Wright, she got on the stand and said it was all Jens's fault. And that, said Updike, sounded almost exactly like what Showalter said when he testified. The reason she changed her story, Updike said pointedly, may be because Elizabeth had been talking to the psychiatrist.

Showalter was incensed. "That has nothing to do with this," he said angrily. "That's an excellent demonstration of sort of an *in vivo* or real life demonstration of what I've been talking about here all afternoon, Mr. Updike. You witnessed a clinical phenomenon!"

Updike was not sure whether to laugh or blow up. "A clinical phenomenon!" he exploded. "So that's what that was."

FIVE MINUTES LATER, WHEN BOTH HAD COOLED DOWN, UPDIKE AGAIN raised the issue about how Elizabeth had changed her story once she got into the courtroom. Why, he asked the psychiatrist, did he think she had done that?

"I wonder why, too," Showalter said, "because she's not asking for mercy. She feels very guilty and feels that probably the rest of her life should be spent as a sacrifice, offering herself as a sacrifice for her involvement in the death of her parents."

It appeared to him, Updike said, that the answer got right back to Elizabeth's interviews with Showalter. Maybe the psychiatrist had not been trying to influence her intentionally, Updike said, but since Elizabeth was so bright she might have picked up on the psychiatrist's feelings on her own.

The inference infuriated Showalter. "I would beg to disagree with that," he said icily.

Updike was surprised. Why is it so impossible that he telegraphed his feelings, Updike wanted to know.

"Simply because we don't fashion defenses," Showalter said haughtily. "That's not my job."

UPDIKE WAS SATISFIED WITH THE WAY THINGS HAD WORKED OUT. WITH one last glare at the psychiatrist, he strolled back to his table. "Thank you, Dr. Showalter. I don't have any more questions."

AS SOON AS UPDIKE SAT DOWN, DREW DAVIS POPPED TO HIS FEET. EAGER to defend his witness, he pointed out that Elizabeth had admitted to Gardner on May 11 that she had made up the story about going with Jens to buy a knife. That was weeks before she had met with Showalter. "Apparently everything the prosecution says about her formulating this afterthought story can't all be accurate, can it?"

"Absolutely not," Showalter said. "I would take strong issue with even the embryonic notion that conveys."

Imagine, Davis continued, that Elizabeth had come to him as a patient off the street and not as a woman charged with involvement in the murder of her parents. What would be his diagnosis then?

"I have a notion," Showalter said, "and this is pure speculation and I want to be very clear about that. But had I met Ms. Haysom as an attending psychiatrist in student health at the University of Virginia in her first semester, I would have been able to make very clearly and unequivocally the diagnosis of a borderline personality disorder."

THAT GOT UPDIKE EXCITED ALL OVER AGAIN. HE PLUNGED BACK INTO THE fight. What did having a borderline personality disorder have to do with the murders of her parents? Updike demanded, springing to his feet.

"It's offered as an explanation," Showalter said coolly.

But Updike was aroused. He had gotten so carried away earlier, he said, that he had forgotten to ask Showalter about his comments on Jens. When the psychiatrist testified that he thought Jens was the dominant figure in the relationship, did he mean before or after the murders?

Showalter said he was not distinguishing.

Updike said he was puzzled. Elizabeth had carefully made the

distinction at one point, saying that she thought she had manipulated Jens before the murders, but afterwards he had manipulated
her. It was important that the distinction be observed, Updike
felt, because Elizabeth had pleaded guilty to being an accessory
before the fact. That meant that she had acknowledged that she
was involved *before* the murders. He asked Showalter why he did
not make such a distinction.

Showalter backed off. "I can't distinguish," he said. "It would
be totally inappropriate for me to speculate further on the personality characteristics of Mr. Soering. I've never met him."

That response made Updike happy. That was the point he was
trying to make. Showalter had just helped Updike weaken his
own testimony. Updike pointed out that the fact that he had
never interviewed Jens did not stop the psychiatrist from testifying that he thought Jens killed the Haysoms because he was
afraid of losing Elizabeth.

"That was a very reasonable interpretation," Showalter coun-
tered. "It fits with this balance between control, maintaining
control, losing control, etcetera. Clinically, it fits together beauti-
fully."

"Clinically?" Updike asked.

Showalter nodded.

"Clinically doesn't do Nancy and Derek Haysom much good,
does it?" Updike said.

"Unfortunately not," Showalter agreed. "You are so correct."

$$53$$

Dr. Showalter was the defense's last witness, but Updike had witnesses to call in rebuttal. The first was Dr. Howard Haysom, Nancy's older son by her first marriage and Elizabeth's half-brother. Updike called him so that Howard could contradict two points Elizabeth had made. The first concerned her allegation that she was raped when she was a ten-year-old attending school in Switzerland.

Howard said he had talked to Elizabeth about that as recently as March 1985, when she went skiing with him in Colorado. He and Elizabeth were riding a lift to the top of a mountain, Howard said, when he remembered the incident in Switzerland. He had not heard the story directly from her before, and he wanted to try to build a closer bond to her, so he asked her about it. She told him that a man had indecently exposed himself to her. She said the man had been standing on the other side of a wire fence at the time.

"She made no indication to you that she'd been raped?" Updike asked.

"No," Howard answered emphatically.

The other point the prosecutor wanted to discuss with Howard Haysom was the statement Elizabeth had made about Howard asking her to help clean up the house in which her parents had been killed.

"Elizabeth Haysom testified that she went there and participated in the cleaning of the house because you asked her to," said Updike. "Is that true?"

He said it was not. "I didn't require that Elizabeth be in the house at all." He said he and Elizabeth's other half-brother, Veryan, had been discussing plans to hire a commercial cleaning crew to take care of the job when Elizabeth interrupted. "She said, 'Why don't we just go out and get some buckets and scrubbing brushes?' I was aghast and shaken by that. I'm a physician. I'm used to seeing a lot of blood. I've seen more than my share, but here was my twenty-year-old sister suggesting something that really astonished me."

He said they did hire commercial cleaners, but Elizabeth was unhappy with the way they did the job and went herself to rewipe the front door.

"If she testified that she went to the house because you asked her to, then that would be an untrue statement, wouldn't it?"

"That's her perception of what I probably said. I do not recall specifically requiring her presence to clean up the house."

As he had done earlier with Veryan Haysom, Updike asked Howard what he thought Elizabeth's punishment should be.

"You know," he said pensively, "I think that this revolves upon one thing and that is, is Elizabeth remorseful. It's my judgment that she is not. The reason for this is that she continues, I think, to tell untrue statements, give twists, spins to pieces of information that are favorable to her but that are not true. I think that she has lied to me in the past and, frankly, continues to lie. I personally am not satisfied with the explanation that her guilty plea provided. I think Elizabeth was in the house at the time of the crime, and I have reasons for that, too."

Updike knew what those reasons were—Howard had told him before. He claimed that he had talked to his mother a few days before she was killed and she had mentioned that she and Derek were expecting Elizabeth and Jens that weekend and that Elizabeth had promised "to do something important for us." She had not elaborated. Also, he had said, he did not think his parents would have let Jens into the house unless Elizabeth were with him. Finally, there was the issue of some documents from Derek mailed to Veryan Haysom in Nova Scotia. The envelope containing the papers was postmarked in Washington on April 1, apparently two days after Derek and Nancy had been killed in Lynchburg, some two hundred miles away. How that document got a Washington postmark on that particular date was one of the unsolved mysteries still haunting the case.

Updike did not want to get into these issues at the hearing. By accepting Elizabeth's pleas to being an accessory before the fact, he had given up claim to trying to establish that she had indeed been present when Derek and Nancy were murdered. Despite Howard's apparent eagerness to discuss those points, Updike cut him off.

ANOTHER OF HIS REBUTTAL WITNESSES WAS RICHARD HAYSOM, AN architect from Calgary, Howard's full brother and Elizabeth's half-brother. Younger than Howard by a year, Richard was ten years older than his half-sister. Richard Haysom said he probably was the closest to Elizabeth both chronologically and emotionally.

Updike asked him the same question he had asked Veryan and Howard, carefully wording it so it would not appear that he was asking his witnesses to usurp the judge's function in setting the sentence. "Do you have any feelings that you wish to express regarding the disposition of this case?"

"Firstly," Richard replied carefully, "I'd like to establish that I'm not here for any vindictive reasons. I also wish to tell the court that today I still love my sister very much. But I feel we have an obligation under the circumstances, and because of the heinous crime that's been committed here, we have an obligation to society to show what the consequences of such crimes are. Therefore, I would want to see the most severe penalty possible."

Elizabeth, who had been sitting hunched over the defense table with her head in her left hand, looking down as though to escape the slap of the words, showed no reaction to Richard's pronouncement. A few minutes later, when she was being led from the courtroom at the end of the day's session, Richard leaned over the rail separating the spectators from the participants and kissed her gently on the cheek. She did not turn or acknowledge the act; she merely kept walking as though it had not occurred.

ON THURSDAY, OCTOBER 8, THE DAY AFTER THE PROSECUTION AND defense made their closing statements, Judge Sweeney was ready to pass his sentence. For the session Elizabeth abandoned her dresses in favor of a striped blue blouse and a bulky blue and beige crew-necked sweater. Sitting with Jones on her right and Davis on her left, she focused on the bare tabletop and ducked her chin as Judge Sweeney, who had remained remarkably silent during the hearing, leaned forward and shuffled the papers in front of him. Slowly and deliberately, he began to read from a typewritten document he had prepared for the session.

In his twenty-two years on the bench, the judge said, it was not often that he lost sleep over a case in his court. But Elizabeth Haysom's case had been an exception; it had caused him considerable apprehension. After reading all the documents that had been filed in the case, including her letters, and after listening to her in court for most of two days he had concluded that she was a "sensitive, poised, gifted, intelligent, articulate person." It was these very qualities, in fact, that made his job more arduous. "It is difficult to pass judgment on someone whose IQ probably exceeds your own," he said.

Still, he added, he had to consider the nature of the charges. She had pleaded guilty to two offenses, each of which carried a maximum sentence of life in prison. The fact that she had pleaded guilty threw a special light on the proceedings. The testimony presented during the hearing dealt only with the background of the case, as it should, and not with the crime itself. "Background testimony invokes sympathy for the defendant, but it cannot be used to lessen the seriousness of the crimes committed and admitted," he said.

Updike and Gardner were not alone in their frustration in trying to find a motive for the murders. Judge Sweeney confessed that he, too, was unable to determine *why* Derek and Nancy were killed. "We are left only with the feeling that the case is a grotesque monument to inappropriate response to parental hatred," he said, implying that he felt that this was an inadequate description but that he was unable to offer a better one.

In reviewing what he had read and heard, Sweeney said, he had concluded that there were three mitigating factors in the case. One was that the prosecutor did not feel that Elizabeth had actually taken part in the crimes. Otherwise he would have charged her with murder. But just because she was physically absent when the murders took place did not mean that she was not culpable. "I am convinced," he said, "that the crimes would not have occurred except for her involvement. Simply stated, I think that her parents would be alive today except for what she did and didn't do."

The second mitigating factor was her decision not to fight extradition and, despite attempts by her lawyers to convince her otherwise, to plead guilty. "This is the first step in rehabilitation," he said.

The third factor had to do with how her brothers regarded her possible punishment. He regarded it as significant that they disagreed. Although they did not question her guilt, each had a differing opinion on how Elizabeth should be dealt with. Veryan was more forgiving, while Howard and Richard were in favor of a long sentence.

He had been impressed, he continued, by Elizabeth's accomplishments and her potential. At the same time, he realized, her punishment must fit the crime, not her background. One thing that still bothered him was that he did not have a clear idea of what type of person Elizabeth was at that time. Before she confessed, she had had a number of perverse attributes. At various times, he said, she had been a liar, a cheat, a manipulator, and a drug abuser. For *that* Elizabeth Haysom, he said, he had no sympathy whatsoever. That Elizabeth deserved all the punishment the law allowed. However, he felt there also had been some changes within her, that maybe there was a *new* Elizabeth. "For that person, if indeed there is one, I feel sympathy as a fellow human being. And I feel sorry that she probably wasted a promising career."

He said that he agreed with witnesses who believed that many of Elizabeth's accusations against her parents probably were exaggerated or untrue. That included the vicious rumors of mother-daughter incest. On that score he did not believe Elizabeth had always told the truth, but he recognized that she had partially conceded her lies when she testified.

Looking over his half-glasses, he fixed his gaze on Elizabeth, who was sitting quietly between her two lawyers, her hands clasped in front of her, almost as if in prayer. In an avuncular voice he told her that he was ready to read her sentence and she could either stand or remain seated. She decided to keep her chair. Sweeney nodded. Speaking quickly and loudly, he sentenced her to forty-five years in prison on each count, a total of ninety years since the sentences would run consecutively. Under Virginia law she would be eligible for parole in 1999. There was no other recourse; guilty pleas cannot be appealed.

Elizabeth did not react when he read the sentence. She sat quietly, staring at her clasped hands.

Still in a kindly voice, Sweeney explained to her that the prison she would be going to was one of the best in the state. "I have visited there several times," he said. "It is a prison, but it is a humane prison where you will be treated well and where you can receive counseling if needed."

When he finished, Elizabeth, still looking down, rose slowly and stuck her arms out, wrists together, for the handcuffs offered by a deputy. Dry-eyed, she walked out of the room and down the steps of the courthouse. On the roofs of nearby buildings, clearly visible against the autumn sky, were sharpshooters Sheriff Wells had posted "just in case."

Epilogue

WITHIN HOURS AFTER HE HAD SENTENCED ELIZABETH, JUDGE SWEENEY'S avuncular feelings began to disintegrate; he began wondering if he might not have let her off too easily. The most he could have given her was two life terms, which on the books was not much greater than the two 45-year sentences he had decided upon. But in practical terms she might, under the sentences he handed down, be back on the street much sooner than he originally had anticipated. With two life terms she would have had to serve at least twenty years before she was eligible for parole. With the sentences he gave her, though, she could be out in twelve years, maybe less if she proved to be an exemplary prisoner. The more he thought about it, the more he was convinced he had to do something. On October 15, 1987, exactly a week after sentencing, Sweeney did an unusual thing. For one of the few times in his entire career he wrote to the state parole board. He was worried, he told the board, that years down the road his intentions regarding Elizabeth Haysom might be misconstrued. He feared that the fact that he had not given her the maximum sentence might be interpreted to mean that he favored some leniency for her. He wanted to make it clear that he did not.

He realized, he wrote, that the most he could do was make a

recommendation to the board because anything else would be beyond his jurisdiction. However, as the sentencing judge familiar with all the aspects of the case, he had strong feelings about the punishment. "Based upon the seriousness of the charges and the heinous nature of the crimes, I strongly feel that Elizabeth Haysom should not receive early release," he wrote. "I think that she should be required to serve a substantial portion of the sentence which I gave her."

AFTER SENTENCING, ELIZABETH WAS SENT TO THE PRISON AT GOOCHLAND where she quickly settled in, ordering some elegant envelopes and embossed letterhead that gave no clue as to the real nature of her current address or occupational status. On heavy off-white paper, in tasteful gray letters, it says simply:

Elizabeth R. Haysom
P.O. Box 1
Goochland, VA 23063
U.S.A.

But the institution dulls the effect by stamping the backs of the envelopes with the message: "Department of Corrections has neither censored nor inspected this item."

Like Holloway, Goochland is a campuslike prison. Except it is more so. There are no high fences or massive buildings that hold tier after tier of cells. At Goochland, there are self-contained living units, each with its own kitchen and dining hall. The prisoners live in "rooms." As recently as the summer of 1989, the population of the prison was 535, which was above capacity. Elizabeth's unit contained fifty-three women, which was too many to allow every prisoner to have a "room" to herself. Nevertheless, Elizabeth managed it. For recreation, there are tennis courts, a gym, a ball field, and, particularly attractive to Elizabeth, a library with more than ten thousand books.

The down side, if it can be called that, is that at Goochland every prisoner has to work. Authorities would not say what Elizabeth's job is. They also would not discuss her conduct or reveal how she gets along with fellow inmates. In other prisons and jails in which she has been held, however, Elizabeth has always been a praiseworthy prisoner, and there is no reason to suspect she is behaving differently at Goochland. Especially not if she is working, despite Sweeney's letter, toward early release.

ACROSS THE ATLANTIC, JENS SOERING CONTINUED TO VIGOROUSLY FIGHT his extradition.

On June 30, 1988, long after Elizabeth settled in at Goochland, the House of Lords in London rejected Jens's appeal of the magistrate court's decision ordering him held pending extradition. Eight days later, with his last appeal in British courts out of the way, Jens filed a motion with the European Commission of Human Rights. It also was intended to keep him from being sent back to Virginia.

Just as Britain has an extradition treaty with the United States, it also has a treaty with the Council of Europe, a group composed at that time of twenty-two Western European countries, including West Germany. Jens claimed that his extradition to Virginia would violate rights that are guaranteed him under the terms of the treaty with the Council. Interestingly, Jens claimed his rights were subject to violation *not* because he might be executed but because he might have to wait for six years or more for the sentence to be carried out. Jens's lawyers called this situation the "death row phenomenon." The real phenomenon was that the claim got as far as it did.

DESPITE THIS NEW APPEAL, ON AUGUST 3, LESS THAN A MONTH LATER, JENS was ordered extradited to Bedford County. The extradition never occurred. Jens was removed from his cell at Brixton Prison and was on the verge of being put on an airplane bound for the United States when he suffered a mental collapse. His extradition was postponed at least until the Human Rights Commission decided whether it would hear Jens's claim.

On August 5 Jens was transferred to a prison hospital. Dr. D. Somekh of Cane Hill Hospital, in the suburb of Coulsdon, Surrey, a psychiatrist who had been visiting with Jens on and off since June 1987, was called in to examine him.

In a report he filed later, Somekh said that Jens had told him several times that he was convinced that if he were returned to Virginia for trial, he would be convicted of capital murder and sentenced to death. Worse than a speedy execution, he said, was the prospect of waiting on death row for his date with the executioner. He feared he would be an outcast among the other prisoners because of his nationality and his social class and that he would be subject to attack from other prisoners because of his race and relatively small stature. He was particularly terrified about possible homosexual assaults because that also would expose him to AIDS, which might kill him before the executioner.

Reacting to these fears, Jens began to behave obsessively. He insisted, for instance, on telling his lawyers at length how to handle his defense and he spent weeks writing down every detail he could remember about his relationship with Elizabeth from the time they met until their arrest. He was beginning to crack under the strain.

Occasionally, Somekh wrote, "Soering has begged me to supply him covertly with means whereby he would be able to kill himself at very short notice if he was informed that he was about to be taken to the United States."

UNWILLING TO TAKE A CHANCE ON JENS COMMITTING SUICIDE, PRISON officials ordered him kept in the hospital on the potential suicide ward. He remained there until November 1988, when the Human Rights Commission's announcement that it would listen to his claim buoyed his spirits.

Two months later the commission issued its ruling. It said by a narrow six-to-five vote that it did not think the alleged existence of the "death row phenomenon" violated the Council of Europe treaty. Instead of clearing the way for his extradition, however, the commission kicked the entire matter upstairs. It recommended that Jens take his complaints to the commission's parent body, the European Court of Human Rights.

ON APRIL 24, 1989, WITH TWENTY OF ITS TWENTY-TWO MEMBERS present, the court held *its* hearing on the complaints at its headquarters in Strasbourg, France, on the Franco-German border. Most of the members of the court are retired judges, lawyers, or academics. The posts are elective, and the terms run for nine years. Unlike rulings from the commission, decisions from the court are generally accepted as binding among the member nations.

Before holding its hearing, the group agreed to allow Germany to have a representative argue its claim that Jens should be extradited to his home country. That marked the first time in the organization's history that a third party not directly involved in the dispute was allowed to participate.

The main issue before the court was the same as that before the commission: If Jens were returned to Virginia, would his civil rights be violated because of the "death row phenomenon?"

All day they argued. The speakers for the three parties involved were Colin Nicholls, one of Britain's premiere experts on extradition, representing Jens; the German representative, Jans Meyer-Ladewig; and Sir Patrick Mayhew, the United Kingdom's attorney general who also represented the United States, which was not a member of the council and could not take part in the discussion.

First of all, Nicholls maintained, if Jens were extradited to Virginia, there was a very good chance that he would wind up on death row. "He has confessed to the murders," Nicholls pointed out. "And the circumstances of the killings strongly indicate that the jury and judge will find them sufficiently vile to result in the applicant being sentenced to death."

Once he arrived on death row, Nicholls continued, Jens could expect to remain there for eight years or more until his appeals were exhausted. "The applicant was eighteen years and four months old at the time of the killings. At the time of the execution, if the proceedings run their course, he will be approximately thirty. The person executed at the age of thirty will be a different person from the eighteen-year-old alleged author of the crime."

In addition to the age factor, Nicholls contended, there was the question of Jens's mental state, the psychiatric syndrome he was suffering from while he allegedly was under Elizabeth's domination. That factor, Nicholls reminded the Court, would not be viable at all in Virginia because the state's courts do not recognize diminished capacity as a form of mental illness. "Atrocious or vile as the objective appearance of the crime was, the applicant cannot be held fully responsible for his behavior. The result is that the applicant risks the harshest punishment known to the law when he may not have been fully responsible for his acts. Punishment of death in these circumstances is disproportionate."

The only way to make sure Jens's rights were not violated, he said, was either to refuse to extradite him at all or to extradite him to his native Germany. "His surrender to the United States is permissible under the convention only if it is legally certain that he will not be exposed to the anguish and the psychiatric torment of the death row phenomenon."

Arguing for the German government, Meyer-Ladewig said the possibility that an accused criminal would be set free if he were not extradited to the United States was hardly the issue in Jens's case. Germany, after all, was readily available. "The United Kingdom can extradite the applicant to the Federal Republic of Germany without violating its obligations under international law towards the United States. And the applicant would receive a just penalty in Germany. The applicant would have no fear of the death penalty, but he would be punished according to his guilt." Naturally, then, there would be no trauma as a result of the death row phenomenon.

Although a prisoner in Virginia can cut short his time on death row by stopping his appeals, Meyer-Ladewig said that is tantamount to suicide and not a viable alternative.

Rising to argue for the British and the Americans, Sir Patrick began by pointing out that while compassion was commendable, "these sentiments must not be allowed to divert the court from its central task." That task, he said, was to determine if Britain, by ordering Jens's extradition to Virginia, would be violating the terms of the convention.

Undeniably in favor of extradition to Virginia, Sir Patrick asked why the court was trying to interject itself into the policies of a nonmember nation. "Put in a nutshell," he said, "the British government's position is this: That it is straining language intolerably to hold that by extraditing a person to a requesting state, the requesting state has 'subjected' him to any treatment or punishment that he will receive following conviction within the jurisdiction of the requesting state."

Look at the issue a little differently, he urged. "Suppose that the part of the girlfriend in the alleged deed had been greater. Suppose that she had joined with the killer in the actual deed. She, too, would then have faced the possibility of being sentenced to death. She, however, is not a German national. If she also had challenged her extradition from the United Kingdom— because, remember, she came together with Mr. Soering—could it reasonably have been argued that, while a violation would occur in the case of Mr. Soering because he is a German national and therefore the possibility existed of returning him to Germany, no violation would exist in the case of Miss Haysom simply because the possibility did not exist of her going to Germany or anywhere else?"

Also filed as one of the documents for the court to consider was Dr. Somekh's report. In summing up his findings thus far on Jens, the psychiatrist said he was worried not so much by Jens's short-term response to the threat of being extradited as by the long-term effects. "The more serious question psychologically is the extent to which Soering has any hope for the future," he wrote. "If things occur which undermine Soering's sense that there is hope of any kind for the future or any reason for him to carry on living, then I fear that the increased severity of the depressive feelings which he is likely to experience will lead either to an overt breakdown or to a successful suicide bid."

AFTER HER TRANSFER TO GOOCHLAND, ELIZABETH KEPT A LOW PROFILE, refusing interviews and visits by photographers. Only once, apparently, did she let that position slip. Early in 1989 she wrote a three-paragraph testimonial for the *Liberty Prison News,* the newsletter published by the Reverend Jerry Falwell's prison ministry, attesting to her conversion to fundamental Christianity. Months later, a Roanoke newspaper, the *Times & World-News,* got a copy of the document and printed it.

In tones remarkably reminiscent of the contest-winning short-story she wrote from her cell at Holloway, "The Sleeper Awakes," Elizabeth wrote feelingly of her latest monomania. Although she was "fed and watered like a beast, trapped in a tiny room for years on end," she had found the path to her personal freedom. "This is in the freedom and the love of Christ," she wrote. "Christ released me from my prison. This time Christ is my defense counsel and the judge is God."

There was no way to gauge whether her sincerity reflects the truth. When she testified before Judge Sweeney during the hearing at Bedford, she appeared sincere, but truthfulness was another question—one that may never be satisfactorily answered. However, given her history of deceiving and manipulating, it is not difficult to be cynical about her latest proclamation. A woman capable of convincingly inventing a contact with the IRA in an attempt to stay *in* jail is equally capable of inventing a contact with God in an attempt to get *out.*

The *Times & World-News* was also dubious. In a biting comment the newspaper noted that it was a useful rule for editorial writers "never to belittle someone else's religion." But in Elizabeth Haysom's case the paper was willing to make an exception. "She now says that after a lifetime of skepticism, she has found Jesus," the newspaper remarked, observing that "signs of an inmate's religious commitment have been known to help convince authorities of the wisdom of parole." Urging prison officials to exercise caution in her case, it added: "Haysom may be reborn [but] her victims still are dead."

On July 7, 1989, the Human Rights Court announced its decision. By a nineteen-to-nothing vote it found in Jens's favor. The judgment, in part, said:

> In the Court's view, having regard to the very long period of time spent on death row in such extreme conditions, with the ever-present and mounting anguish of awaiting

execution of the death penalty, and to the personal circumstances of the applicant, especially his age and mental state at the time of the offence, the applicant's extradition to the United States would expose him to a real risk of treatment going beyond the threshold set by the Convention.

Also of importance, the court added, was the fact that Germany was conveniently available as an alternative trial site. "In the particular instance the legitimate purpose of extradition could be achieved by another means which would not involve suffering of such exceptional intensity or duration."

The result of its decision, the court added, was that Britain could not extradite Jens to Virginia until the Bedford County prosecutor promised not to seek the death penalty.

THE DECISION PUT BOTH BRITAIN AND JIM UPDIKE IN UNCOMFORTABLE positions. Britain could send Jens to Germany or it could ignore the decision and send him to Virginia. For his part, Updike could drop the death penalty charge and agree to try Jens for first degree murder with a maximum sentence of life.

Needless to say, Updike was not pleased with his options. Already frustrated because he had been unable to take an active role in any of the extradition battles, he announced that he would not give in; he would not voluntarily drop the capital murder charge against Jens. To surrender, he said, would be the same as submitting to "international blackmail."

At a news conference in the Bedford County courthouse Updike told reporters: "We have this red herring that Jens can be tried in Germany as a German national. That's ludicrous. They have no evidence to conduct a meaningful prosecution. All the evidence is here. I can't see spending thousands of dollars of taxpayer's money for a restricted prosecution dictated by a foreign government. If it occurs that this case becomes Germany vs. Soering, then as far as I'm concerned, Germany can go to hell."

The *Lynchburg News & Advance,* not surprisingly, supported his position a few days later. A July 13 editorial fumed: "The ruling is contemptible, utterly divorced from reality and arrogantly abusive."

The London *Times,* in a more restrained and erudite way, took much the same stance. It said the decision stemmed from a "most perverse reading of the Convention" and predicted "it will do nothing but harm to the principle of extradition [the purpose of which] is to ensure that fugitives from justice cannot escape due process in the country where the crime was committed." It continued: "The Court's justification is expressed in terms which suggest that it wishes to disapprove of extradition to any country which retains the death penalty." Worst of all, the newspaper said, the decision promised to create an unfortunate precedent. "This could in time produce a situation in which fugitive European nationals could be certain of evading extradition to the U.S. for capital crimes, providing they took care to move to Europe ahead of the police."

In Virginia, Updike sat tight, waiting to see what Britain would do. The answer came on August 1, 1989: Home Secretary Douglas Hurd said Britain would extradite Soering to Virginia only on the condition that he not be tried for "any offense, the penalty for which may include the imposition of the death penalty."

Updike glumly accepted the decision, pointing out that it was a compromise made at the federal level under the terms of the treaty between the two nations. The decision, he said, was equivalent to federal law, and he was bound to obey it. For the record, though, he told reporters there had been no bargaining on his part. "I would like to think that if I'd negotiated, I'd have done a better job."

Again, the British cranked up the machinery to extradite Jens. And again it ground to a halt almost before it got going. As soon as Hurd announced his decision, Jens's lawyers filed another motion with the British High Court claiming that the home secretary had waited too long to make up his mind. Under the terms of the Anglo-American extradition treaty, the brief said, Britain had sixty days either to extradite Jens to Virginia or to set him free. In actuality the decision was not made for two years after the first extradition order was issued. But that was because Jens was appealing. Whether the judge would decide that the clock began ticking as soon as the original extradition order was signed or if it would factor in the various legal moves that ate up the months had not been determined when this brief was written. In any case, it did not appear that Jens would be tried in Bedford County at least until early 1990, if at all.

ON THE ONE HAND, UPDIKE WAS FRUSTRATED AND ANGERED BY THE delays. "This could go and on," he said, reaching across his desk and digging in his brass box for a fresh cigar. "But on the bright side, I know he *is* going to be back. One day he's going to be tried right here," he said, pointing over his shoulder in the direction of the courtroom.

His mood lightened. His frown surrendered to a tiny smile. "If there's one thing I've learned from all of this," he said, flicking the wheel on his lighter, "it's patience." He paused, touched the end of the cigar to the flame and inhaled. "I've developed the patience of an oyster," he said, breaking into a grin that was all but hidden by a cloud of blue smoke. "I think I'm going to need it."

Afterword

DID SHE? OR DIDN'T SHE?

In her testimony Elizabeth tried to persuade Judge Sweeney that she had not wanted Derek and Nancy slain. Only removed. Transported outside her realm. Taken off into space somewhere, like the characters in the movie *Cocoon*. Elizabeth had been trying to draw a distinction between wanting to be rid of her parents and wanting to be *rid* of her parents. It did not work. In the end, it does not even matter. The issue is moot. Elizabeth Haysom pleaded guilty. As far as the law is concerned she helped plan Derek's and Nancy's murders, no matter her evasiveness, her splitting of hairs. But such equivocation is typical of Elizabeth. She is the consummate obfuscator. The inveterate fabricator. In her mind, obviously, there is no discernible line between fact and fantasy.

Actually, the evidence that she wanted them murdered is stronger than I have been able to indicate in the preceding text. Her letters to Jens are more explicit than she was willing to admit in her testimony, and considerably more candid than I have been able to demonstrate. The reason for this is both simple and frustrating: The federal appeals court for New York, in two recent rulings, has misinterpreted the U.S. copyright law and subverted it to such an extent that the public's right to know has been severely damaged. In essence, the law as misconstrued by the court—but which will continue to be the law until that court changes its mind or it is reversed by the supreme court—calls into question an author's right to quote from unpublished letters and diaries. Apparently, that means *all* unpublished letters and diaries. The court, either through shortsightedness or a deliberate attempt to befog, has failed to make clear if these puzzling new standards apply as well to documents that are part of an official record. In other words, legal scholars have so far been unable to determine if the court intended to make a distinction between letters ferreted from someone's attic and correspondence that is part of a public file. In this case, letters from Jens and Elizabeth are not only part of the court history (some were entered into evidence by Elizabeth's lawyers; some were read on the stand by Elizabeth herself), but have been published in newspapers and broadcast on radio and television. Yet the law, as distorted by the appeals court, is such that their reproduction in this format may well be prohibited under threat of injunction. The result is that the reader of this book is placed at a definite disadvantage. Anyone anxious to decide for himself whether Elizabeth wanted her parents murdered, as evidenced by her own words in her letters to Jens, is hampered in making that determination because the evidence (i.e., the letters themselves) cannot be printed, either in whole or in part.

But that is only one of the considerations in this strange but fascinating case. At question here is not only *whether* Elizabeth wanted her parents killed but *why*. And that may never be answered.

Rare, indeed, is the child who has not at one time or another harbored a desire to do away with one or both parents. Happily for the parents, very few actually do so. Elizabeth was an exception. Of course, there have been others. History is replete with instances of parricide. Everyone knows about Oedipus, who killed his father and married his mother. And there was Electra, who, obsessed with her relationship with her father, encouraged her brother, Orestes, to kill their mother. And as recently as yesterday's headlines there was the case of Cheryl Pierson, the Long Island teenager who hired a classmate to kill her father.

But Elizabeth's motive or motives are not nearly as apparent. Cheryl Pierson had her father killed, she said, because he had been sexually abusing her since she was eleven. Elizabeth passionately denied on the stand that Nancy sexually abused her. Significantly, she did not specifically deny that an incestuous relationship existed. But that does not mean that one did. At one time she said there was such a relationship. At another time she said there was not. Elizabeth is the only one still alive who knows for sure, and she is not likely to say any more at this stage. In any case, who would believe her now, no matter what she said on the subject? It is not inconceivable that her intention all along has been to obfuscate. Certainly she is intelligent enough to appreciate the benefits that confusion could offer her.

WHY ELSE WOULD SHE WANT TO BE RID OF HER PARENTS? BITTERNESS, perhaps. Elizabeth is a child of privilege. Derek and Nancy gave her everything but a steady, loving relationship. To Elizabeth that could have been reason enough. Undoubtedly, the circumstances were eating at her for years. Since at least her midteens she had been telling classmates at Wycombe Abbey that she was adopted. Still, that is not unusual. A number of children, particularly those with imaginations as active as Elizabeth's, have uttered those same words. But most of them did not go on to arrange for their parents' murders.

At one point she said she wanted to be free. Unquestionably, Nancy *was* domineering. Undoubtedly, the relationship with both Derek and Nancy *was* frequently suffocating. But Elizabeth could have left. Simply walked out the door. She was almost twenty-one years old. She did not have to repeat her European experience with Melinda to escape from Derek and Nancy. She did not have to starve in the streets or subject herself to sexual abuse. If she had approached the issue in a mature way her siblings more than likely would have been supportive. But Elizabeth also was greedy. Walking out would have meant the end of her subsidized education. She wanted the benefits a continuing relationship with her parents could offer her, but she did not want the concomitant responsibilities. She wanted Derek's and Nancy's money, what little there was left of it, but she did not want to earn it.

WAS ELIZABETH INSANE? EMPHATICALLY NOT. *Insanity* IS A LEGAL TERM, not a psychiatric one. For her to have been judged legally insane—and that is the only thing that counts in this instance—certain specific criteria would have had to have been met. In Virginia, as in twenty-five other states, those criteria are set forth in what is called the M'Naghten Rule, which holds that a person shall not be held responsible for criminal acts if, because of a "disease of the mind," he or she is unable to know the "nature and quality" of his or her acts or does not know that such acts are wrong. Not even Dr. Showalter tried to claim that she met those standards. She had a personality disorder. She was obsessed. But she was not insane.

WHEN ELIZABETH WENT OFF TO THE UNIVERSITY OF VIRGINIA, SHE WAS full of suppressed rage. In her first days there she met someone who is, by all accounts, as potentially explosive as she. He, too, is a child of privilege. He, too, was smothered by his parents' devotion. Klaus and Anne-Claire Soering, like Derek and Nancy Haysom, sought only the best for their child. Jens went to a good school; he never wanted for anything. Anne-Claire often went to considerable trouble and expense to arrange parties for Jens, hoping that these would make him more popular with his classmates. Her attempts failed, not because of her, but because Jens is a personally disagreeable fellow. On his desk in the German consulate, Klaus kept a large framed photo of Jens and Kai—none of his wife, just of his sons. In his own way he was as captivated with his children as was his wife. As were Derek and Nancy with Elizabeth.

Elizabeth emerged deeply scarred from her relationship with her parents. So, apparently, did Jens. He was as bitter and full of fury as she. Elizabeth once described the two of them as kindred spirits. They fed on each other's insecurities. They played to each other's weaknesses. They led each other on. They were searching for "pure" love, a love, as Elizabeth called it, "beyond reason." It was a sick relationship. What they found instead of love was hatred. Of their parents. Of authority. Eventually, of each other.

WE DO NOT YET KNOW WHY DEREK AND NANCY WERE MURDERED. But so far, we have heard only one side of the story. We will not be able to say with any certainty what motivated Jens and Elizabeth to plot and ultimately carry out the murders until we have listened to Jens. Judgment about motive has to be postponed until Jens has his day in court. That should be in a Virginia court. To try Jens in Germany would be a travesty.

When and if the day of Jens's trial comes, it will be interesting indeed to hear his explanation. And it will be just as interesting to see if Elizabeth, when she is called as a witness against her former lover, will change her story yet again. If she does, it will hardly be a surprise.

As this book was going to press, Jens Soering decided to abandon his long fight against extradition, and was returned to Virginia to face first-degree murder charges in the deaths of Nancy and Derek Haysom.